*Fragile Families, Fragile Solutions*

*Fragile Families, Fragile Solutions*

A History of Supportive Services
for Families in Poverty

Robert Halpern

Columbia University Press
NEW YORK

Columbia University Press
*Publishers Since 1893*
New York   Chichester, West Sussex
Copyright © 1999 Columbia University Press
All rights reserved

Library of Congress Cataloging-in-Publication Data
Halpern, Robert, 1951–
    Fragile families, fragile solutions : a history of supportive
services for families in poverty / Robert Halpern.
        p.      cm.
    Includes bibliographical references and index.
    ISBN 0–231–10666–1 (cloth). — ISBN 0–231–10667–X (pbk.)
    1. Family services—United States.   2. Poor—Services for—United
States.   I. Title.
    HV699.H28   1998
    362.82'8'0973—dc21
                                                                98–16738

Casebound editions of Columbia University Press books are printed on
permanent and durable acid-free paper.
Printed in the United States of America
c 10 9 8 7 6 5 4 3 2 1
p 10 9 8 7 6 5 4 3 2 1

This book is dedicated to Alfred J. Kahn.
"We stand on the shoulders of giants."

# CONTENTS

ACKNOWLEDGMENTS

I would like to acknowledge the helpful feedback of Brenda McGowan and John Schuerman; the wonderful editing of Susan Heath; and the support of John Michel at Columbia University Press. Financial support for research and writing was provided by the Ford Foundation and the Annie E. Casey Foundation (for chapter 9). Equally important were the support and encouragement of the exceptional program officer, Janice Molnar, formerly of Ford, and Janice Nittoli, of Casey.

*Fragile Families, Fragile Solutions*

Social services emerged as a distinct institutional realm in American society during the twentieth century, as a particular way of addressing families' support needs and influencing family and community life. Services have been an important component of American society's efforts to address the causes, consequences, and correlates of poverty. Over the course of the century, services and service providers have worked to socialize poor families into dominant childrearing norms (and sometimes to protect poor children from their parents). They have striven to integrate immigrants more fully into American life and to help them adapt to societal demands. Service providers have tried to help families get basic needs met, to help them address obstacles to self-sufficiency, and to prepare them to take advantage of economic opportunities. Yet after a century of development and numerous cycles of reform, social services for poor families in the United States remain far from coherent and responsive.

In this book I examine the history of supportive social services to examine the ways in which those services have been helpful, and sometimes unhelpful, to poor families; the factors that have constrained service provision and reform; and what would make the service enterprise viable in the coming years. I will discuss formative influences on the development and evolution of supportive social services; their objectives and underlying assumptions; approaches, achievements, and dilemmas faced by providers; and lessons learned from experience. I will also examine selected current reform initiatives and innovative service approaches in relation to those lessons. Finally, I will offer a modest set of prescriptions for the future.

The focus of the book is those services designed to support and as necessary strengthen childrearing and family life and to a lesser extent those designed to help poor families move toward economic independence. I will be looking at social or family casework; the full range of community-based models, agencies, and programs that provide social services, including settlements and today's "family support" programs; and certain child welfare services. I will examine both who has provided services and how they have been organized.

The general plan of the book is chronological. Chapters 1 and 2 analyze the emergence of services as a distinct institutional and social realm, beginning with their nineteenth-century roots, Progressive era concerns and strategies, the settlements, the emergence of family casework (its assumptions, tasks, and roles), Mothers' Aid, and formative dilemmas in purpose and practice. Chapters 3 and 4 discuss developments during the 1920s and 1930s—including early organizational trends, the introduction and influence of psychoanalytic theory, responses to the depression, and the elaboration of a national social welfare framework—and in the 1940s and 1950s the consolidation of services as a social realm and efforts to respond to changing inner-city populations and communities.

Chapters 5 and 6 examine the struggle to rethink and reform services for poor families during the 1960s: the assumptions underlying reform efforts, the goals and approaches of the renewed push for neighborhood-based services, the changing relationship between service providers and poor families, some of the innovative service models, and, in the public aid arena, the brief rise and rapid fall of casework. Chapters 7 and 8 look at the complicated mixture of developments in supportive services during the 1970s and 1980s: the continuing crisis in authority; the first concerted efforts at organizational reform; new service models and ideas, including early childhood intervention; efforts to respond to escalating crises in child welfare; and the deteriorating conditions of service work.

Chapter 9 discusses developments during the 1990s: emergent ideological debates; the situation of poor, urban families; developments in social welfare policy; and current service reform trends, approaches, and specific initiatives. I include among the initiatives I discuss a few concerned primarily with system reform and a number concerned with shifting the locus of organization, planning, and provision to the community level. In this chapter I will also consider efforts to integrate supportive social services into broader community development efforts.

In a concluding chapter I will attempt to summarize the lessons learned from historical experience with supportive services and discuss tasks for the future—the conceptual one of reconstructing a more positive vision of social services and their potential structure and roles and the concrete one of designing and supporting good services on the ground. I will discuss the kinds of external and internal supports that make good frontline practice possible and sustainable and will offer recommendations for conceptualizing and approaching reform itself.

## Background

Social services emerged around the turn of the century out of a simultaneous sense of loss, crisis, and optimism. There was a sense of loss of the idealized family and community, with their strong informal support systems, clear moral codes, and procedures for enforcing those codes. There was a corresponding sense of crisis regarding the damage that urban life, particularly urban poverty, was doing to families. Massive immigration, deepening economic inequality, and labor unrest also affected social cohesion and social order. But people also felt a sense of optimism regarding both the potential of the new disciplines of sociology and psychology to explain the causes of these problems and the ability of the new helping institutions and intervention strategies to address them.

The new institutions and approaches were of two sorts. One, embodied in the settlement movement, was community-focused. (This also included such supportive and/or developmental services as day nurseries and youth programs.) The other, found in the emerging discipline of social casework, focused on individual and family adjustment. Both approaches seemed to proponents more powerful and constructive than charity and moral exhortation. Their mission—to strengthen the domestic practices of poor immigrant families and generally help them to adjust to American society; to identify and address community and social conditions that undermined family well-being; to organize and build a sense of mutual support within poor neighborhoods; to reconcile cultural and class conflict; to address the consequences of, and when possible reign in, the worst excesses of industrial capitalism—was both ambitious and diffuse. It also set the stage for internal disagreement over purpose, emphases, and methods-that would plague the service provision community throughout the century.

During the first decades of the twentieth century the service enterprise grew largely from the bottom up. Local helping agencies and institutions proliferated, and the new helping professionals—nurses, social workers, visiting teachers, home economists, settlement workers, and child development specialists—claimed an ever broader array of social concerns. These included concerns about which they were deeply ambivalent, such as the provision of material assistance and poor women's struggles to balance work and family demands.

The new helping institutions were not the "state." Some local juvenile courts played a role in the elaboration of services, as did local overseers of the poor. But the federal government would not begin to play a significant role in social control, social problem-solving, and economic redistribution until the 1930s. Rather, services early on were perceived by proponents and providers as a "social extension of humanity's best individual instincts" (Glasser 1978:106), tempered by scientific method. They were seen also by some as a counterweight to the market, with its glorification of predatory behavior.

Nonetheless, services became gradually more tied to the state through a growing social welfare framework in state Mothers' Aid programs, and later the federal Aid to Dependent Children program. Two principles underlying this framework were particularly relevant to services. The first was that there were moral distinctions within the community of poor and vulnerable people and therefore some groups were more clearly deserving of public support than others. The deserving included those who made a social or economic contribution to the country—the families of war veterans and disabled workers (Skocpol 1992)—and those whose poverty could in no way be attributed to their choices or behavior, primarily children (who, it was felt, were both inherently vulnerable and deserving of protection from their parents' market failures [Testa 1985]). Widows fit both deserving categories, since motherhood and family life were viewed as important "foundations" of the state and society (Garfinkel and McLanahan 1986:98). The less deserving (or at least more worrisome) poor included unwed single mothers, families deserted by husbands, and families in which husbands could not or would not find work.

The second principle underlying the emerging social welfare framework was that, regardless of cause or situation, the poor had to be helped carefully, not wholeheartedly, in order to prevent long-term dependency and reinforce the work ethic. This principle included the corollary ideas that regardless of the reasons for poverty, people were personally responsible for doing something about their condition and that state assistance should be a last, and temporary, resort.

Assessing and categorizing the poor, calibrating assistance to them, supervising their use of assistance, and encouraging responsible behavior created important new semipublic roles for social service providers, who argued that they were best trained to undertake such tasks. The new roles began to tie social services more closely to the state (Polsky 1991), eventually making them an important expression of state interest in poverty. Social service providers themselves continued to identify new purposes, including helping poor families adjust to and prepare for the demands of a changing society and economy.

The emerging premises and practices of social services—particularly the goal of helping individuals adapt to prevalent social conditions—could have been severely damaged by the Great Depression of the 1930s. As one casework theorist noted at the time, asking poor people to "adapt to a psychotic society" was a "cruel burden" (Grace Marcus, quoted in Ehrenreich 1985:114). But for the first of many times services themselves proved adaptive to the realities of their era, reemerging stronger and more entrenched. From the New Deal to the mid-1970s the purview of the social services and the roles of service providers steadily expanded, first in Depression-era programs and later in the growing Aid to Dependent Children program, an array of new programs for vulnerable ("multiproblem") families, and the growth of state child welfare systems.

Optimism about the potential of social services, and confidence in their societal role, peaked in the 1950s (Rochefort 1981). During that same period, two trends were setting the stage for later crisis. One was a fundamental shift in the locus of economic activity in the United States, as workplaces became dispersed from older urban neighborhoods to the suburbs. As jobs the cities were losing jobs, enormous numbers of poor African Americans, Puerto Ricans, and Mexicans were migrating to those cities, expanding traditional minority ghettos and leading to massive racial turnover in formerly white ethnic neighborhoods. Such racial turnover was tremendously disorienting to many established private social service agencies and some simply abandoned neighborhoods in which they had worked for decades; the majority, however, struggled to adapt to new populations and tasks. These two trends changed the context for service provision. The traditional goals of integrating poor families into the economic and social mainstream and helping them through temporary economic downturns made less sense when that mainstream was receding from view.

When significant amounts of federal dollars flowed to the cities in the 1960s, with the purposes of increasing economic opportunity and preparing poor children and adults to take advantage of new opportunities, the social services once again reinvented themselves. Older service approaches such as settlements and community health centers were revived. Preventively oriented parenting and child development programs, neighborhood social service centers providing a wide array of supportive services, and employment and training programs were introduced, and optimism about the potential of services was briefly refueled. Growing public concern over exploding public aid case rolls and long-term dependence provided social casework with a new lease on life. Casework proponents "[pronounced] themselves ready to take on a clientele even more difficult than that which had faced their Progressive forebearers" (Polsky 1991:160).

At the same time social forces were emerging in poor urban communities that would lead to questions about the most basic premises of formal helping services for poor urban families. These forces included the civil rights movement and its offshoots, particularly welfare rights, and the efforts of minority leaders to create pride in ethnic identity. The focus on civil rights and pride in racial identity led to a questioning of the rights of helping professionals to define, label, and categorize poor people and of the ability of helping professionals to "grasp their clients' experience and aspirations" (Polsky 1991:176).

The federal initiatives of the mid-1960s were politically disavowed, and some were all but abandoned within a few years of their inception. As a reform movement they left a mixed legacy: on the one hand new service institutions, at least some of which (Head Start and community health centers) would take permanent root; on the other hand new doubts and questions about services among the public and the service providers themselves. By the late 1970s public frustration with the inability of social services to effectively address poverty-related problems was beginning to harden into a permanent feature of the social landscape. The 1980s brought, among other things (e.g., a nine-year freeze in the minimum wage, a dramatic decline in the value of Aid to Families with Dependent Children (AFDC) payments, and the first efforts to end public aid as an entitlement), repeated budget cuts in social services for poor families and a deepening sense of frustration within urban child and family service systems (Orfield 1991:519).

## The Current Moment as Fulcrum for the Future

This is a particularly critical time in the historical development of supportive social services for poor families. From the outset, there had been periodic criticisms. In the 1920s Hyman Kaplan, the head of Cincinnati's Jewish social agencies, warned that social service providers were turning into "technicians" (Kirschner 1986:84). In the early 1940s C. Wright Mills attacked what he called "professional social pathologists" and their tendency to "slip past structure to focus on isolated situations" (Mills 1943:170). But in recent years services have been under almost constant attack as poorly conceptualized and designed, ineffective, wasteful of public resources, self-serving, and even harmful to those they are intended to help, as well as to society in general.

It has been argued that "there is no need to worry about sufficient services because services have no real value" (Orfield 1991:525; this is not Orfield's own position); that "the record compiled by the human services is dismal" (Polsky 1991:5); that "our efforts to deal with distress themselves increase distress" (Glazer 1971:xx); and that formal helping efforts are "nothing more than power in disguise" (Gaylin, Glasser, Marcus, and Rothman 1978:x). It has also been suggested that social services ought to be evaluated not on the basis of the good they might do but on the basis of the harm (Glasser 1978:145–146). The predominant images of service providers in the press are of the defensive bureaucrat and the overworked, undertrained, cynical case worker; both images are caricatures of the compassionate professional helper.

Critics have also argued that services and helping professionals have slowly but steadily appropriated family and community functions, thereby weakening both spheres. Lasch (1995:98) claimed that "neighborhoods have been destroyed not only be the market . . . but by enlightened social engineering . . . The atrophy of informal controls leads irresistibly to the expansion of bureaucratic controls." In taking over family and community functions, services have been accused of weakening the "self-healing" forces in society and of replacing "natural duties"—such as those of family members to each other—with artificial ones that are more contingent (Hardin 1990:530).

It is particularly striking that the attacks on services are coming not just from the left of the political spectrum, which has long criticized services as witting or unwitting tools of social control, but from the center and the right as well. A recent editorial by a political moderate describes social services as "expensive, coercive programs of institutionalized compassion" (Dennis 1994:36). Writing in *The Public Interest*, a conservative policy journal, McDonald (1994:60) argues that "there is no evidence that social services can compensate for the lack of personal responsibility that is fueling America's epidemic of illegitimacy."

To an extent, services have been a lightning rod: for a sense of the failure of major social institutions to fulfill their responsibilities, and for a general "feeling of chaos in public arrangements (Schorr 1986:11). Yet not all criticism directed against services is displaced from elsewhere. As worrying as external attacks has been a growing sense of futility within the social service community. In discussing the state of child welfare services, one writer notes that they have "a Sisyphean quality—no matter how many innovations are introduced, there seems to be little, if any progress" (Anderson 1990:82).

At the same time that faith in social services has reached a low point, some argue (again) that we now, finally, have the knowledge and experience to design and implement effective services, at least for particular families in particular places. In *Within Our Reach* (1988) Lisbeth Schorr described twenty well-conceptualized, funded, and implemented human service programs for particularly vulnerable children and families and identified the principles of good practice common to those programs. Since the publication of Schorr's book there have been scores of reports, case studies, and the like describing principles of "best practice" in social services and programs or initiatives that seem to embody those principles (see, e.g., Milton Eisenhower Foundation 1993).

Partly in response to the belief that prevailing services are not helpful, and partly in response to the belief that we now have the knowledge needed to provide good services, there is renewed interest in some states and many localities in fundamentally rethinking the prevailing service system for poor families. The theses and elements of this renewed push for reform are varied—in some cases complementary, in others tangential, in still others contradictory. For example, there is a push for greater accountability within the human services and a simultaneous interest in structuring services to give frontline providers greater flexibility and discretion. (A few proponents link the two ideas by arguing that discretion should only be provided in exchange for willingness to be evaluated by predefined outcomes or progress indicators.) There is an interest in creating friendlier, less "formal" helping arrangements and a simultaneous interest in using standards and credentialling to assure quality in service areas that seem less well-developed (e.g., family support programs, home visiting).

Three larger, and in some instances related reform trends are: (1) a renewed effort to break down the categorical and systemic walls separating services (described as service "decategorization" or as making services more "child-focused" or "family focused"); (2) a renewed push for community/neighborhood-level organization, governance, priority-setting, administration, and provision of services—and as part of this multifaceted decentralization, an effort to create a full continuum of services within discrete community areas; and (3) an unprecedented push for integration of social services into broader community economic, physical, and social development strategies.

There are a number of rationales behind these reforms. One is the idea of "concentrat[ing] and integrat[ing] resources and program knowledge in particular communities over a sustained period of time," yielding a more comprehensive and coherent attack on poverty-related problems (Kubisch, Weiss, Schorr, and Connell 1995:2). A second is the idea that the residents of poor communities (or at least the leaders of such communities) know best, and have the right to determine, their own priorities and support needs. Related to this is the idea of viewing services as a vehicle for community-building and "empowerment." A third rationale derives from the value of redirecting service dollars: by-passing seemingly unreformable bureaucracies; viewing those dollars as potential investments in poor neighborhoods and as a form of economic redistribution; and, relatedly, viewing services as a potential form of social capital. Underlying discrete human service reform trends is the likelihood of a fundamental realignment of federal/state/local relations in social welfare responsibilities. As I write, Congress has passed legislation that dismantles the fragile web of federal entitlements woven over the past sixty years to protect and support poor families. The Aid to Families With Dependent Children (AFDC) program will be replaced by a new program (Temporary Assistance to Needy Families), which, in its preoccupation with moving mothers into the workforce makes no mention of federal responsibility for protecting and supporting vulnerable families; it also gives states significant discretion with respect to how and for whom poverty-related social welfare funds are used. Responsibility for the design and administration of social welfare policy will devolve to states and municipalities. These changes are being accompanied by strict budgetary constraints that will increase the already great strains on both state and local social service networks.

The dramatic shifts in our social welfare framework are themselves related to a reignition of longstanding societal debates about the locus, extent, and nature of public responsibility for our society's most vulnerable members; about why families are poor; the extent, meaning, and consequences of dependency; and about how best to help (or compel) people to escape poverty. Particularly notable is an intensifying attack on poor, single mothers. Like critiques of services, this attack is coming from a variety of points on the political spectrum. In testimony to the House Ways and Means Committee on January 10, 1995, Donna Shalala, President Clinton's Secretary of Health and Human Services, warned that "if able-bodied women refuse to comply with work requirements, they should should lose their welfare benefits, and the children could be taken away from the parents by state authorities and placed in foster care or group homes or put up for adoption." This attack extends beyond mothers of children born out of wedlock. A report by two Heritage Foundation staff members argues that regardless of the reasons or circumstances, divorce has "an element of personal choice and responsibility that widowhood does not" (Butler and Kondratas 1987:138).

Resentment and anger toward single mothers is mingled with a new level of distrust of poor people in general. Mead (1994:33) argues that welfare recipients who are placed in jobs or job preparation activities should be monitored closely, not because they might need ongoing support and encouragement but because if not monitored they might give in to "contrary temptations . . . If that pressure [close supervision] is absent, deviance will occur, even if the poor themselves disapprove of the behavior." (In another paper Mead argues that welfare recipients interpret close monitoring and supervision as "caring" and communicating high expectations; 1995:36–42).

A final factor making the current moment in social services seem unusually fateful is the worsening economic and social situation of poor urban families. More than 40 percent of poor families with children now live in urban neighborhoods characterized by high concentrations of poverty, profound social and economic isolation from the larger society, and the weakening of the institutions that hold a community together and sustain its residents. What has served historically as the paradigm of highest-risk family life—chronic financial and material hardship, vulnerable and overwhelmed parents, overburdened social support networks, and an unsupportive community context—is rapidly becoming the norm for young families in urban poverty. The large and growing numbers of multiply vulnerable families are overwhelming the capacities of even the strongest community social service agencies.

Given the current climate questioning the assumptions and value of social services, the simultaneous claims that we now know what good services are, the renewed pushes for service reform, the rethinking of our fragile social contract with poor families, and the difficult situation of poor families, it is useful to step back a bit more than we customarily do. It is important to examine—or perhaps to remind ourselves—where assumptions stem from; what ideals and tensions underlie particular policy purposes and service approaches; and what we have learned from past reform movements. It is important to clarify what social services can be and do, and what resources they need to fulfill their appropriate tasks; to articulate a basis for helping that can accommodate the contradictions, dangers, and pressures impinging on services; and to construct a positive, commensurate, balanced vision of services and their potential role in social problem solving. We do not lack an armament of "best practice" principles, approaches, and models; rather, we lack a way to figure out their use, place them in a coherent conceptual and ethical framework, and link them more closely to the realities of family and community life.

## Roots of Current Dilemmas: A Mixed History of Achievement and Struggle

Services have been an important expression of our sense of responsibility toward vulnerable families and social groups. They have simultaneously reflected the ambivalence and contradictory beliefs that define that sense of responsibility. Services have played a critical if modest role in helping families cope with the correlates and consequences of poverty. They have provided emotional support; encouragement, guidance, and feedback; and practical assistance with every kind of imaginable problem. They have helped countless individuals and families in discrete, small, difficult to measure (and often unnoted) ways: no one has counted the number, let alone measured the effects of thousands of home visits and phone calls to inquire as to how someone is doing and feeling, whether a referral worked out, or whether a family member is feeling better. No one has measured the contribution to community life of the hundreds of small, community-based agencies that provide early childhood services and after school programs, adult literacy or language classes, emergency food or rent money, or a place to turn when problems turn into crises. No one has captured the effect of thousands of acts of mediation with welfare agencies, schools, hospitals, housing authorities, and utilities on behalf of families (Piven and Cloward 1971).

Services can be simple supports that make inherent sense: a primary care clinic in a high school, an after school program, a program providing support and assistance to newly employed welfare recipients to help them remain in the labor force, or a program providing a few hours respite care for the children of an overwhelmed parent. Services can also involve the most complex and subtle of interventions; for example, the effort of a therapist to strengthen a troubled parent-infant relationship. One can go into any low-income community in the country and find providers struggling under difficult conditions to meet family needs, improve community life, and find a useful role.

In spite of their reputation for conservatism, service institutions have been among the quickest social institutions to recognize and respond to changing family and community circumstances, as well as to emergent social problems. They have acted as "the canary in the mine," alerting us to the conditions of life for poor families and in poor communities, to emerging problems and issues. Social service agency staff were among the first to observe evidence of the coming depression in the late 1920s; the first to recognize the growing destructiveness of urban racial segregation in the 1950s and the first to note the growth of homelessness in the 1980s. From the mission churches of the mid-nineteenth century, which struggled to find new ways to deal with joblessness, hunger and homelessness (Leiby 1978:77), to today's "family preservation programs," and "comprehensive community initiatives," innovation in social services has been constant, almost relentless.

Supportive services have acted as "mediating institutions" (Bergert Neuhaus 1977). They have linked families to new social networks and provided a vehicle for civic participation and, occasionally, a path into the mainstream. They have constituted in part a series of natural experiments into the means of rebuilding the deteriorated social fabric and replenishing the "social capital" of poor communities (i.e., a sense of common interests and identity, a degree of public social interaction, and civic association; see Putnam 1993). They have been a key element in American society's struggle to find a workable basis for social relations, mutual responsibility, and the expression and enforcement of social expectations.

And yet services have struggled almost from the time of their emergence a century ago. Some dimensions of this struggle are inherent to formal helping, especially under conditions of poverty and social exclusion. Others derive from choices made by service providers: a history of presumption and misreading has existed alongside the history of practical, immediate assistance, of creativity and innovation, of subtle, unrecorded, and unnoted helpfulness. Still other sources of struggle derive from the societal context in which services have had to operate. Social services have been a key arena for American society's efforts to express, contest, and occasionally reconcile contradictory values. More than anyone else except poor people themselves, human service providers have had to contend with the concrete, everyday expressions of these contradictory values.

## Challenges Inherent to Formal Helping

Some part of the struggle experienced by social services over the course of the century is inherent to formal helping itself. Formal helping relationships are paradoxical and ambiguous. They cannot be unilateral, and at the same time they are neither equal or reciprocal. In trying to address peoples' vulnerability and strengthen their autonomy, formal helpers make them more vulnerable and dependent by asking (or requiring) them to become clients. Formal helpers face the challenge of finding shared bases, purposes, and boundaries for helping relationships. People are invited, required, or choose to enter into helping relationships for often vague reasons. Even when the initial bases and motives are clear, they change and evolve as the relationship deepens.

Formal helping involves the challenge of simultaneously applying one's own theoretical and experiential lens to help guide interventions and make sense of what one is learning and trying to adjust that lens to the client's own way of looking at the world and his or her life. It involves the challenge of seeking understanding across chasms of class, race, and life experience (Perez-Foster 1996). It also involves the challenge of finding a constructive stance; of balancing societal, one's own, and the client's interests; of balancing "technique" and caring, skill and empathy (Halmos 1970). Difficult ethical issues are involved—notably determining one's responsibilities as a helper in exchange for the "privileges and exemptions . . . [the invasion] of the privacy, freedom, dignity and civil protections not normally accorded any human being by another" (Rein 1983:150).

Other inherent dimensions of the struggle within services derive from the distinct additional challenges of helping problems under conditions of poverty. The problems being addressed under conditions of poverty are often complicated and intertwined. The tools of interpersonal helping are modest in relation to the hardships and difficulties associated with poverty in American society. Poor people do not usually see social services as central to addressing their concerns and preoccupations. (At the same time, services provide the principal contact some poor families have with the larger society.)

Providers themselves sometimes question the relevance of services under conditions of poverty. As McGowan (1990:196) notes in her study of innovative child and family service agencies in New York City: "all the administrators at our study sites talked at length about their frustrations in being able to accomplish so little" in relation to the totality of families' support needs and difficulties. Further, the inherent ethical issues in helping—especially issues of problem definition, power, and authority—seem to be heightened in work with poor families, especially when there are consequences for access to basic necessities, or for privacy and autonomy in family life.

## Challenges Stemming from Service Providers' Premises and Assumptions

Kunzel (1993:5) notes that those who are the objects of social concern often have seemed "peripheral to the cacophony of voices raised to represent, redeem and treat them." The history of services is in part a story of the ways in which others have conceptualized, defined, and categorized the lives of the poor; put differently, a history of poor families' loss of control over self-definition. Service providers' motives for seeking control over how poor people and their lives are interpreted have been complex. Hirschman (1991) points out that they originally sought control not, as is argued today, for malevolent or selfish reasons but in reaction to the nineteenth-century tendency to view poor people as an undifferentiated, "vaguely threatening" mass. Nonetheless, it has been argued that helping professionals quickly learned that they could draw power and self-definition from the right to define others, particularly the determination that those others required professional guidance (Grubb and Lazerson 1980:99).

Service providers too often have interpreted families' situations and difficulties in ways that fit their own world views, as well as what they themselves had to offer. As a result their responses to families' difficulties have sometimes gone beyond what families "brought to" the helping situation or acknowledged as support needs; instead, they have aimed to restructure families' lives in basic ways (Gordon 1994:46). Formal helpers often have been slow to recognize their own self-interest and subjectivity. Discussing the history of services to unmarried mothers, Kunzel (1993:139) writes: "The amount of ink spilled and the number of conference hours spent by social workers discovering casework to be a process in which their own ideas, desires, and pre-conceptions figured as strongly as those of their clients would have been ironic, even laughable, to most unmarried mothers."

The tendency to define and categorize poor people has been destructive in part because it has contributed to "the shrinkage of experience" associated with poverty in the United States (Kelly 1995:6). Too often labels have determined the communities, housing, learning experiences, and jobs to which poor people have had access. Labels and categories are overly reductive, denying the complexity of human beings. Lenrow (1982:67) notes that "once established, a categorization defines what is relevant about the people labelled." This is especially damaging when, as is frequently the case, the categories used are based on vulnerabilities or dependencies. In a very different vein, categorizing and sorting have led to the individualizing—and therefore the weakening and fragmenting—of American society's conception of poverty. As poor peoples' common difficulties—their experience of discrimination, their inability to make ends meet, or their humiliating treatment by welfare bureaucracies—are individualized and viewed on a case-by-case basis, they lose their impact. They are no longer seen as systemic or patterned (Piven and Cloward 1971).

If service providers have struggled to hear and acknowledge the social implications of poor families' common experiences of hardship, at times they also have genuinely misread poor families and their communities. They have mistaken parental exhaustion or survival-related adaptations for neglect. They have failed to see the heterogeneity in a population of families. The most vulnerable individuals or families in a particular group have been held up as characteristic of that group. Providers have also failed to see the richness of support structures in putatively disorganized communities.

While social service providers have at times been controlling, paternalistic, and intrusive, they have at times been too nonjudgmental, displaying a kind of clinical humanitarianism that itself undermined clients' sense of agency and integrity. Keith-Lucas (1957:124) noted that " 'Thou shalt not impose,' which can be a genuine moral principle guiding the social worker, becomes transmuted into 'Thou shalt not let the client become imposed upon by the pressures of society.'" One crack-addicted mother said of a program that took care of her children, helped find housing, supervised the children's health care, and provided extra food, clothing, and household supplies when she was strapped for money, "they made it too easy for me to get high" (Stone 1992:65).

## Problems with the Organization and Reward Structure of Services

A different source of struggle for services has been related to their organization and reward structures. It has become a truism that those most in need of supportive services are precisely those least likely to have access to or to participate in them. It has also become a truism that categorical and fragmented service delivery systems undermine frontline providers' inclination to recognize and ability to respond to families' support needs. Many vulnerable families "fall between the cracks" of the prevailing service system (Kamerman and Kahn 1988). Problems are not identified and addressed until they become critical. Even when problems are identified early, families may not be linked to services for a variety of reasons.

One reason may be the lack of consonance between the organization of services and the ways in which communities and families manage their lives, meet needs, experience and struggle to address difficulties. Problems and support needs arise unpredictably and often do not fit the categorical mandates of those who happen to be serving families at the moment. Individual providers are physically and administratively isolated from each other, creating barriers to cooperative work. Categorical fragmentation creates "an overwhelming managerial burden for those families who are not yet too discouraged to go on seeking help" (Schorr 1988:260).

Different dimensions of families' lives—for example childrearing, economic security, and the personal development of parents—are intertwined. Yet there has been an almost complete separation in policy and practice among services addressing adults' roles as parents and nurturers, services addressing their roles as providers, and, not least, services addressing their roles as partners in relationships. Mutually isolated, fragmented policy frameworks complicate poor parents' efforts to manage different demands, partly through lack of attention to the impact of their prescriptions on domains outside their purview. To cite just one example, public aid programs rarely provide for gradually increasing participation requirements (in terms of weekly hours) as people's children get older. Rather they use blanket, all-or-nothing rules, which ignore both individual capacity and family situation.

Bureaucracies' rules, procedures, and priorities create an aura of indifference to families' support needs. Staff are rewarded more for accurately following procedures and for avoiding mistakes (e.g., in eligibility determinations) than for responding flexibly and creatively to the uniqueness of each helping situation. They are often forced to spend significant amounts of time creating self-protective paper trails, at the obvious expense of direct helping services to families. Frontline providers at the Center for Community Life in New York City told observers that it was both exhausting and demoralizing to constantly have to fight and beg (schools, welfare, housing, and other bureaucracies) for the most basic resources for the families they served (Hess, McGowan, and Meyer 1995:19).

## A Difficult Societal Context

Services are often considered in a vacuum, as if they were a discrete and isolated strategy for supporting people and addressing social problems. In reality, in all their aspects—from funding patterns to objectives to helping relationships—services are strongly shaped by and are reflective of the ideals, beliefs, and myths, the tensions, contradictions, and ambiguities of the society in which they are embedded.

Particularly relevant in the U.S. context have been American society's ambivalence about key social issues, the sometimes inappropriate social tasks services have been given, and the lack of a coherent guiding philosophy or model have been particularly relevant to services' struggles in the context of the United States. Supportive services to poor families have been shaped, buffeted, and occasionally paralyzed by Americans' moral and ideological uncertainty—about human nature; the causes and meaning of poverty, inequality, and dependence; whether pluralism is a strength or a problem; the role of the state in problem-solving; and the nature of collective responsibility for vulnerable members of society and of those members' own responsibilities in return. American society has made only modest progress over the course of the century in its debates about the values, priorities, and assumptions it holds regarding both poor people and poverty itself, and therefore about what should guide the provision of services.

Poor families have been viewed alternatively as the barometer of society and as marginal to it; as the source of many societal problems and the key to improving it. We acknowledge that forces outside of poor families are critical to their well-being, but we direct our interventions inside those families. We have tended to interpret family difficulties as exceptional phenomena, rather than as a characteristic result of our social priorities and arrangements. Yet we accept, and at times glorify an economic system that inherently creates extreme inequality in earnings and wealth. The poor have been viewed simultaneously as unable to cope on their own and as responsible for "bearing up," for making the best of a difficult situation (Leiby 1978:69). They have been viewed simultaneously as childlike, and therefore in need of guidance and supervision, and as fully adult when it comes to responsibility for their situations. We argue that the poor will not work unless forced to, and that the poor are no different than anyone else, wanting only the opportunity for a decent job and health insurance.

We have been both sensitive to and uncomfortable with the stresses and difficulties experienced by poor families. We have been particularly uncomfortable with poor women's struggles to balance work and family responsibilities. Early in the century poor women were criticized because they worked outside the home, thereby violating the "domestic code" and failing to attend properly to their children. Now they are stigmatized for not working. (In reality, poor women have always juggled both, and they continue to do so today.)

Largely due to our ambivalence about the most basic issues of our common life, services have been given competing, sometimes contradictory purposes: to enable and at the same time to control recipients; to support parents and at the same time to protect children from their parents' negligence or harm; to start from poor peoples' own understanding of their lives, and at the same time to define, categorize, and interpret their lives using external standards; to link poor people to mainstream norms, institutions, and opportunities and, at the same time, to highlight their difference from the mainstream by diagnosing them and sorting them into categories.

Our sense of social responsibility motivates us to provide services and supports to poor families, but our ethos of personal responsibility leads us to do so in a grudging, conditional, and occasionally dehumanizing manner, defeating whatever sense of belonging and community might have resulted from the process. Thus we provide financial supports and then accuse people who use them of laziness and of living off society. We require people to become clients in order to receive support, and then accuse them of clientlike behavior. We require poor people to meet difficult expectations without providing the supports and scaffolding that would help them do so, or allowing for setbacks. We do little to provide families with the supports that might prevent particular problems, and then "set up rescue missions to undo the damage to those we have placed in jeopardy in the first place" (Scheper-Hughes 1987:351).

Another important thesis of this book is that, given their limited means, too much has been asked (explicitly or implicitly) of services and service providers. As I have already implied, local service agencies and programs, and their frontline providers, often seem to end up with de facto responsibility for reconciling our competing beliefs about the poor and dependent. Moreover, services have had to bear a disproportionate share of responsibility for addressing the correlates and consequences of poverty, and more broadly for establishing a basis for social relations, mutual responsibility, and the expression and enforcement of social expectations. They have been asked to buffer families from the damaging effects of both changing economic conditions and the economic system itself. They have been asked (and to be fair, sometimes themselves claimed the capacity) to change people, and sometimes their life situations, without any alteration of the larger social ecologies in which those people are embedded. Services have been asked to function as the primary vehicle for helping American society achieve its ideals of equal opportunity and full social participation. (Ironically, service recipients themselves often have modest and limited expectations of what constitutes a successful helping experience; Rees and Wallace 1982:147.)

Inappropriate approaches to measuring success exacerbate the effects of inordinate expectations. This is not simply to blame evaluation or evaluators. There is much insight into the achievements and limitations of services in the program evaluation literature. But in my view, most frameworks for assessing services have been too blunt, failing to account for contexts and constraints; for the efforts that go into laying the groundwork for good outcomes (i.e., relationship-building, dealing with immediate, concrete priorities); and for the accumulated effects of what Carl Weick (1986) has called "small wins." Prevailing frameworks have not allowed room for the iterative, unpredictable process of growth and change in both poor families and those who help them. They have not accounted for the immediacy and unpredictablity of helping processes; the idea that services, while having a modest role overall, are often critical to particular families at particular moments in time.

Inordinate expectations of services, combined with little public sense of what service providers actually accomplish (however modest), have led to disappointment, especially when social problems being addressed have persisted or worsened. This disappointment in turn has led to doubts about the usefulness of services, the motives of service providers, and the value of trying to provide support to poor families. Those doubts have been particularly acute during times of heightened value conflict, such as the present. In recent years doubts about services and service providers have been connected also to a larger loss of belief in the legitimacy of traditional authority in the United States. This loss is not necessarily a bad thing. Traditional authority has been as much abused as used constructively and equitably. Nonetheless, rejection of it has tarred all those charged with authority, regardless of their beliefs, purposes, or practices.

At least some of the pressures impinging on services are due to the lack of a coherent philosophical framework to shape and protect them. Today we have hardly any better conception of the role of services in social problem solving, and more generally in our social life, than we did earlier in the century. American society continues to waver between a narrow, instrumental, and residual conception of services and a belief that they should be woven more fully into the social fabric of society. When minority groups rejected the "caring parent" as a model for services in the 1960s, service providers found that they had nothing to replace it with. The lack of touchstones—about identity, purpose, expectations—has heightened services' vulnerability to American society's schizophrenic attitudes toward poverty and poor families.

## Impact of These Broad Factors on Service Provision

Taken together, the inherent challenges, self-imposed complications, and difficult societal context impinging on services undermine the conditions needed to support the development of solid, trusting, helping relationships and good, thoughtful services. Frontline providers' ideal conceptions of their work are under constant assault: from the contradictory tasks they are given; the promises they feel compelled to make; the things they have to do that contradict their ideals (e.g., determining eligibility or denying that someone needs or would benefit from a certain kind of help because they lack time to provide it); and the messages they get from society. At times providers have been forced "to take actions that have wholly forseeable consequences for further harm to already vulnerable clients" (Orfield 1991:521).

In a form of vicious cycle, doubts about services contribute to lack of adequate and reliable resources, leading in turn to further pressure to reduce frontline discretion, increase frontline accountability, and concentrate services on those most at risk. Lack of adequate resources has been found to lead to less outreach to families, the weakening of "satellite" branches of mainstream service agencies, and to "hit and run" helping (Perlman 1960). It has led to less supervision of frontline staff and less interest among senior staff in mentoring (Bocage, Homonoff, and Riley 1995). Lack of resources has led also to pressure to constantly respond to new fads and movements, thus undermining stability and the ability to focus on improving existing services.

One result of the pressures on providers, and their resulting responses and adaptations, has been the gradual "separation of meaning and action" in human services and a breakdown in service providers' faith in their work (Rein 1983:140, 152). Frontline workers, struggling to make sense of the pressures they feel and forced to suppress their own legitimate doubts and worries, experience a barely recognizable, but nonetheless painful, sense of dissonance. In the words of Kamerman and Kahn (1988:267) social service providers "do what they can and must" to support and strengthen families. One of the great paradoxes, and protective aspects, of services is that although they are powerfully shaped by broad social forces, in the end they are defined by very specific relationships. Nonetheless, the difficulties of "doing the job well" in supportive social services seem in good part related to "society's ambivalence about having the job done at all" (Rees and Wallace 1982:3). As one frontline provider in a highly respected community-based program tells Hess, McGowan, and Meyer ((1995:13): "It is appalling how little people know about this kind of work and how little they recognize the importance of it. I find that very hard."

## Experience with Reform

The history of reform efforts is an important part of the history of supportive services for poor families. Reform has been motivated by dissatisfaction with prevailing services, new ideas, knowledge, and approaches, the rediscovery of old ideas and approaches, changing social conditions, newly identified social problems, and shifting public concerns. Reform movements have often reflected an effort to renew the ideals underlying social services, renew public confidence in the service enterprise, and signal responsiveness to public concerns. They have reflected an effort to take marginal but energized elements of the human services and place them at the heart of the service enterprise. Not least, reform efforts sometimes have served as a form of social safety valve when social pressures and disjunctions were high.

Different historical eras have had characteristic or paradigmatic reform strategies. One thinks of the settlements of the Progressive era, clinical casework in the 1940s, the delinquency prevention and multiproblem family initiatives of the 1950s, the assorted community action programs and services of the 1960s, and the family support and family preservation movements of the 1980s. Yet in each era there has been much borrowing and reinvention, both witting and unwitting. As I have already noted, the mid-1990s seem characterized by an uneasy mixture of reform ideas, including a renewal of neighborhood initiatives; an effort to rationalize scarce resources through careful targeting and accountability; and the use of certain broad (and relatively ill-defined) themes—family-centered, comprehensive, and so forth—to shape service approaches.

Again, a key question is why persistent efforts to reform services have not brought us closer to a coherent and responsive service system for poor families. I will argue that there are a number of different reasons. At a practical level, reform often is introduced at the worst time, when a system is in crisis and has the least capacity to take risks, question itself, and mobilize the needed energy for change. As McGowan (1990) notes, discrete reform proposals and plans often run against the grain of larger systemic responses to fiscal or political crises. Thus in New York City in the late 1980s, reform panels and commissions suggested that in order to improve its troubled child and family services the city should move toward a "neighborhood-based family service system that could provide a comprehensive range of support services" to families. In practice, city officials "responded to the crisis by moving—perhaps inevitably—toward increased regulation, tighter management, and more categorical targeting of services" (McGowan 1990:6).

Reformers have tended to try to by-pass bureaucracies, rather than analyze their functions—for instance, protecting service providers and clients from patronage politics—and then acknowledge and address those functions in their reform efforts. Yet bureaucracies repeatedly have demonstrated the capacity to absorb reform efforts into their ongoing practices by outwaiting them, "turning" them, coopting them, and occasionally simply sabotaging them. To some extent, reform has been constrained by simple bureaucratic gravity: the demands of day-to-day routines are stronger than the ill-defined promise of new approaches (Hagedorn 1996).

As with services themselves, reform is often burdened by overly ambitious or contradictory objectives. Discrete approaches (for example, community planning and governance, family preservation programs, or family support programs) or discrete clusters of principles (for example, comprehensive, family-centered services) are seen as somehow powerful enough to completely remake the service system. For instance, Nelson (1991:217) noted that "family preservation works, in some measure, because its workers assume responsibility for the broad range of problems that may threaten family capacity, and because they have resources to respond to multiple and often changing needs . . . In their most extreme formulation, the implications of family preservation practices probably point to a thoroughly reorganized service system." Certainly family preservation services are a helpful component in a continuum of services for vulnerable families. But they do not embody anything like a complete basis for reforming services.

Reform proposals rarely consider implications beyond the domain with which they are immediately concerned. For example, current efforts to push or pull poor mothers into the workforce are likely to have more complex effects on those mothers and their children, on the social fabric of poor communities, and on corollary services (such as after school programs) than are currently discussed. (Whether or not mandating mothers of young children to work will succeed in linking them and their children to the social mainstream, it may very well make poor women and their children more vulnerable to oppressive family arrangements; Hirschman 1991:41.)

Once a reform initiative is begun, no one seems to feel that he or she has permission to alter inappropriate objectives. Most reform initiatives fail to acknowledge the legitimacy and allow for the working though of mixed motives, interests, and perspectives. Most fail to allow room for uncertainty, doubt, learning from experience, and then making mid-course corrections. Observers also misframe the actual outcomes of reform initiatives in a way that prevents them from building constructively on experience. Indeed, we do not view reform efforts as building experiences; rather, hope they will be definitive in one or another sense.

In a related vein, reform has been constrained by the difficulty of figuring out how and where to use existing knowledge and experience in each new reform effort, as well as the lessons from prior reforms. When particular services are helpful, and sometimes when they prove unhelpful, it is partly due to their inherent soundness and partly due to the interaction of particular ideas with a particular setting. In some instances promising ideas from the literature or other initiatives tend to become frozen when they are introduced into a new setting, losing the flexible, iterative, developmental quality that helped get them developed and may have made them valuable in the first place. Ideas, models, approaches need continued development and evolution in each new setting.

Reform is often imposed on communities, agencies, and frontline providers from the outside. Those most affected by reform proposals—frontline providers and families—are brought into the process too late and too ambivalently. Both groups are too rarely consulted about how well particular services are working and what would make services more effective. In discussing the Annie Casey Foundation's "New Futures" initiative, designed to improve services for high risk youth and their families, White and Whelage (1995:25) note that while in theory the case managers "were to function as the eyes and ears of the collaborative by informing those at the top of the organization about frontline conditions, in practice no mechanisms were created for them to do so; and even where feedback mechanisms were in place, policymakers were not inclined to value the knowledge of case managers as useful."

At a deeper level efforts to reform services have been shaped by the same ambivalence about poverty and dependence that has shaped service provision. Almost every problem-solving impulse in American society, every choice made, is soon accompanied by a contradictory one. We try ideas, and even as we are working them out we abandon them; or we undermine them in more subtle ways by underfunding them, loading them with inappropriate expectations, or changing or expanding the target population. We rarely seek the middle ground between opposite poles of reform (e.g., to preserve families at all cost or to protect children at all cost).

Handler and Hasenfeld (1991) argue that one reason reform usually does not lead to significant changes in practice is because it is intended to be largely symbolic—to reaffirm certain values and reassure the public that services providers support those values. The paradigmatic example of this is the repeated efforts to introduce work requirements into welfare programs in the past thirty years. Each effort, from the Work Incentives Program (WIN) in the late 1960s to the Family Support Act of 1988, to the current welfare reform proposals, has made work requirements a centerpiece. But not one has been funded at a level remotely adequate to putting in place the supports and supervision necessary to implementing work requirements.

From an historical perspective, reform has had a repetitive, often circular quality: reformers keep making the same promises, rediscovering and re-circulating the same ideas, with similar consequences. Ideas that once were viewed as the key to solving particular social problems are repudiated, and then are championed again. Institutions that were once hailed as the key to saving children and young families, then criticized as harsh, regimented places that undermined initiative and individuality (Gittens 1986:40), are now resurrected as one alternative for teen parents and their children. Over time we have shifted from a preference for subsidizing foster families to care for poor children to that of financially supporting poor parents—and now back to the former idea.

I will explore the puzzlingly repetitive quality of reform in this book. It may be that strong underlying societal continuities shape and constrain services, and problem-solving generally, even as reform has given the impression of evolution and change. Reform can be seen as repeated responses to chronic concerns that are periodically reactivated: about dependency among the poor, out-of wedlock childbearing, the adequacy of childrearing practices in poor families, the social threat posed by the behavior of poor youth. The nature of such longstanding concerns may explain why "measures claimed as 'reform' often were in line with traditional values and strategies" (Chambers 1992:501). For example, for all that mothers' pensions seemed a genuine reform in the early decades of the century, the idea in fact reflected historic beliefs in the primacy of motherhood and the need to supervise poor families. The nature of our longstanding concerns also may explain why it is often the more idealistic, humane dimensions of reform efforts that fall away first, leaving bare the social control skeleton underneath (Ryerson 1978:33).

A second reason for the repetitive quality of reform may be the reconceptualization of old strategies through the use of new theories and knowledge. Social casework has been repeatedly renewed, through psychoanalytic theory, behavioral theory, and various systems theories. The old goal of family preservation was reinvigorated using family systems and crisis theory. (New theories have often also been used to explain why past reforms were not more successful; Polsky 1991:113).

Still another reason may be related to the ways in which successive reforms interact. Each new reform effort is undertaken without regard to lessons learned from previous efforts that addressed similar problems with similar purposes and strategies. Because of the frequent failure to see reform efforts through, each new reform effort has to cope with a very real residue of unresolved contradictions, half-developed or semi-abandoned ideas, and a long legacy of disappointment resulting from promises that cannot be kept.

## Current/Emergent Reform Initiatives

In a later chapter I will examine all the above issues in relation to current reform initiatives, particularly those concerned with creating integrated, coherent, and responsive frontline services; moving away from a problem-focus; shifting the locus of governance, design, and accountability to the community level; and embedding social service reform within broad community development initiatives. (These strategies are found both separately and combined in different initiatives.)

Reorganizing services, decentralizing and "decategorizing" them, and returning them to their neighborhood roots have been recurrent themes in social services almost from the time social services first emerged. The generalist and neighborhood approaches in services persisted, even as services steadily became more professionalized and bureaucratized in the middle decades of the century. They were kept alive in scores of discrete initiatives in the thirties, forties and fifties, and then were a centerpiece of the major federal programs of the 1960s. Neighborhood-based service strategies were seen to meet many needs that bureaucratic services did not—bringing services together in a more integrated fashion, providing social supports and recreational opportunities, reaching out to families unwilling or unable to seek help and support, making services more accessible and "friendly," creating a "community" as opposed to a "case" focus, and creating opportunities for community members to participate in service design and provision.

The historical rationales for conceptualizing and organizing services at the local community level continue to be relevant. If anything, the pressures on public social services have made them more rigid, fragmented, and crisis-oriented. Yet current initiatives raise a number of questions. What does it take, and what are the costs as well as the benefits of transferring public sector functions to private, neighborhood organizations? Can services be made more coherent in purpose, mission, and so forth, at the local level—in particular in communities—without greater coherence at other levels; in state human service systems; and, more fundamentally, in beliefs, assumptions, and structures at the societal level? What is the relationship between community control and accumulated knowledge and understanding of social issues (whether codified as best practice, principles, guidelines in requests for proposals, or in reform legislation)? What is it, exactly, that service clients and community members can best contribute to the understanding of problems beyond their own experiences? How can and should policy makers make sense of the variability in priorities, and thus in outcomes for families that is likely to result from neighborhood-based services systems? Is it possible that a neighborhood-based focus might serve inadvertently to heighten the social isolation of poor, urban neighborhoods, even as it strengthens a sense of community? (Indeed, poor neighborhoods are also service ghettos, with their service providers experiencing the same isolation and exclusion as their residents.)

In many respects the present moment is a particularly difficult one for service reform. As I have already noted, a growing proportion of poor families are vulnerable in many domains. The continued isolation and continuing resource depletion of many poor neighborhoods complicate the desire to create strong, community-based service systems, and to use those as launching pads into the mainstream for community residents. In spite of the worsening situation of poor families and their communities, the public, and therefore the politicians who follow its lead, seems to be in a particularly ungenerous and insecure mood. Elected officials chip or hack away at human service budgets that long ago lost any "bureaucratic" excess they might once have had. Federal budget cuts in social service block grants and other programs could indirectly undermine the financial resources that new reform initiatives are counting on from public service budgets, not to mention the specific services they see as elements of their initiatives.

The impact of continued budget cuts simply heightens the dilemma in current reform initiatives of what to do with existing organizations, as well as the responsibilities and tasks of services. Existing structures cannot be wished away. There is in some measure an inherent tension between innovating to meet the unmet needs of poor families and communities and assuring that one also devotes adequate resources to existing tasks and responsibilities. Berlin (undated:5) describes the worsening of poverty-related problems as "a tidal wave surging over the decks of the [social service] agencies charged with responding." Yet each new reform effort undertaken "draws funds away from ongoing policy initiatives, and creates turmoil in the social agency network" (Lipsky 1984:19). When funding is no longer tied to specific services and to specific types of clients, how will increasingly scarce funds be apportioned across and within local service networks within a community-based supportive service system? Which neighborhoods would get priority, and why? Should some funds go to nonservice activities that promote community development aims?

## A Word About the Historical Approach of the Book

Historical approaches to studying social issues bring risks. Looking backward produces the desire to create coherence, to find greater continuity over time in assumptions, beliefs, and preoccupations than may actually have existed. There is a tendency to filter the past too much through the lens of current preoccupations and concerns. Not least, there is the temptation to succumb to the wisdom of hindsight. As Kirschner notes, "nothing comes more easily than judgments against our ancestors for underestimating their task and leaving the mess for us to clean up" (Kirschner 1986:39).

Historical approaches also bring the risk of didacticism. Rather than letting the historical experience shape a story and its messages, history is interpreted and used primarily to teach lessons designed to lead to specific action. To illustrate the dangers of didacticism, Grob (1973) uses the example of persistent efforts to attribute what most would agree to be the destructive effects of America's public welfare system to either too harsh or too generous a view of the poor. In reality, intentions have been more complex and contradictory. Moreover, there may not be such a close relationship between intention and effect in social welfare. The relationship is weakened by changing circumstances, experience, and the local actions of many participants, from frontline providers to families. (A central challenge of writing about supportive social services is that of capturing this decentralized and multifaceted body of experience.)

Yet an historical approach does provide perspective. It reminds us of what Polsky (1991:8) describes as the "long buried compromises" that underlie many of the chronic tensions and difficulties in services. It helps us understand why, as Katz (1983:239) puts it, a social welfare system that no one likes is so resistant to change.

An historical approach also helps or induces us to think more deeply about whether there has been (and by implication how best to measure) progress over time in the prevailing social service system for poor families. It has often been the case in the social services that innovations in method have given providers a basis for arguing that they have made made progress. Certainly there are things that we know, understand, can do better than in the past. Many principles of good practice seem reasonably stable at this point. But it is less clear that there has been progress in wrestling with basic challenges to good services—for example, articulating a coherent and constructive framework of underlying assumptions, purposes, and expectations, and then working through the implications of these for the design of services. An additional function—and value—of a historical perspective is to create a narrative that is realistic about the past and present but that allows us to move forward in a constructive way. That is the core purpose of this book.

# CHAPTER ONE

# The Emergence of Supportive Social Services

Although never more than a modest sphere of social life, and granted only a relatively modest share of public and private resources, social services have been described as the twentieth century's religion. More modestly, they have been part of a century-long struggle to create new forms of authority compatible with a pragmatic, scientific outlook and new forms of social care and control compatible with the complexities of urban life. This struggle began in the last decades of the nineteenth century, as observers of American society became aware that "the assumptions and values of tradition were succumbing to the forces of modernity" (Diggins 1994:111). It enervated the social reform movement known as Progressivism, which provided the soil in which services were first nurtured and grew.

Supportive social services emerged distinctly yet idiosyncratically in the first two decades of the twentieth century. They were stimulated by the concerns of certain groups of established Americans about the societal effects of massive immigration, the living and working conditions of the urban poor, and a variety of social problems associated with urban poverty. Social services were shaped in reaction to, and yet they also clearly grew out of and borrowed from, predominant nineteenth-century problem-solving approaches, particularly the use of institutions. As Allen (1994) suggests, helping services represented in part a shift from old, concrete and physical forms of social control to new, more abstract ones, with the same purposes and effects.

Services were one expression of the powerful reform impulses of the Progressive era. They were an expression of a growing belief that science and technology could help solve social problems. They were also a response to the felt need for new models of social relations appropriate to an increasingly urban, industrial society. Not least, they reflected a growing tendency in American reform to transform political and economic problems into cultural and psychological ones. The helping relationship would be a new means for reforming society.

Services created, and themselves were elaborated by, a new profession: that of professional helper—settlement worker, case worker, home economist, visiting teacher, child psychologist. As Rein (1983:139) puts it, "people appeared whose main business was to help other people develop and adapt to the complexities of modern society." The new helping professionals gradually staked out certain social territory, notably family and community life, and then wrestled with the local political machines, religious institutions, and charitable organizations for control of that territory. These new professionals did not just react to evident problems associated with poverty, they identified new ones. They focused more than had past reformers on the psychological life of families and the reasons for the decisions and behavior of family members. They argued that poor families could not raise their children properly without outside help, nor use material assistance appropriately without guidance and supervision.

The new professional helpers had what Sullivan (1995) calls a civic view of the professional's role in society. Expertise was to be used in the service of broad social ends—not just addressing specific social needs and problems but strengthening democracy and reconstructing urban society. At the same time, in order to establish themselves as a profession, they strove to develop a "monopoly of credibility" (Wenocur and Reisch 1989:7). They argued for the inherent superiority of their specialized knowledge and its accompanying method over moral exhortation. They argued that professional social service agencies were best equipped to embody "all the organized helpfulness of their communities" (Kahn 1928:185). And they argued that only those within the profession were qualified to evaluate its work.

Even as services were emerging, proponents of different visions were fighting over their assumptions, purpose, and organization. Many of the contrasting impulses and dilemmas that would be part of the service experience throughout the twentieth century were present from the outset. Providers argued about what model services should be built on: caring parent, fellow community member, or disinterested technical specialist. They struggled with the question of how to interpret and respond to families' economic vulnerability. They struggled with the issue of whether to respond straightforwardly to obvious support needs or to view those needs as an opportunity to intervene more dramatically in families' lives. They argued about whether they should be agents of society, of families served, or both.

Conceptual debates within services would become an important vehicle for working out a twentieth-century ideology regarding poverty: its meaning causes, and individual and social consequences; its types and categories; the best way to address it; and the distribution of responsibility for doing so. As a vehicle for interpreting poverty, the developments and struggles within services were also a vehicle for interpreting single motherhood, ethnicity, and cultural difference. Beyond the debates, the conceptual frameworks, institutions, and approaches established by the first formal helpers provided a template for addressing poverty that would prove enduring, even after it came to be seen as problematic in many ways. The therapeutic view of the poor established in the early decades of the twentieth century would shape poverty-related social policy for the remainder of the century. (This policy would evolve into a perception that the poor were inherently vulnerable. In turn this perception would lead to the ambivalence about expectations of the poor that has plagued poverty-related social policy since the 1950s.) The therapeutic view also would lead, albeit indirectly, to inordinate expectations of helping services as a vehicle for addressing poverty and related social problems.

## Nineteenth-Century Roots

Twentieth-century approaches to service provision for poor families have been shaped in part by nineteenth-century interpretations of and responses to the growth of urban poverty. These themselves derived from a lethal combination of late eighteenth-century economic theory and a religious ethic preoccupied with the weaknesses—and at the same time the malleablity—of the human character. This combination of theories held that each individual was responsible for his or her own interests and fate. Inequality was not just natural, but was one of the costs of progress, tempered by an invisible hand in which the wealthy "without knowing it, advance the interests of society" (Smith 1759: IV.1.10). Hard work was the key to moral improvement, personal salvation, and social progress. There was no room in the "busy world" for "social drones who prey upon the industry of others" (Lubove 1965:8). If one (or one's family) was poor it was due to personal character deficiencies. Although some groups of people were inherently superior to others, individual deficiencies were nonetheless not fixed. They could be addressed through will power, personal effort, and working harder (regardless of how hard someone was already working).

English poor law principles and practices were added to the mix of ideas underlying early efforts to address urban poverty. These principles included the idea of compassion as a moral sentiment, rather than a political principle, and therefore something that had to be watched over carefully (see Himmelfarb 1991); the belief that providing material assistance to people led inexorably to dependence; the practice of localized responsibility for the poor, embodied by public representatives (superintendents or overseers) who would guard community interests; and a preoccupation with distinguishing between deserving and undeserving poor, and between poverty and pauperism. The provision of "indoor" relief through poorhouses became the dominant programmatic response to urban poverty. A new form of outdoor relief (i.e., material aid) emerged, but it was viewed as a last resort. When provided at all, it involved modest, one-time grants of food, fuel, and occasionally money. Like the poorhouse, it was designed and administered as much to discourage and dissuade people from becoming dependent as to provide support to them.

Early nineteenth-century social reformers, many of whom were ministers or had strong religious ties, were preoccupied with the loss of moral authority and influence over the poor that occurred in urban settings (Polsky 1991:36). They recruited female parishioners to provide assistance and instruction to poor families. Women involved in work with the poor banded together to form the first benevolent societies. In Philadelphia, for example, women from a number of Protestant denominations formed the "Union Society" (Degler 180:300). These early women's organizations nurtured social activism in women that would grow throughout the century and eventually provide the ingredients for the emergence of formal helping services

The prototypes for later outreach approaches within services also can be found in the efforts of early nineteenth-century religious reformers to instruct and supervise the poor. One such effort involved "districting" combined with outreach, intended in part to recreate the informal social control arrangements of small communities in large cities. In 1818 a report of the New York Society for Prevention of Pauperism proposed: "Divide the city into small districts and appoint district visitors who would acquaint themselves with indigent families to advise them with respect to their business, the education of their children, the economy of their houses, and to administer encouragement and admonition" (in Leiby 1978:44).

By mid-century, fundamental changes in the nature of economic activity were laying the groundwork for the later focus of service providers on the interior lives of families. Wage labor shifted the locus of economic production out of the home. With that shift, childrearing, which had been embedded in family economic activity, emerged as a distinct, identifiable function, one reserved for women. In Lasch's (1977) terms, the bourgeois family model (private, child-centered, structurally isolated) emerged as a refuge from the increasingly harsh, uncontrollable, and incomprehensible world of industrial capitalism. The ideal of the protective family was nonetheless belied by the horrendous living and working conditions most families experienced. It was proving harder for poor families to lead decent lives in urban communities than it had been in rural ones. The heightened expectations that women would provide a proper home, which resulted from a growing cult of domesticity, simply added one more source of stress to poor mothers' lives. Moreover, the same forces that were undermining the conditions of family life were undermining the traditional means families and communities had used to cope with problems (Katz 1983 1993).

Childrearing among the poor was added to laziness, improvidence, and godlessness as a focus for reformers' scrutiny and worry, and would remain so for the next century and a half. Intervention emphases would alternate between strengthening, supplementing, and supplanting the family, with the emphasis at any moment a function of prevailing social preoccupations and reaction to previous efforts. No matter what the emphasis of the moment, it was assumed that those in authority had a right to scrutinize and monitor childrearing in poor families and when necessary intervene to instruct and even discipline parents.

Periods of more intense social reform in the United States have often been set in motion by a rise in public concern about particular social trends. Such concern was stimulated in the mid-nineteenth century by a wave of immigration from Europe to major cities in the East and Midwest. This migration was mostly caused by a combination of rapid population growth and economic displacement associated with industrialization in Europe (Kennedy 1996:57–58). With this migration the deeply rooted ambivalence toward immigrants that would shape immigration policy and social welfare assumptions more generally first appeared. Immigrants were viewed simultaneously as the source of America's economic and social vitality and as "degraded, freeloading louts, a blight on the national character and a drain on the economy" (Kennedy 1996:56).

Initially, responding to the support needs of immigrant families fell to existing modest structures, including benevolent societies, women's clubs, and city missions. The latter shifted their emphasis (somewhat) from religious instruction to more practical actions, such as providing food, fuel, and clothing (Chambers 1985). Yet even such expanded efforts seemed an inadequate response to the problems brought by and associated with exploding numbers of poor immigrants—congested slums, illicit behavior, intemperance, crime, unsupervised and vagrant children, epidemics of disease. Social observers warned of the negative internal effects, as well as the threat to social order and stability, posed by large numbers of poor people concentrated together in particular neighborhoods (Katz 1995:67).

Reformers pursued a number of courses in addressing what was seen as the crisis of slum life. Some reformers urged the poor to leave the cities for the countryside. This had little effect. Scrutiny of childrearing among the poor increased, and became the self-appointed responsibility of numerous private organizations, most notably Societies for the Prevention of Cruelty to Children (SPCCs, modeled on and at times departments of local Societies for Prevention of Cruelty to Animals). More fundamentally, reformers decided that the environment had to be changed for as many poor families as possible. To prevent immediate transmission of disease and intergenerational transmission of harmful parental and neighborhood values and behaviors, children had to be separated from unhealthy influences, which could mean their parents as well as their neighborhoods. Deviant adults should be removed from the community, rehabilitated, and returned to it.

Thus emerged the perceived need to build institutions. Poorhouses existed in urban areas, but they had proven an inadequate vehicle for meeting the specialized needs of different populations. Of particular concern, children often ended up in poorhouses by default, since the rule that entering parents give their children up for adoption was unworkable and sometimes resisted by parents (Silberman 1990:9). A more differentiated institutional network was created, to separate different populations and to achieve the differing combinations of protection, socialization, education, rehabilitation, control, and punishment viewed as appropriate for each. Orphanages, half-orphanages, foundling hospitals and foundling homes, infirmaries, workhouses, industrial schools, homes for unwed mothers, reform schools, refuges, asylums, even police stations became vehicles for achieving these different purposes.

Nonresidential institutions continued played a modest role in efforts to educate and protect subgroups of the poor. Some city missions began specializing—in widows with young children, pregnant teens, half-orphans, or street children (Chambers 1985:10). Infant Schools were started, to serve young children of poor working parents. Their aim was not only to provide child care, but to "remove children [sic] from the unhappy association of want and vice," and place them "under better influences" (Cahan 1989:9). The first day nurseries emerged in New York and a few other cities (although most would not provide full-time care until the 1880s. For instance, the New York Nursery primarily provided room and board for the young children of wet nurses, a group at particular risk of infant mortality because their mothers could not breast feed them; Prochner 1996:9).

Most specific institutions were founded by private, religiously rooted, reform organizations, filling a void left by the lack of a public social welfare framework and response. Since they argued that they were meeting a public as well as a religious purpose, these organizations eventually sought some public funding for their activities (Sutton 1988:46). In this they were helped by their argument that institutions were efficient, concentrating people in need of supervision, behavioral change, health care, or other services together. They were helped also by their visibility, which (at least superficially) made them seem real and "comprehensible" as problem-solving vehicles (Monkkonen 1993).

What began as reasonable, if not adequate efforts to deal with problems of urban poverty quickly lost perspective or were overwhelmed. Local Societies for the Prevention of Cruelty to Children (SPCCs) made a contribution to the articulation of children's rights. However, they were as preoccupied with the normative childrearing behavior of poor, immigrant parents as they were with extreme cases of child abuse; they were also as enamored of their own power. SPCC agents "acted like police in countless small ways . . . They threatened families with arrest or with taking custody of children. They regularly interviewed neighbors and relatives, attempting to entrap them into damaging statements about those under investigation" (Gordon 1988:55). They sometimes "tried to persuade local judges to take children from parents on the slightest pretense, frequently in opposition to the views of other agencies" (Katz 1983:193–194). Not surprisingly, SPCC agents were both feared and hated by the families who were the focus of their attention.

The great majority of specialized institutions gradually lost whatever protective, educational, or rehabilitative ideals they had begun with. Their superintendents were very budget-conscious (Morton 1993:32). As the proportion of public funding increased, every decision was viewed in light of consequences for taxpayers. This led to such cost-cutting efforts as reducing the amount of fruit and milk in resident children's diets. Rather than serving as havens against unhealthy influences, institutions became breeding grounds for them. Overcrowding, close quarters, and inadequate diet contributed to frequent illness and high rates of mortality. (Some foundling hospitals were little more than places to which infants were sent to die of neglect and disease.) Little rehabilitation or education went on in many institutions, and the environment of many was cold and harsh. For example, it was common for children to be forbidden to speak at meals. Institutions' excessive regimentation and harsh treatment of residents came to be viewed as "destructive of [those key American traits] initiative and individuality" (Gittens 1986:41).

Institutions' visibility became more of a liability than an asset, since the gap between their rhetoric and their actual practices and conditions was easy to see. Observers documented incompetent and corrupt administration. Institutions that started out for specific purposes and populations over time became undifferentiated "catchalls" for any type of marginal community member (Garten and Otto 1964).

A few institutions worked reasonably well. These became "integral parts of their communities," involving community leaders in their oversight," working to keep siblings together and children in touch with their parents (Zmora 1994:7). The networks of residential settings run by Evangelical women for young, unmarried mothers were also relatively helpful (Kunzel 1993), as, more selectively, were infant schools. But even these latter two institutions experienced problems. Some residential homes for teen mothers could be warm and accepting; many others were cold if not harsh settings, with "long confinements, religious instruction, domestic chores, [and] rigid rules" (Morton 1993:13). Physical and social conditions in the majority of infant schools were inadequate. The large number of young children enrolled in some centers, combined with long hours—often from early morning till dark—resulted in little more than custodial care for a good part of the day.

Families tried to use institutions to their own ends, for example asking them to care for their children during a period of extreme hardship. Orphanages, for example, were as likely to care for destitute as for orphaned children. Yet it proved difficult for families to use institutions to meet their own self-determined needs without becoming ensnared in the logic and practices of the institutions from which they were seeking help. In some instances, destitute mothers who wished to place their children in orphanages were required to give up their parental rights. When, as was not uncommon, they were reluctant to do so, this was seen as evidence that they lacked love for their children and perhaps should have them forcibly taken away (Gittens 1986:24). A few orphanages acknowledged the importance and supported the maintenance of parent-child bonds. For example, Chicago's Nursery and Half Orphan Asylum viewed its mission as providing a kind of extended respite care for some children. It not only did not insist that parents relinquish their rights, but insisted that parents visit at least bi-weekly (Cmiel 1995:22). Such institutions, however, were the exception that proved the rule.

It was hard to know how long particular institutional experiences should last and who should determine lengths of stay. If the idea was to remove children or adults from unhealthy environments, that would seem to require long stays, so those children or adults would simply not return to those environments. Yet long stays limited the number that could be served and was costly. Conversely, some institutions designed to provide temporary refuge found themselves sheltering children or adults for months or even years, since providing refuge did not address the causes of peoples' difficulties.

In spite of their growth, institutions never replaced public and private outdoor relief, which continued both to meet needs and to serve as a target of many reformers' fears and feelings about the poor. The rapidly industrializing economy was throwing off ever larger numbers of marginal and dependent people, increasing the pressures on local public assistance programs (Skocpol 1992:95). Criticism of outdoor relief was fueled by its growing cost, by the fact that it was so visible as a public expense, by its haphazard administration and abuse as a form of patronage, and by the fact that many of those in need of temporary assistance were immigrants. It seemed to some observers that assistance was granted too freely and easily and that the same families were seeking assistance over and over (Monkkonen 1993:341). It seemed to some that use of public assistance was "contagious," spreading from household to household on a particular block (Kusmer 1973:661).

For neither the first nor the last time, public assistance at the end of the nineteenth century was criticized not just as misguided but as worsening the problems it was intended to address. Josephine Shaw Lowell, a leading advocate of private charity, wrote in 1884 that "poverty and suffering are increased and even caused by the relief intended to cure them" (Lowell 1884:58). Public assistance, she argued, led poor people to expect more than they were actually given, thereby "relaxing their habits." Responding to cases of real hardship served to let into the system "a whole class of fraudulent cases." In general the moral and spiritual harm caused by providing relief was greater then the economic benefit of such provision (ibid.:59). Charles Loring Brace (1872:22–23] argued that government was unable to administer aid with sufficient discretion and that financial and other material assistance was "useless" if it did not affect poor peoples' character and habits. (While Brace railed against public aid, he gladly accepted government dollars. Over half the 1887 budget of his Children's Aid Society—

$109,000 out of $200,000—came from various government funding sources; Bush 1988:71).

## Scientific Charity

Criticism of institutions and of prevailing public assistance practices contributed to the rise of the scientific charity movement and the Charity Organization Societies (COSs). Providing charity scientifically meant discriminating between those individuals more and those less deserving of assistance, and careful calibration of relief, so as to promote thrift and self-denial and to prevent dependence and moral corruption. It required balancing individual needs with a more abstract common good. And it meant sometimes curbing one's compassion and generosity in the best interests of those asking for help (Himmelfarb 1991). Proponents of scientific charity contrasted it with the unpredictability and excess of social reform. Lubove (1965:11) cites COS leader Mary Richmond, who warned COS workers not to be "swept away by enthusiastic advocates of social reform from that safe middle ground which recognizes that character is at the very center of social problems."

One principal line of action of the Charity Organization Societies was the development of central registries of those seeking assistance from different agencies and institutions within a city. These registries were intended to coordinate and monitor (in effect gain control over and reduce the municipal government role in) relief. In at least a few cities they were intended also to serve as a vehicle for "confidential communication among agencies . . . interested in a family," for the purpose of coordinating advice (Reynolds 1963:29). COS agents also carried out thorough investigations of all relief-seekers. These investigations included interviews with neighbors and efforts to determine if there was any extended family to help provide relief.

A third line of action involved efforts to reach out to individual families to provide instruction, guidance, and supervision through "friendly visiting" by well-to-do women. The friendly visitor was not just to "expound" such virtues as thrift but to "demonstrate" them; for example, planning a future outing that the family could look forward to, thus teaching family members to delay gratification (Boyer 1978:153). The other side of friendly visiting was an implicit and sometimes explicit threat: cooperate, follow our advice, express deference, or we might use our influence to recommend denial of assistance or even removal of children from the home. Local COS offices also provided some concrete services, for example "labor bureaus" and day nurseries.

The various efforts of COS practice were linked by a desire to bridge the gulf between social classes and the belief that provision of relief by strangers somehow deepened the gulf—in fact that it actually caused the separation of society into classes (Kusmer 1973:661). This desire to reconcile social classes certainly stemmed in part from the unprecedented labor conflicts of the era, both the anger and militancy of the strikers and the violent responses of the large corporations. Gettleman (1963:313) argues that COS workers "recognized [sic] in practice the gulf between social classes," but nonetheless pursued "its bourgeois vision of a classless society dominated by norms of middle class gentility."

The COS strategies appealed particularly to small businessmen interested in both fighting local government fraud and corruption and reducing public expenditures. Although the Charity Organization Societies did gain a measure of control over distribution of relief in many cities, their abstract ideology and intent was not implemented uniformly. Proponents of scientific charity criticized the assistance provided by local political machines as too idiosyncratic, but the quality and quantity of COS assistance also varied. The personal dispositions of local charity agents interacted with the variety of family situations to shape the amount and kind of relief granted. In general, what material relief was provided was doled out in small amounts, enough to keep a family "just above starvation" (Katz 1983:42). New forms of "fraud" replaced old ones. In some cases the moral calculus used by a COS for providing aid forced people to lie, mostly out of desperation. Thus, in order to increase her chances of being approved, a deserted mother might say she was a widow (see Katz 1993:60–61).

Other child and family welfare organizations, such as the Catholic and Jewish charities, worked with local charity organization societies in particular cases, but maintained their independence. These other organizations wanted to preserve their primacy in serving particular religious or ethnic groups. They also wanted to maintain their own funding. As a result, relief and other forms of support to poor families remained extraordinarily decentralized in many cities. For example, in addition to municipal government programs in Philadelphia at the turn of the century, there were still "103 relief societies, 62 children's charities, 96 hospitals and health agencies, 78 homes for adults .. not to mention the 865 churches and missions and 265 other religious associations" (cited in "The Family," February 1929:329).

The COS movement was not monolithic. Edward T. Devine, the general secretary of the New York COS, wrote that poor people seeking relief "should not be set the problem of analyzing the psychological eccentricities of possible donors (Devine 1904:17). The COS emphasis on self-help sometimes had positive dimensions. In 1905 the COS in Indiannapolis donated a large plot of vacant land and seeds to a group of seventy-five African-American families associated with a local settlement house. The project yielded a productive communal garden (Crocker 1992:81). Nonetheless, the majority of COS leaders, if not always their frontline agents, seemed to have an inherently "critical spirit" (Leiby 1978). They displayed a distrust for the poor that had nothing to do with the facts of poor families' lives. This distrust was due in part to the influence of their own religious background and beliefs and in part to the fact that many of the growing number of urban poor were Catholic and foreign-born. Bremmer (1972:11) notes that the charity community's preoccupation with immigrants' mores and behavior "tended to obscure fundamental economic questions in a fog of religious and national prejudices."

The premises and practices of scientific charity were dealt a severe setback by the depression of 1893–94, in which over three million workers were thrown out of work. The depression made it starkly clear that unemployment, hunger, and homelessness were not caused by overly generous relief or deficient personal character. Lane (1973:39) points out that for the first time, some involved in helping the poor let "empirical evidence, rather than their philosophy . . . dictate their actions." Still, many in the COS movement resisted what they were observing and criticized the emergency relief efforts that mobilized to help destitute families. One COS leader noted that "the results of years of work by the COS may be swept away in one season of unusual distress by sentimentalists" (Olasky 1992:127).

The principles of scientific charity would be harshly criticized by the Progressives who came to dominate reform between the turn of the century and World War I. Yet as Kusmer (1973:657) points out, scientific charity was not a "detour" on the way to the modern welfare state. The COS movement introduced the idea of the helping relationship as a means of reforming society, family by family. The experience of firsthand work with the poor affected some COS workers and leaders who went on to play a role in the formation of social services. The Charity Organization Societies as institutions provided the infrastructure for emergent child and family casework agencies. Not least, the beliefs underlying scientific charity—particularly the fear of creating dependency, and the view of work as a kind of salvation—would constrain social welfare debate throughout the twentieth century.

## Social Change and Social Reform at the Turn of the Century

The two decades surrounding the turn of the century were unsettling in a host of ways. Deep economic recessions and depression, continuing, periodic labor unrest, new political movements, widespread government corruption, massive immigration, and chaotic urban growth all contributed to a feeling that America's economic and social life was out of control. The nineteenth-century faith in the potential of industrial capitalism to increase the economic well-being of all, or even the majority of Americans was dissipating, at least for the moment. It was clear that corporations' interest in the well-being of their workers extended no further than the boundaries of corporate self-interest. Almost half of all Americans still lived in poverty; only now as wage laborers they had even less control over their working lives. Neither urging the poor to leave the cities, nor rehabilitative institutions, nor the calibrated relief and moral suasion of charity workers had proven effective in reducing poverty-related social problems.

It was not only persistent, ubiquitous poverty that was so problematic. It was also the hardening patterns of economic insecurity and hardship associated with industrial capitalism—dangerous working conditions leading to frequent injury and illness, subsistence-level wages, periodic, unpredictable joblessness—complicated by urban living conditions and immigration. Families were increasingly vulnerable to broad economic cycles. Katz (1993:56) notes that many working-class families "experienced recurrent spells of dependence" and all lived "on the verge of dependence." In an analysis of 300 case records of families that had had contact with the Minneapolis family service agency, Stadum (1990:89) found that three fourths of family heads had work only intermittently.

Half the population of some major cities were immigrants (Wenocur and Reisch 1989:22). Immigrants seemed willing to subject themselves and their children to anything in order to gain a toehold in American life. They often lived under horrible conditions, in congested, airless, lightless apartments, and accepted exhausting, low-paying, debilitating work. Patterson (1986:4) quotes from a 1905 article in "Charities," a COS journal by charity agent Anne Daniels: "I attended [in her home] a woman ill with tuberculosis, finishing trousers. . . . Three years of life in this apartment killed the woman. . . . The other day a little girl of 8 years was dismissed from the diptheria hospital after a severe attack of the disease. Almost immediately she was working at women's collars, although scarcely able to walk across the room."

The poor immigrant neighborhood embodied all the concerns of those worried about social disorder. Beyond the congestion and filthy streets, life in such neighborhoods was seen to lead to the breakdown of family life and the weakening of the social fabric. Mobility was high, mothers frequently worked long hours, children were unsupervised, and desertion by husbands appeared to be common. Studies around the turn of the century reported that "up to one fifth of women with children seeking relief assistance had been deserted by their husbands (Chase-Lansdale and Vinovkis, undated:17). Such desertion was not always permanent and was sometimes tied to men's search for work. It did however contribute to the impression of family and community instability.

In reality, immigrants residing in poor neighborhoods did what they could to recreate traditional institutional forms of mutual assistance and support and to invent new ones. They turned the family once again into a collective economic unit of sorts—for example, contracting as a unit for piecework. They created mutual assistance societies and relied on landlords, merchants, and social agencies, as well as friends and relatives (Katz 1995:166). But these economic strategies and social resources, while helpful in staving off destitution, were fragile, shifting, and unpredictable.

## The Response of Progressive Reformers

Progressivism highlighted the core issues—and limitations—in American social problem solving more clearly than any reform movement before or since. Progressivism encompassed diverse groups of reformers, with diverse visions of society and and specific concerns. The latter included reigning in corporate monopolies, reducing municipal corruption, securing the vote for women, banning alcohol and saloons, assimilating immigrants, restricting immigration, protecting workers, regulating tenements, public health reform, child labor reform, and family preservation. Yet underlying the specific emphases and preoccupations were common concerns and clear limits.

Progressives were dismissive of nineteenth-century problem solving efforts, not just because of their harshness but because of their narrow objectives. The charity organization societies, and to a lesser extent the residential institutions, viewed themselves as providing limited, temporary aid and support until families could get back on their own feet. Progressives claimed that this approach avoided the heart of poverty-related social problems, which they in turn would not avoid (Cmiel 1995). In this they were disingenuous, for Progressive reform involved an effort to find apolitical explanations for and approaches to addressing the essentially political problems experienced by the most vulnerable members of American society. It involved a search for problem-solving objectives and approaches that did not question the basic tenets of American life: the primacy of the marketplace, individual responsibility, the value of work in shaping character (and conversely the harm of nonwork); adherence to middle-class norms in domestic life; and, in the civic sphere the existence of a public interest that transcended the interests of specific contending groups.

Finding nonthreatening objectives and approaches required rationalization. Thus Progressives argued that social and economic problems were due not to American ideals but to the distortion of those ideals. Working conditions and wages were so abysmal because employers simply lacked understanding that good working conditions and wages were in their own, as well as in workers' interest. Until those with economic power recognized this community of interest, the most useful thing reformers could do was was to strengthen vulnerable families' capacity to accept their situation and to cope with and adapt to existing arrangements. Because many vulnerable families were immigrants, this rationalization was couched in terms of the need for cultural assimilation.

The majority of Progressive reformers were more interested in reconciliation among groups than in fighting for the interests of any particular group. For example, when organized labor chose to focus on the needs of its members rather than more broadly on the conditions of life for working-class Americans, that left no obvious interest group to do so (Ehrenreich 1985). The Progressive movement could have filled this void; yet it did not. It was too diverse in composition and interests, and its leaders had a distaste for the violence and disorder that sometimes accompanied workers' efforts to secure decent wages, greater job security, and improved working conditions. Progressives were supportive of workers in specific ways—for example, providing material aid to workers and their families during strikes or helping to organize women's trade unions. They were concerned about issues of economic exploitation and distributive justice. But their primary strategy was to address these issues indirectly, by protecting children and families from the consequences, by shaping and supervising family life in poor families, and by preparing children to compete in a competitive economic system. Progressives tried to create a counterweight to the marketplace and its values, by strengthening what they viewed as the noneconomic spheres of society, particularly family and community.

It has been argued that Progressivism was strongly shaped by the world view and preoccupations of the middle-class women who played key roles in that reform movement (Lasch 1965; Skocpol 1993:18). Broad concerns about regulating corporations and over general working conditions were translated into the types of issues to which women were attuned. Thus a central focus of labor law reform was protection of female workers' "capacity for motherhood" (Skocpol 1993:4). Women reformers focused on issues that they assumed most affected poor women's and children's lives—tenement reform, public health campaigns, maternal and child health services, compulsory schooling, Mothers' Pensions, child care. Progressive "maternalists'" reform agenda derived from a complex mix of beliefs and fears: a longstanding belief in separate spheres for men and women; a belief that the quality of home life was the key to societal well-being; fear of the social consequences of too many mothers working; and fear of the social effects of immigration. Ladd-Taylor (1994:50) cites Hannah Schoff, president of the National Congress of Mothers, and a reform leader, who argued that "every wrong condition that confronts our nation . . . infant mortality, juvenile delinquency, increase in divorce, race suicide, municipal and political corruption . . . has its root in the kind of care and training received in the home."

Concerns about motherhood and poor mothers were bound in contradictions that would shape supportive services for the rest of the century. While clearly committed to supporting poor families in their efforts to cope and meet family needs, Progressives lacked faith in those same families, both generally in their ability to define and meet their own needs and specifically in their childrearing goals and capacities. Progressive reformers, especially those involved with the settlement movement, viewed the lives of poor families in a more complex fashion than had their predecessors. They saw and commented on the coping and adaptation, and on parents' sacrifices for their children. The literature of the time is full of descriptions of poor immigrant women working long days at exhausting jobs—as domestics, washerwomen, seamstresses—while simultaneously managing inadequate budgets, keeping their homes clean and their children fed, and dealing with constant problems and emergencies.

At the same time these reformers viewed the coping strategies of poor families—taking in boarders, pulling children out of school to work, moving frequently (to stay one step ahead of constables or to find more affordable housing)—as more harmful than helpful. They focused on "parents too busy and too insensitive to supervise their children properly," vulnerable children, and adults exposed to immoral influences (Ryerson 1978:24). Poor families' practices did not reflect prevailing prescriptions for toilet training, child management and discipline, feeding, care of illnesses, and household budgeting. Poor parents were viewed as lacking the capacity to prepare their children for the demands of a democratic society and a complex industrial economy.

In a kind of mental trick, coping strategies that were the result of inadequate income were converted from consequences to causal factors, explaining why certain groups were poor and struggling. Reformers shifted their attention from broad problems such as working conditions to specific, visible ones, particularly the often alien behavior of immigrants: "Russians preserved their Old World custom of nailing windows shut; Italians built shelves in already cramped flats to serve as beds for their lodgers; and various immigrant fed their infants beer, wine, or garlic water to ward off disease" (Kirschner 1986:30). Reformers argued that tenement reform would be fruitless without making people "capable of using a better tenement" (Ladd-Taylor 1994:50).

Progressive reformers did sometimes raise basic questions in their writings: They asked who benefited from the conditions of work and of daily life experienced by the poor; why so many were squeezed between unaffordable rents and low wages; why whole families were forced to work ten- or twelve-hour days doing piece work. At the same time they typically argued that poverty was due to the fact that the United States was a socially "misorganized" or "misarranged" society, or was due to lack of communication between groups (Levine 1971:137, 160), Progressives occasionally acknowledged more fundamental reasons. Edward T. Devine wrote that "the sting of modern poverty in prosperous communities is precisely that it is not necessary, that it is the result of social neglect, of industrial exploitation, of maladministration in government, or an obsolete system of education" (Devine 1907:463).

Yet at heart Progressives reflected American society's basic ambivalence about poverty and poor people. The well-known reformer Jacob Riis embodied in one person many of the contradictions in Americans' feelings about poverty at the time (Lane 1973). Riis recognized the broad forces acting on the poor but still mistook coping and adaptation for laziness or worse. He was both wary of the harshness and coldness of scientific charity and disdainful of the seeming inability of the poor themselves to act wisely. He believed simultaneously that those who would help the poor should trust them, and that the poor should make more effort to help themselves. While skeptical of the motives and means of private philanthropy, he believed that it kept helpers closer to their clients.

Progressives consistently failed to acknowledge the full implications of their social critiques. At one level they continued to insist that the solution to economic exploitation was a new social ethic to which all groups and classes would subscribe. At another level, even while acknowledging that social and economic conditions made an ideal family life impossible for poor families, they continued to focus far more on those families' mores and behaviors than on the social conditions affecting them (Grubb and Lazerson 1980). Remaking people became the central approach to remaking society. And, as would be the case throughout the twentieth century, addressing inequality became partly, if not largely, a matter of by-passing the well-being and prospects of the present generation and focusing on those of the next.

Rothman (1978:69–70) describes the Progressives' approach as more focused on poor families' needs than on their rights. He argues that "a reform platform that looked to needs expanded the boundaries of political intervention, legitimating a wide range of ameliorative action. . . . But the concept cut two ways: those in need of help were more or less like children." This view of poor families could be found in some reformers' descriptions of them. The author of a 1910 study of living conditions in immigrant neighborhoods of Indiannapolis observed that "Like young children, they [immigrants] should have their actions regulated by authority until they reach a point of understanding" (Leander Adams, cited in Crocker 1992:50). While no longer judged in nineteenth-century terms (i.e., as innocent or guilty), poor people still were seen to need guidance by others who knew what was best for them. They required such parentlike supervision not because of a specific transgression but because of their general status.

## Intellectual Foundations

Two other threads in Progressivism—threads that contributed to the emergence of social services in a variety of ways—inadvertently reinforced the prevailing reluctance to view and address poverty as a political problem. These were Progressivism's experimental spirit, complemented by faith in scientific knowledge and method as keys to social progress, and the unusual role played by the philosophical school known as Pragmatism. Scientific method offered the hope that problems of distributive justice might be resolved through technical means. Moreover, it was seen to be ideologically neutral; it could as easily be harnessed for good as for evil purposes (Wenocur and Reisch 1989:88). Pragmatism, whose best known proponent was John Dewey, mixed with the ideas of Charles Darwin, provided the intellectual foundations for Progressives' approach to reform.

The basic thesis of Pragmatism was that the truth of an idea or belief depended on "its usefulness in making sense of experience and guiding action, not on its correspondence to an ultimate reality that exists outside or beyond our existence" (Sandel 1996:35). This thesis in turn promoted the idea of facing social problems practically, nonhistorically, and nonideologically; of trying to find whatever worked, based on the exigencies of the immediate situation (Diggins 1994:2). Although Darwin's ideas permeated intellectual culture at the turn of the century, different people focused on very different aspects of his work. The Progressives focused on two related ideas. The first was that the physical and social environment was critical in shaping behavior. This implied that the cause of social problems, and therefore the appropriate focus of problem-solving, was not faulty character but bad environments. The second was the idea of adaptation: human beings and human groups were capable of change as they "adapted to [changing] conditions around them" (Levine 1971:94).

Together, these two sets of ideas suggested to Progressive reformers that since society was changing rapidly, and traditional sources of authority (and problem-solving) were weakening, the best response was to experiment with new ways of maintaining social order, promoting democracy, rearing children, and helping people find their proper place in the industrial order. The city would become a laboratory for the creation of new institutions and the reform of old ones (Sullivan 1995:72). Social science knowledge and methods, employed by a growing network of dispassionate but socially engaged professionals, would find new solutions to social problems.

The Pragmatists also believed that intellectuals, by virtue of their intelligence, had an important role in and responsibility for improving society. In part what Dewey an his colleagues meant was that adherents of their intellectual ideas were better suited than eighteenth-century liberal economists or nineteenth-century religious philosophers and charity organizations to develop a constructive social welfare framework. Neither Adam Smith's perfect market nor religious authority provided adequate bases for understanding and addressing social problems. Individuals acting in their own self-interest were not being guided by an invisible hand to promote the common good. The "scope and complexity" of urban problems was "too vast to be handled by the impulse of benevolent individuals" (Lubove 1965:158).

In retrospect, Pragmatism has proven to be just as inadequate a tool for social policy development as liberal economic theory (and moral conservatism). It turns out that while social problem-solving does indeed have to be partly inductive, some firm set of beliefs and assumptions still has to guide the choice of problem-solving approaches. The question then becomes who has the power to name and explain the problem. There are genuine differences in the interests and values that shape problem-solving that cannot be glossed over. Also, as Sullivan (1995:75) points out, Dewey's vision of "a future of public-spirited experts seeking to assist the lay public in discovering itself" and solving social problems was naive. The new professionals would quickly become preoccupied with their own survival and growth. (Citing Edward Devine, the COS leader, Lasch [1965:148], notes that the new helping professionals were just as excited about the "mutual discovery of one another's existence" as they were about their actual work with poor families.) Moreover, what poor Americans needed was not self-discovery, nor scientific rationalizations for assembly lines in which they repeated the same small task hundreds of times a day.

Levine and Levine (1992:7) argue that social services "did not start out as conscious extensions" of intellectual currents or scientific theories. In their view, services originated primarily as those involved in work with the poor struggled to find practical responses to family problems. Nonetheless, service providers' ambitions and approaches were indirectly influenced by the broad intellectual currents of their era and directly undergirded by the concerns, knowledge base, and methods emerging in sociology and psychology. These disciplines provided "a set of instructions for family life" that was far more precise than that provided by moral prescriptions (Meyer 1977:12). They provided the rationale, concepts, and language for sorting and categorizing people and therefore individualizing the experience of poverty.

The "contributions" of social science underlay the helping approach that emerged as social casework. One writer would liken social caseworkers to "social microbe hunters" patiently observing to find the causes of social ills and then experimenting to remedy them (Johnson 1926:232). The view of motherhood as a science (as well as a profession) fueled the various forms of parent education that thrived during the early decades of the century. Information on scientific home management and correct childrearing was purveyed through "a flood of pamphlets, articles and books" (Grubb and Lazerson 1980:22). Organizations such as the National Congress of Mothers and the Child Study Association of America brought mothers together for "study groups." In some locales, experienced study group members would make home visits to poor parents to share state-of-the-art childrearing information (Thomas and Thomas 1928:309). Meanwhile, a different kind of more inductive, situation-specific experimentation was emerging in the settlements, which, though drawing on social science, was more grounded in community life.

# CHAPTER TWO

# Formative Strands: Settlements, Casework, and Mothers' Aid

*At first the helpers used the words that everyone used. But as they helped
they began to notice peculiarities among the poor, and they gave them
names. The world of the helped was transformed . . .*

*[The poor became] more and more dependent on the rule makers, but
they themselves no longer knew their reality. Besides being poor, they were
ignorant of the ways in which their lives were conceptualized.*

—Salvador Minuchin, 1995

*The mother of five or six children may, with some reason, be inclined to
think that she knows a little more about how to bring up children than the
young-looking damsel who insists on trying to teach her how to do it.*

—a pastor who worked with Italian immigrant families,
cited in Ruth Crocker

## The Settlement Response

As the paradigmatic institutions of the Progressive era, settlements embodied the energy and contradictions of Progressivism. They were innovative and conservative. Their practices reflected "social control with a conscience" (Borris 1992). Settlements strove to recreate in urban settings the
healthier forms of civic life, social organization, and control characteristic
of small towns and rural communities. At the same time, some settlement
leaders, such as Jane Addams, believed that what the immigrants they
served needed were not the "old pieties of small-town America" but a better "understanding of the industrial metropolis" (Sullivan 1995:76). The
most vulnerable among the poor—mothers and children—also needed a
measure of protection against the negative or harmful influences of the
urban environment.

It has been argued that settlements had no clear mission or theoretical
framework for helping others, beyond the general notion of acting as neigh-

bors and the "whatever works" of Pragmatic philosophy. As the head resident of a settlement in Minneapolis noted, "a settlement is democratic, scientific and practical" (Karger 1987:xii, 57). Lack of a preexisting theory was almost a point of pride in the settlement move ment. Settlements viewed themselves as laboratories for the creation of new problem-solving approaches. Programs and activities evolved from trial and error, the realities of family and neighborhood life, what was learned through research by settlement staff, and what families brought to the settlement. Echoing Dewey, settlement staff argued that in a rapidly changing society, the new members (i.e., immigrants) had "as much to teach their teachers as to learn from them" (Lasch 1965:159). Strong informal networks among settlements allowed ideas that worked in one setting to be "quickly taken up elsewhere" (Chambers 1963:112). Local governments picked up on settlement ideas as well (e.g., playgrounds, lending libraries, and school nurses).

Settlements' pragmatism, and their workers' desire to be useful, contributed to the array of practical services they provided—day nurseries, employment bureaus, English classes, dispensaries, primary health care services, pasteurized milk (which ordinarily was unaffordable to poor families), a place to take a shower, information on local relief policies and procedures and on workmen's compensation, legal assistance, and emergency financial and material relief (including housing). Settlement staff responded to countless emergencies and crises—women in labor, a life-threatening illness in an infant, asthma attacks, abandoned children, job loss, evictions, desertions, children's school problems, husbands' alcoholism, and domestic violence.

Surrounding the practical and emergency assistance were an array of developmental supports for children and adults—sports and hobby clubs; summer camps; dance, drama, and art classes; theatre and other cultural events; and libraries. Settlements pioneered what is today the diverse field of youth work. Their boys' clubs and clubhouses were designed to provide constructive, safe, and yet youth-controlled alternatives to street life for youth prone to join gangs. A variety of other community providers "colocated" themselves at settlements, including public and visiting nurses, Juvenile Court probation staff, and counselors. Community groups, including ethnic associations, used settlement facilities for meetings and sporting events.

Underlying the specific services provided were broader ambitions that derived from the social disorganization and deterioration settlement staff perceived around them, and the deficiencies they perceived in families served. Settlements strove to inculcate "American" childrearing norms in participating families, through activities at the settlement itself and through home visiting by settlement workers and ancillary nursing staff. They took a "two-generation" approach to this task. Day nurseries and kindergartens run by settlements were viewed in part as vehicles for Americanizing immigrant children directly—for example, by teaching them how to wash themselves and brush their teeth and eat new foods, as well as teaching them table manners, bed-making, and the like (Crocker 1992:65). School-aged children ("future mothers") were socialized through clubs for cooking, gardening, housekeeping, sewing, and child-training (sometimes through the use of dolls). Immigrant women were shown "model" apartments and offered classes in home management, hygiene, nutrition, discipline, and toilet training. These classes were sometimes organized by ethnic group, so that parents could receive instruction in their native language. In a practice that foreshadowed the staffings and team meetings seen today in many social agencies, the Henry Street settlement in New York had a "family council," which met to make and review plans for "difficult [family] situations" (Levine and Levine 1992:54).

Settlements also sought to use their institutional presence to stabilize their neighborhoods. They worked to build a sense of public spirit, community, and even local tradition, believing that these were absent (Chambers 1963:112). Settlement leadership and staff campaigned for tenement reform and improved public services for poor communities, and in specific cases advocated for broader reforms in government and corporate practices. Yet although a handful of settlement leaders were politically active, most shared a sense of disenchantment with politics, desiring instead to create "social democracy," people "acting together in a common life" (Leiby 1978:129). Most viewed settlements not as a voice for the powerless but as interpreters, mediators, and reconcilers—between social classes, workers and managers, bureaucrats and clients, tenants and landlords. Settlement staff would interpret the norms and demands of American life to immigrants and the realities of immigrants' lives to the larger American public.

Almost as important as what settlements were and did was what they could not do and see. Although settlements were located in the middle of very poor neighborhoods, their staff were constantly surprised by the extent of the hardship experienced by neighborhood residents. Wukas (1991:12) cites the example of Mary Wilson, a resident in Chicago's Northwestern University settlement, who taught art appreciation classes, at the end of which she would give framed pictures to each child, to take home and have hung on the wall:

One child refused the picture, insisting that she had no walls. Perplexed at the child's repeated claims, Miss Wilson visited the home and found that the family lived in a fourth floor loft, which was occupied by five families. Four of the families occupied the four corners, leaving the center to the child's family, hence, no walls.

Although settlement staff claimed that they were guided by families in their practice, families had little influence on the staff's basic assumptions and goals. Settlement staff prided themselves on their self-reflective and culturally sensitive approach to service provision. They tried to keep their arguments—e.g., for the importance of adopting American childrearing practices—pragmatic, so as not to seem to be attacking immigrants' sense of self and identity. They tried to work from the principle of creating a bridge between immigrants' immediate lives and concerns and the new ideas they wished immigrants to adopt. Yet they never really accepted immigrants' powerful desire to hold on to their ethnic identities (Lissak 1989:182). They never came to question their central goal of Americanizing immigrants. In spite of their sensitivity to social change, settlement leaders and staff viewed American culture as "something already fixed" (Crocker 1992:214).

For their part, immigrant families resisted the Americanizing goals of the settlements in a variety of ways. Attendance in classes designed to teach correct domestic practices was variable (Crocker 1992:59). Of the many areas of their lives, immigrant women felt the least need for instruction in childrearing and home management. The advice and instructions provided by settlement staff and visiting speakers often seemed to contradict what they knew through experience. Husbands also played a role in limiting attendance, viewing supervision of their wives' domestic behavior as their prerogative (Crocker 1992). Even when immigrant mothers attended classes, their domestic practices continued as before.

The efforts of the settlements to Americanize immigrants did not, for the most part, lead to explicitly negative reactions. Participating children and adults were accustomed to treating those with power and education with deference. Immigrants needed and appreciated the settlements' many concrete services and critical assistance with problems. Not least, they too wanted to become American, to master American ways. They simply wanted to become so on terms that allowed them to hold on to their identities, as well as to the security provided by tradition. Thus immigrants tolerated settlement workers' naivete, and worse.

Settlements' pragmatism sometimes meant going along with problematic societal practices rather than challenging them. For instance, they participated in the trend toward development of separate social services for African Americans (Philpott 1978). Settlement leaders argued that there was little point in trying to force people together reluctantly, even though ecumenism was a fundamental principle in immigrant neighborhoods with many ethnic groups. The focus of settlements on work with African Americans often exacerbated racial stereotypes and demonstrated the occasional contradictions of Pragmatism. Flanner House in Indiannapolis developed special programs to train African-American women in scientific domestic practice. This activity was designed to lengthen the life of the job market for domestic servants (the largest for African Americans), which was threatened by the automation that came with new electric appliances (Crocker 1992:90–92)

The decline of Progressive reform after World War I affected the settlements strongly. Settlement leaders became caught up in, and sometimes were targets of, the fears, anger, and xenophobia unexpectedly released by the end of the war. As the number and types of service agencies multiplied in cities, settlements were gradually nudged first off-center and then to the margins of local services networks. Their broad mission, focus on cultural and community activities, lack of helping procedures, and perceived identification with the labor movement all contributed to this marginalization. In order to compete for funds from the emerging local funding federations, settlements gradually converted themselves into (or at least stressed their role as) social service agencies. They created departments and hired specialists. They adopted the language and problem-focus of the emerging social services. (Borris 1992 argues that in reality, settlements' public presentation as community organizations had always masked their simultaneous efforts to become part of the new helping professions.)

Settlements did, however, manage to maintain important parts of their identity as community-based institutions, as well as their generalist approach, well into the 1930s. They continued to provide a variety of practical services to immigrants and continued to serve as a place to go in emergencies. They maintained and even strengthened their commitment to the arts, which they viewed as an "antidote to the mechanical, passive conforming habits of industrialized communities" (Chambers 1963:127). Settlement leaders argued for the central role of settlements as the preventive end of the service continuum. Lea Taylor (1935:474) wrote that "the informality of a settlement approach brings to light many minor problems [such as incipient delinquency or domestic trouble] where early service is essential to prevent the development of major problems." Not least, they continued to serve as sentinels of emergent social problems.

## The Emergence of Social Casework

Social casework, which emerged in the first two decades of the century, was another central strand in supportive social services. Casework grew out of the scientific charity movement—casework leader Mary Richmond had herself been a key COS figure. Although the preoccupations of the charity organization societies had remained the same between the 1880s and the early 1900s, their agents were developing more complex views of poor people (Katz 1983:43). Casework proponents such as Richmond nonetheless chose, perhaps had to choose, to argue that the approach of untrained charity workers was wholly inadequate. Richmond (1917:130) described the interviewing technique of charity workers as a "stupid compiling of misleading items."

Spurred in part by the growing presence of social workers in hospitals, and clearly in search of scientific credibility, Richmond and her colleagues adopted medical terminology for the new field of practice, describing the work in terms of diagnosis and treatment. (Germain 1970:13, speculates that Mary Richmond's close association with two physicians at Johns Hopkins "contributed to her development of the medical or disease metaphor.") Like charity agents, caseworkers would still conduct interviews and collect corollary information about families. But they would do so more skillfully, thoroughly, and objectively; would filter the information through a more sophisticated lens (i.e., one that asked a specific, predetermined set of questions of the information collected); and would strive to be more disciplined in their thought processes. Families' own stories were not to be taken at face value, especially when they led to the obvious conclusion that a family needed financial assistance. Presenting problems or specific requests were to be viewed as doorways into the lives of families rather than as ends in themselves. Describing one illustrative case, in which a family approached a caseworker for help in securing health services, Richmond (1922:101) wrote: "What did the family caseworker responsible for this particular treatment find, in addition to opportunities for health services? She found a husband and wife estranged, a woman discouraged and overburdened, a man worried and unable to make ends meet." Beyond more thorough assessment, caseworkers would work more intensively with families, over a longer period of time, than had their predecessors.

The casework approach and methods clearly differed from that of the settlements. At the same time, like settlement workers, caseworkers were supposed to be nondogmatic. They were not to stereotype or over-general-ize based on social status or ethnicity. The caseworker's initial goal was to try to understand why a particular client thought and acted as he or she did. This was the beginning of the paradoxical idea that peoples' behavior, no matter how seemingly wrong or destructive, should be viewed as their best effort to cope, adapt, and meet basic needs. The caseworker's job, however, was also to "help people see their responsibilities and opportunities" more clearly (Leiby 1978:122). This was in part a euphemism for transmitting so-cietal norms and expectations, and asking poor people to bear up, to accept limits as well as pursue opportunities.

Two broad goals for poor families shaped early casework practice—that of adjustment and that of assimilation. These derived in large part from the fact that services emerged during a period of large-scale immigration; it was seen as immigrants' responsibility to adjust and assimilate to Amer-ican society. (The centrality of these goals was heightened by the nation-alism and nativism that accompanied the World War I and continued into the 1920s.) The focus on adjustment derived from the Progressive preoc-cupation with the rapid changes occurring in American life, a belief in the importance of adjustment and adaptation to these changes, and generally in the importance of looking ahead rather than looking back (Diggins 1994:20). Not least, it derived from the belief that people had to find, and accept, their individually suited place in in the industrial economy. Ad-justment was not just focused outward on society, or inward on the self. Richmond (1922) argued that it included relatedness to others within the family, for that was where one learned what one needed to succeed in the larger world (from Leiby:123).

The goal of assimilation was seen as critical to social order and har-mony. It would help overcome the "inertia" of traditional practices and start families on a new track. It would help assure that immigrant children were prepared adequately for their future as citizens and workers. It sup-ported the Progressive belief that all families could "belong" to society, if they learned to conform to its norms. To a few service providers, assimila-tion implied that immigrants could add their new cultural identities to, and eventually integrate them with their old ones. To many others, it re-quired repudiation of those older identities. Regardless, the domains on which caseworkers often focused were those most resistant to fundamen-tal change.

If the settlements strove to achieve their goals through many means—literacy and language classes, vocational training, civics classes, primary health services, as well as classes in homemaking and childrearing—caseworkers focused almost exclusively on immigrants' domestic life, particularly on childrearing (Mink 1995:8). Problems of adjustment and lack of assimilation among immigrants were seen to have their roots in childrearing practices. Mink (1995:28–29) argues that "maternalist policies defined ethnic motherhood in opposition to 'American' childhood." Although altering mothers' values and behavior was seen as difficult, it was deemed worth the effort because of its potential benefit to children.

Caseworkers' helping efforts typically included some social support, as well as supervision—the latter expressed through pointed questions, instruction, and advice, and sometimes through the formulation of treatment plans. There was an element of what would later be called client- or family-centered helping in some early social casework. This probably derived from an acknowledgement that families served knew their own realities better than did the helper, and also from the residue of Progressive enthusiasm for learning from the disenfranchised. (John Dewey had argued that in a rapidly changing society the young and the new members of society had "as much to teach their teachers as to learn from them"; cited in Lasch 1965:159).

The regularity and duration of contacts with families varied enormously, depending on caseload, the nature of family problems, family cooperation, and mobility. From the outset there was concern about the inability to reach and/or adequately serve certain families. One writer (Sears 1926:255–258) identified a "gap" between families and services that she called a "resistive zone." Families in this zone "fail to profit from the social program . . . because their difficulties are too subtle, as yet, to be aided . . . [or because they] resist the encroachments" of service providers.

While the rhetoric of casework leaders suggested a change in intervention philosophy and methods from those used by charity workers, their practice often did not reflect this change. Notes and records of casework through the 1920s mostly described the broad facts of clients' lives, the specific requests for assistance, and the caseworkers' responses, including recommended plans of action (Garton and Otto 1964). There was little reflection in the records of the process of work with families, of gradually deepening helping relationships, evolving goals, and the like. In return for linking families to needed resources, case workers assumed the right to intervene as fully as they wished in families' lives. A Jewish immigrant, Anna Yezierska, relates the following incident, in a 1920 short story, "The Free Vacation House" (from "Hungry Hearts," included in Freeman et al 1992:207). A few days after a visiting teacher finds Anna, the mother of six children, exhausted and near a breakdown, she receives a home visit from a worker for an agency that arranges country vacations:

> "I am from the Social Betterment Society," she tells me.
>
> "You want to go to the country?"
>
> Before I could say something, she goes over to the baby and pulls out the rubber nipple from her mouth, and to me she says, "You must not get the child used to sucking this; it is very unsanitary."
>
> "Gott in Himmel!" I beg the lady. "Please don't begin with that child, or she'll holler my head off. She must have the nipple. I'm too nervous to hear her scream like that."

The visitor then proceeds to ask Anna a series of questions about her background, her family, how she uses her money.

> "My goodness!" I cry out. "For why is it necessary all this to know? For why must I tell you all my business? What difference does it make already if I keep boarders? If Masha had the whooping cough or Sonya had the measles?" . . .
>
> "We must make a record of all the applicants and investigate each case," she tells me. "There are so many who apply to the charities, we can only help those who are most worthy."

Caseworkers struggled as much as had charity workers with immigrants' values and coping strategies. A few casework educators and writers urged frontline workers not to ignore immigrants' histories and reasons for clinging to traditional practices. One noted that "for most of us, foreign-born families seem to have sprung into being, full-armed, at Ellis Island" (Hull 1924:78). Such warnings, however, had little effect on caseworkers' distaste for immigrants' behavior, home conditions, even their difficulties. The gap between case workers' and immigrant women's view of the world was constantly exposed. Case workers frequently were angered at their clients' refusal to heed advice, and their seemingly irrational fears (for example, the not uncommon fear of hospitals, or the reluctance to ask a landlord to fix a problem in an apartment building).

Kunzel (1993) argues that case workers were particularly predisposed to view unmarried mothers as inherently unfit: "Although social workers professed a belief in the fundamental right of unmarried mothers to make their own decision, in practice they often pressured them to place their babies for adoption" (p. 129). The new tool of "differential diagnosis," purportedly designed to allow the caseworker to make individualized determinations, usually led to a recommendation to put the baby up for adoption (pp. 128–129). Widows, whose situation was theoretically more acceptable and understandable, were sometimes treated no better than unwed mothers (Gordon 1990:12).

From the perspective of poor families themselves, caseworkers and their agencies were both intrusive and another resource, one requiring its own peculiar compromises to gain access to. Moreover, families were not just passive recipients of (or resisters to) services. Stadum (1990:94) argues that early family casework was both "haphazard and controlling," and that at the same time "recipients set some limits." Families sought to use services to their own ends. They cooperated or feigned cooperation to the extent necessary, followed or ignored advice as they deemed appropriate. When needed assistance or resources were not forthcoming they sought out other agencies, gradually learning where to turn for which types of support. At the same time, poor families had no expectation that caseworkers were there to "render social justice" (Stadum 1990:94).

At least some intervention occurred at the request of family members, usually mothers seeking emergency relief, protection from an abusive husband, or help with a family health problem or with a child's problems in school. Katz (1983:18–19) cites a 1909 letter to Philadelphia's Society for Organizing Charity that asked, "Will you please call and see Mrs. William Sullivan 2726 Oakdail I have two very sick children and my husband has no work and I am sick myself so I would like you please for god sake not for me." As Gordon (1988:295) notes, "this does not mean that the inviters kept control of the relationships, or got what they wanted. The guests usually did not leave upon request. . . . But it is a mistake to see the flow of initiative . . . in only one direction."

## Supportive Services and the Emergence of Mothers' Aid

The emergence of supportive social services in the first decades of the twentieth century was interwoven with, and in some ways propelled by continuing steps toward the development of a social welfare framework. The first steps toward that framework had been taken in the nineteenth century, with pensions for the widows of Civil War veterans (Skocpol 1992) and with modest municipal programs of outdoor relief. As I have already noted, the Progressives' focus on poor women and children shifted and enlarged the canvas of American social reform. This shift was reflected in almost every item of the Progressive reform agenda, but most of all in the push for the establishment of Mothers' Aid as an entitlement.

The establishment of Mothers' Aid programs in most states was itself interwoven with larger secular trends in society, including changing perspectives on the roles and rights of women, a changing economy and shifting labor markets, and the chronic preoccupation with the decline of the family. Piven and Cloward (1971), Kessler (1982), and others have argued that throughout United States history, welfare policy has been an important tool for regulating the supply of labor. Clearly, welfare policy has also been designed to address perceived threats to the idealized family model, to "normal" family life and roles.

Throughout the nineteenth century, poor single mothers were lumped together for some purposes in the minds of the charity community and the public, and differentiated for others. Widows were respectable, women deserted by or separated from husbands less so. Unmarried mothers formed a distinct group, with a distinct network of supports. Regardless of category, all poor single mothers were "caught in a . . . contradiction" (Handler and Hasenfeld 1991:23). They were expected to work to support their children, preferably such home-work as sewing, taking in laundry, and, when necessary, taking in boarders. At the same time they were criticized for neglecting their children or for overworking them (since for some home-work, such as piece work, the only way to survive was to involve the children). When they worked outside the home, single mothers were accused of neglecting the home itself. Some in the charity community also believed that single mothers posed an inherent threat to society, by virtue of their status and visibility.

Except for the subgroup of young, unmarried mothers, single mothers were left largely on their own to reconcile these contradictory expectations. Modest amounts of material aid from charities or municipal public aid departments did little but take the edge off their struggles. The overwhelming majority had no choice but to work, and low wages forced them to work long hours. Further, men and women were "played off against each other in many occupational areas" (Kessler 1982:68).

In the first three decades of the twentieth century there was a gradual shift in perspective on single mothers, maternal employment in working-class families, and children's needs, creating a climate that made possible the enlargement of support. This shift was linked in part to changing perspectives about how best to respond to child neglect in families in which a lone parent or both parents were forced to work (Gordon 1988 ch. 4). When child neglect had been discovered by child protection agencies such as the Societies for the Prevention of Cruelty to Children in the nineteenth century, it had been viewed as critical to remove children from the home. Now it was seen to make more sense to support and supervise mothers. The shift in perspective was linked also to a growing belief that families, specifically mothers, had to be involved in efforts to prepare immigrant children for American life. They could not just be supplanted by schools and related institutions. As Mink (1995:30) puts it, "mother-directed policies [would travel] through women to children."

Research by public health workers, settlement staff, and others was also illuminating the dangers of maternal employment for young children. New mothers who worked were found to have disproportionately high infant mortality rates (Ladd-Taylor 1994:31). Studies found that many poor women with young children were forced to use terrible child care arrangements, with large number of children crowded into cramped, airless settings for long hours (Cahan 1989). Some children were taken to the factory, where dangerous machinery limited their movements. Many young children were simply left alone in their apartments for long hours. Day nurseries, which had grown from a handful in the early 1880s to some 700 by 1916, were designed to address child care problems (Cahan 1989:13). But they themselves often provided little more than minimal custodial care in barely sanitary surroundings; and in any case, they were inconveniently located for the great majority of families.

Not least, changing perspectives on maternal employment in poor families was linked to growing concerns about child labor. These concerns had diverse roots: the interests of organized labor in restricting competition for jobs; the belief of industrialists that immigrant children needed a good, formal education to prepare them for work in an industrial economy; and changing perceptions of children, in particular a societal sentiment that children needed nurturing and protecting in order to grow into healthy citizens. If children were not to work they would need supervision, which also implied that mothers should not work. Cahan (1989:22) quotes from a 1911 article in "Good Housekeeping" in which the author uses a case study to warn of the various costs of forcing single mothers to work: "Three years of superhuman effort on her part, and a weekly expenditure of five dollars for the care of her children. Result, what? Overwork is slowly killing the mother, while for the lack of her control by day the older boy is getting into juvenile court."

Concern about the effects of poor women's work on care and supervision of children extended to concern about family life in general. A 1910 Senate report on women's and children's labor found that "the so-called normal family—father with wife and children dependent on him for support—is not found" (cited in Kessler 1982:122). Advocates of expanded

Mothers' Aid argued that it was the key to normal family life, itself viewed as the "foundation of the state" (Garfinkel and McLanahan 1986:98). Society could be seen to owe widowed families payment for their husbands' contribution to the community; it could even be seen to owe mothers "payment" for the critical service to society of raising children (Chase-Lansdale and Vinovkis, undated:19). From a narrower economic perspective, poor, unskilled mothers' efforts in the home were deemed to provide greater returns to society than their equivalent efforts at work. (In the 1920s a new economic argument for Mothers' Aid appeared: industrial management engineers argued that single mothers brought their worries and difficulties to work, limiting their effectiveness as workers and infecting the whole climate of the workplace; Todd 1927.)

Finally, proponents of Mothers' Aid argued that private charity was inadequate in many respects as a basis for assistance to families. Charity organizations often took too long to investigate in situations in which families had pressing needs for relief; at the end of their investigation they might provide inadequate or no relief to a family. Moreover, their punitive and stigmatizing spirit made them more destructive than helpful.

In its turn, the charity community fought against the establishment of state Mothers' Aid programs for the same reasons it had fought public outdoor relief in the late nineteenth century. Municipal relief programs were still viewed as corrupt or incompetently managed. There was a fear that poor families would come to see Mothers' Aid as an entitlement. Another old argument, revived for the new debate, was that helping already deserted wives and children would simply encourage more desertion. Energy would be better spent tracking down deserters and forcing them to pay support. (In fact, some social agencies such as SPCCs did spend resources on this task, often with the assistance of juvenile courts.) Yet another argument was that the focus of helping efforts should be on either reconciling wives and husbands or encouraging women to find new husbands. This ignored the reality that many men who had deserted their families could not or would not pay any support. Many couples could not or would not be reconciled. (A modest portion of desertion was deliberate, arranged by married couples to increase chances of receiving some assistance.) Not least, some single mothers did not want husbands; they were already "embittered and exhausted from the efforts of holding together a two-parent family" (Gordon 1988:105).

One new argument against Mothers' Aid was that the resources targeted for aid would be better spent preventing the causes of widowhood; for example on a public health campaign against tuberculosis, or even on improving working conditions (Leiby 1978). This argument was ironic because most of those who made it made little or no effort to push also for national health insurance and significant reform of working conditions.

Underlying the arguments made by the charity community against Mothers' Aid was a fear of being pushed aside by new public bureaucracies. The private child and family service agencies that were evolving from local COS offices wanted to maintain what they viewed as their central role in emerging supportive services for poor families. Ironically, although the private charity community lost the fight against Mothers' Aid, it succeeded in assuring that its philosophy and approach to providing assistance to poor families would be be the one embraced by the new public programs (Ladd-Taylor 1994:138). Moreover, private charity agencies were not pushed aside as states established their programs. They continued to offer their own assistance to many families, and played a variety of roles in the new public programs.

Mothers' Aid legislation was passed by state after state, starting in 1911; by the late 1920s almost all states had programs, at least in name. Although its proponents viewed Mothers' Aid as support for women and for healthy family life, many programs were framed as child welfare programs. The Director of Pennsylvania's Mothers' Aid program stated that the purpose of the program was "not wholly and primarily the alleviation of material distress but also the well-being of the children under supervision, as expressed in terms of adequate mother care, health . . . [and] school progress" (cited in Mink 1995:29).

Viewing families receiving Mothers Aid' as child welfare clients provided a rationale (if such was needed) for careful investigation and then continued monitoring, on child protection grounds. In many cities Mothers Aid was lodged in juvenile courts or child welfare agencies, rather than in relief agencies. It was viewed as an expression of the juvenile court's role as "superparent" to poor and vulnerable families (Van Waters 1925). This administrative arrangement made programs susceptible to the whims of individual judges and to the "particularistic, punitive, and/or rehabilitative judgments in which the courts specialized" (Gordon 1994:45).

Most early Mothers' Aid statutes included not only a means test but a morals test, excluding mothers found unfit by character, behavior, and even intelligence (Patterson 1986:27). Many programs also excluded specific categories of single mothers. For example, early amendments to Illinois's original Mothers' Aid legislation excluded women who had been deserted by their husbands, "aliens," women whose husbands were in prison, and women who had illegitimate children (Gittens 1986:76). Over time statutes became more inclusive, although a variety of factors resulted in continued discrimination in program practices. One was the almost complete discretion granted local program administrators over who was approved for aid. A second was the simple lack of funding. Many states provided no funds to the local jurisdictions charged with implementing the program. The federal government did not participate in provision of aid. (Berkowitz and Mc-Quaid 1989:92 note that "as late as 1928, 96 percent of total federal welfare expenditures went to war veterans.")

A third factor contributing to discriminatory program practices was the continuing reliance on moral and behavioral criteria in judging individual worthiness for aid. Factors as idiosyncratic as language spoken at home, family diet, household composition, and children's household roles all fed into determinations of approval for aid (Skocpol 1992:469; Mink 1995:41). In some jurisdictions particular ethnic groups were more likely to be approved for aid than others. Some jurisdictions included such criteria as the number (e.g., three or more) and age of children in their eligibility determinations.

The key vehicle for sorting applicants was investigation. The investigation process tended to expand or contract (in length and thoroughness) as a function of funding and demand for relief. In a comparison of cases opened in a family service agency in Minneapolis first from 1900 to 1910 and then from 1920 to 1930, Stadum (1990:78) found a decrease in approvals for relief and an increase in assessment, partly tied to increased applications for relief. In a 1917 study in Chicago it was found that the juvenile court, which administered the program there, typically took two to four months to decide on a request for aid (Abott and Breckinridge 1921:22). In some cases the application process was so drawn out and intrusive that applicants simply withdrew from the process. As a result of the extensive investigation that often occurred, over half of applicants were eventually deemed ineligible (Orfman 1996:101).

The lengthy investigation process and efforts to sort people by moral category, combined with limited funding, meant that only a small percentage of female-headed households—from 5 to 10 percent, depending on jurisdiction—actually received Mothers' Aid. The overwhelming majority of women approved for Mothers' Aid in the early years of state programs were widows, even though the number of widows was declining and the number of deserted and "unmarried" mothers increasing. As late as 1931, over 80 percent of recipients were families in which the father had died, even though this group constituted only 38 percent of single mother families (Cmiel 1995:98). Grants to those approved invariably were inadequate, and thus more than half of recipients had to work, contradicting the basic purpose of the program (Handler and Hasenfeld 1991:71). A study in Pennsylvania found that Mothers' Aid grants provided 39 percent of recipients' family income, mothers' own earnings 21 percent, and older children's earnings 27 percent (Skocpol 1993:476?). When mothers did work, at exhausting, low-paying jobs, they were accused of neglecting their children and threatened with loss of the small amount of aid they received.

Acceptance of the supervision of one's family's personal life was the quid pro quo for receipt of financial assistance. The analogy of hiring and firing employees was used: "mothers were hired by the state to care for children, and their continued employment was dependent on satisfactory performance" (Gordon 1994:52). The inherent tendency toward close supervision of recipients was reinforced by the inadequacy of funding for public aid programs, combined with ever increasing applications for aid. Social workers also were trying to prove to a skeptical public that they were careful guardians of its money (Skocpol 1993). Together, these factors increased the pressure to apply discretion in maintaining as well as approving grants.

Caseworkers working for or on behalf of juvenile courts conducted periodic home visits to families receiving assistance. They checked on the cleanliness of the home (and its inhabitants), who was living there, and how money was being used. They issued instructions and offered advice. In some locales women receiving aid were required to join parenting classes. One parenting group in Detroit, organized by the Mothers' Pension Department, focused partly on "teaching the use of milk to Italian women . . . When [the class] was completed a prize was given to the mother who had introduced the use of milk most extensively to her family" (Thomas and Thomas 1928:319). This class was subsequently extended to focus on citizenship and on explaining to mothers the meaning of American national holidays and national heroes.

Most women put up with demands, intrusiveness, or arrogance from case workers, with lectures about spending, hygiene, or care of children, as well as questions about relationships with men. In a few instances distrust, depradation, or requirements seemed too much and women simply withdrew from the program (Ladd-Taylor 1994:157). If they could have, more women might have rebelled openly.

Mink (1995:3) writes that Mothers' Aid "offered political tribute to motherhood while requiring poor women to earn their tribute through cultural assimilation." Mothers' Aid practices reflected the mixture of empathy and disapproval that upper-middle-class women felt for poor, immigrant women. Like most supports to poor families before and since, Mothers' Aid was viewed with ambivalence even by those who fought for, managed, and

implemented it. Proponents and providers could not shake the deeply rooted American belief that being in need of support made a person or family
morally suspect, no matter what the reason for that need. Providers also
feared that the very act of intervening to support and strengthen families
would weaken them by making them more dependent. (This fear was contradicted by testimony from frontline workers that, far from creating dependence, financial aid fostered self confidence, initiative, and a desire to be
free of aid as soon as possible; North 1931:30.) Not least, ambivalence toward
Mothers' Aid stemmed from the simple fact that it was needed at all, a fact
that threatened a variety of the myths underlying American life.

Ambivalence about the very basis of Mothers' Aid undermined the
whole enterprise. It contributed to inadequate grants, which simply extended rather than resolved the historical dilemma faced by poor single
mothers between trying to earn income and caring for their children. It
contributed to the assumption that if a family needed financial assistance,
it automatically needed supervision and guidance as well. It undermined
helping relationships, leading to mixed messages, contradictory behavior,
and a pattern of doing and then undoing (Halpern 1991). And it destroyed
families. Parents who could not get Mothers' Aid and could not cope were
forced to turn to foster care and orphanages, which came to be seen as a
refuge for unworthy parents (Cmiel 1995:103).

Although Mothers' Aid broadened the sphere of government responsibility, it did not challenge traditional ideas about women, families, and economic relations. It supported and reinforced both the idealization of motherhood and the notion that the quality of mothering underlay both social
progress and social problems. It reinforced the nineteenth-century doctrine
of separate spheres for men and women. It established the principle that a
primary goal of public policy for families should be to strengthen their ability to meet private responsibilities (Grubb and Lazerson 1980). And, in its
argument that good maternal care prevented social problems, it reinforced
the tendency to argue that the only legitimate rationales for family support
are instrumental ones.

Mothers' Aid also reinforced the idea that the family and the marketplace were unconnected spheres, to be considered and dealt with separately. Family well-being could be achieved without addressing the economic
factors that undermined families. The state could and would intervene in
family life for putatively benevolent purposes (i.e., to reinforce middle-class
family norms), even as it refrained from intervening in the marketplace.
Government's few interventions in the latter were themselves strongly conservative. Thus the federal government was strongly resistant to legislating

a minimum wage, preferring to focus on workmen's compensation. None of the strategies developed to help poor and working-class families during the formative decades of the twentieth century had the purpose of directly reducing poverty, or creating a universal social security framework for working Americans. Of all the many arguments marshalled to support Mothers' Aid, there was one that was conspicuously absent: It should be provided simply because people needed it.

### Early Patterns: Dilemmas of Purpose and Practice

Andrew Polsky, Christopher Lasch, Norton Grubb and Marvin Lazerson, and many others have argued that the new forms of family intervention that emerged in the first decades of the century were largely destructive. Polsky writes (1991:9) that "the first social practitioners invented a different form of power, one that penetrated to the most minute level of every day life" in poor families. The fact that this power was masked, and was justified by the invocation of scientific method and individualization based on differing needs, made it particularly insidious. Substantively, the power of the new helping professionals resided in their assumption of the prerogative to recommend (if not determine) who would receive what kind of support and assistance, and conversely who might be subject to sanctions, loss of assistance, and even loss of privacy rights. In other words, professionals' power—and to an extent the source of the damage they did—resided in their self-proclaimed right to label and categorize the poor.

Lasch (1977) saw the new helping professionals as perversely undermining the very institution they claimed they were to trying to strengthen. At the same time that they insisted on the importance of the family as the core unit of society, they insisted that some—if not most—families were incapable of knowing their own needs and caring for their own children. He wrote that "having monopolized the knowledge necessary to socialize the young, the agencies of socialized reproduction then parcelled it out piecemeal in the form of parent education." Lasch saw a parallel in the way industrialists had "expropriated" workers' technical knowledge, broken it down in small units, and created the assembly line, and the way in which the new professional helpers expropriated childrearing knowledge and wisdom, and tried to reframe it in scientific terms (p. 18).

In the same way that producers of material goods created demand for their goods through advertising, helping professionals were seen to manufacture demand through the message that parents needed their help in childrearing. Thus Thomas and Thomas (1928:301) wrote that "some parents are becoming more and more conscious of their inability to handle the problems that arise [in childrearing]," in effect creating that reality by suggesting it. The Children's Bureau was particularly influential in suggesting to parents that there was one correct way to rear children and that deviating from it could lead to great harm.

Lasch (1977:15) argues that "in order to justify their appropriation of parental functions, the [new] helping professionals [told themselves that they were] doctors to a sick society." At least some helping professionals strove to gain control over the whole sphere of reproduction and helping. Lasch (1977:16) cites Judge Ben Lindsey of the Denver juvenile court as a case in point. Lindsey argued that the state (more specifically helping professionals representing the state) should have a role in deciding who could and should become parents.

### Too Simplistic a Critique?

There certainly was much that was problematic in the purposes and approaches of early "professional" helpers. They presumed that poor families' own stories were untrustworthy and required verification. They had little self-doubt. Stadum (1990:83) notes that "unmarried middle class social workers appear to have had few qualms about telling wives and mothers what constituted proper homemaking, childrearing and family relations." The early professional helpers expressed disdain for nonprofessionals, whether charity volunteers, community leaders, or appointed officials. (Orfman 1996:991 cites Edith Abott's judgment that some rural judges lacked the "social intelligence" to administer Mothers' Aid and were too informal in their practices.)

The new helpers tended to view their work in the framework of an abstract common good—whether cultural assimilation, adjustment, social stability, or democracy. Providing concrete supports, meeting clear needs somehow was not purpose enough. As a consequence, helpers sometimes sacrificed specific families' well-being in the service of consistency in adhering to their abstract principles (Stadum 1992). They also did not ask what poor immigrants were owed in exchange for adjusting to the demands of the industrial order. Particularly problematic was the way that helping professionals took advantage of poor families' vulnerability in order to exert their influence. The use of parents' requests for assistance as opportunities to explore all aspects of families' lives, and to make families submit to supervision, at times verged on the unethical. Although this quid pro quo had existed throughout the nineteenth century, it seemed to contradict the basic tenets of professionalism.

In retrospect, then, early helping professionals appear over-confident, and sometimes arrogant, with too great a faith in their methods. Formal helpers' behavior sometimes contradicted their professed ideals. But the completely negative view of the emergent social services held by Polsky, Lasch, Grubb and Lazerson, and others is an over-simplification. The growth of the role and purview of helping professionals was as much incidental as deliberate. It was a function of the complexity and seeming disorder of the urban context, the social organization of cities, the variety of unmet family needs, and the abuses of institutions and charity organizations. The rights that helping professionals claimed for themselves—to intervene in poor families' lives, to name and categorize the poor, to orchestrate relief—were not usually wrested from the poor; rather, they were wrested from others who had previously claimed those rights.

Settlements (as well as school social centers, neighborhood health centers, and other neighborhood agencies) certainly provided an enormous amount of practical assistance, supplementary child care, and education to large numbers of families. They could be a physical and psychological refuge from the hardships and strains of daily life, and a reliable last resort when all other efforts to solve problems had failed. Although provided with the aim of assimilation, their English language, citizenship, basic literacy, and other classes helped many adults with the challenges of adjusting to demands in the United States. Casework played a more specialized and limited role, although it increasingly became a correlate of all requests for emergency assistance or public aid.

Services and service institutions were from the very beginning an expression of the mixed sentiments underlying Progressive reform—religious and scientific, nativist and pluralist, intrusive and protective, idealistic and realistic. Services were conceived in part as a means of preparing families for industrial capitalism, and in part as a means of protecting families from capitalism's worst effects. Early helping efforts, like subsequent ones, were not monolithic. They were complex in motive and heterogeneous in practice. Responses to families depended on the specifics of a family's situation or the predisposition of the particular helper. Gordon (1990:194) suggests that at times early helpers were able to circumvent their own prejudices and procedures, whether by quickly approving small amounts of material aid or by providing a "hint as to how to 'work' the relief agencies." Responses depended also on how well a helper knew a family and could put a particular problem or crisis in perspective. Settlement staff, for example, often had a better chance to observe the "ups and downs" of families' lives over time and might therefore have a more balanced view of their strengths and vulnerabilities (Reynolds 1963).

As I will discuss in the next chapter, there was at least a measure of self-questioning. Numerous articles in *The Family*, the main casework journal, struggled with the purpose and basis of casework and warned against cultural insensitivity, presumptuousness, and related behaviors. Thus one writer warned her colleagues that "we [are falling] into the habit of regarding parents as a necessary evil, as mere trustees of their children, not as valuable human entities in and for themselves" (Palevsky 1926:68). From early on, service providers struggled with the question of how to respond to the basic realities of their clients' lives. It was difficult to ignore the connection between most family problems and inadequate wages, irregular work, and bad working and housing conditions. It seemed less clear what to make of this connection: whether to treat these basic problems as a given, as one focus of the helping efforts, or as evidence of family inadequacy; whether simply to respond to obvious support needs or try to identify and address latent issues that might underlie those support needs.

Some providers recognized that counselling and modest material assistance were not enough to alter family circumstances: "in family after family even the child's physical needs cannot be decently satisfied unless the earnings of his father are to be supplemented over a long period of years" (Moore 1927:186). Others chose to focus on the gap between what they observed and domestic ideals that were unrealistic given poor families' lives. They focused in on adults' or children's unkempt physical appearance, a husband's drinking problem, or a mother's failure to bring a child in for health care sooner. Gordon (1994:46) has pointed out that some poor mothers indeed experienced difficulties that provided a rationale for intervention, for instance feelings of depression, of being overwhelmed and unable to cope with parenting demands. But, she argues, the response by case workers and others often went far beyond these difficulties. Moreover, the presence of other difficulties did not lessen the centrality of poverty itself as the problem in families' lives.

In part, service providers' (often limited) response was due to the limitations in what they had to offer. When there was nothing more to be provided or arranged, helpers counselled patience. This could mean that "we have done all we can for the moment," "do not act impulsively," or both. In part it was due to the providers' limited identification with those they served. It is also possible that service providers chose or felt compelled to bridge the widely divergent views held by more advantaged Americans concerning social problems, poor people, and the role of government.

The weight of families' own concerns had some impact on early professionals' empathy, understanding, and presumption—though not as much as it might or should have. Settlement staff, caseworkers, and others struggled to reconcile their sense of expertise and insight with poor families' own right to self-determination. Although the claim of specialized expertise was an important underpinning of the new helping professions, this claim conflicted with helping professionals' belief that helping also had to be democratic. To reconcile these two values, helpers made a number of arguments that themselves were not consistent. They argued that they were putting their knowledge and expertise in the service of clients' own goals and priorities. They argued that the helper was not (and should not perceive herself as) superior to the client, and that the helper and client each had something to teach (and learn from) the other.

Challenges to the legitimacy and approach of the emerging social services did not come just from poor families. Polsky (1991:19) points out that there was a modest challenge from reformers who viewed "collective action" as the route to "social membership" for poor people. These reformers included settlement leaders such as Robert Woods. In a different vein, trade union leaders worried about the role services were playing in meeting the needs of industrial capitalism for compliant, efficient, socialized wage labor, and the effects services were having in weakening workers' will. Samuel Gompers (1919:16) warned that services would undermine workers' sense of initiative: "Doing for people what they can and ought to do for themselves is a dangerous experiment . . . Let social busybodies and professional public morals experts reflect on the perils they rashly invite under this pretense of social welfare."

Emerging social services, then, both fit well into larger social currents and struggled for an identity, as well as a place in society. Helping professionals' pretensions toward scientific method fit the excitement about the potential of engineering solutions to problems. Their promises to funders and the public that they had the tools to address the sources of poverty complemented a strong societal wish that poverty would disappear. By focusing on the poor as individual cases with unique characteristics, formal helpers lost sight themselves, as well as helping the broader society lose sight of the common—and continuing—forces shaping poor families' lives. Thus the optimism of the new helping professionals was undermined in tiny measures, day in and day out, by their actual experience of working with families.

# CHAPTER THREE

*Trial by Fire*

Supportive services during the 1920s and 1930s were shaped by powerful external events, as well as being marked by continuing internal turmoil. After World War I, public sentiment about poverty, inequality, and immigration shifted dramatically. Nativism, hysteria about communism, fear of moral (and genetic) decline, and an emphasis on conformity created a turbulent public climate for those involved in social problem solving. Workers saw their rights to freedom of speech and assembly curtailed. Immigrants, long viewed as a threat to social order and cohesion, were now viewed as potential subversives as well. (Being unemployed also was subversive, in the minds of some.) As Crocker (1992:122) notes, "no aspect of foreignness was above suspicion."

Those who worked with immigrants and the poor, and were seen (accurately or not) to represent their interests, also became targets of suspicion and hostility. When they were not being attacked as un-American, settlements were recruited, and when necessary pressured, by corporations to intensify their work in the Americanization of immigrants. Crocker (1992:108) describes how Campbell House and Neighborhood House in Gary, Indiana, were urged by local steel companies to work with mothers to assure a healthy, happy family life for their male workers and to help prepare immigrant children for their future work in the steel mills.

The 1920s also brought a strong backlash against Progressive aspirations and reforms. Support for Mothers' Aid programs (described in the previous chapter) barely outlasted their passage. By the mid-1920s the spirit under-lying the legislation was gone (Ladd-Taylor 1994). One can argue the same for almost all the legislative and programmatic accomplishments of the era. For instance, the Shepherd-Towner Act of 1921, a major initiative of the Children's Bureau, which provided grants to states for maternal and child health, steadily lost support through the 1920s and was allowed to lapse in 1929. Attacks on the act came from the organized medical establishment (including the U.S. Public Health Service), which perceived a threat to its prerogatives and income, and from critics of the Children's Bureau, worried about socialist influences and the incursion of the federal government into family life.

The growing social service sector itself became a target of the public backlash against Progressive reforms. By the late 1920s the media was re-flecting (and itself contributing to) public concern about escalating expen-ditures on services. Social service providers were accused of contributing to the growing demand for relief among poor families and of inventing de-mand for their own services. One social work writer noted that "family so-cial work is under urgent necessity to capture the imagination of a long-suf-fering public" (Kahn 1928:187).

Many of those who had led and participated in the reform activities of the prewar period were gradually turning into bureaucrats and agency-bound staff. Social service providers were not abandoning the poor and working class and were certainly not "frauds," as one Buffalo labor leader described them (in relation to the gap between their rhetoric and their ac-tions; cited in Levine 1971:142). Indeed, much of their daily work with poor families continued to focus on responding to health, financial, housing, and other crises; assistance in locating and gaining access to resources; and as-sistance in addressing family problems such as desertion and children's school difficulties. Still, the social service community played only a modest role in efforts during the 1920s to promote national health insurance and old age security. (They would only join the fight for social security at the height of the Depression.)

Internally, the emergent service system already was taking on the charac-teristics for which it is criticized today. It was becoming both overcentralized and fragmented, with simultaneous duplication and gaps in services, compe-tition for control of families, and insistence on discretion in who would and should be served. One study noted that an increasingly crowded agency en-vironment in some cities was creating a sense of competition and mutual an-tagonism among agencies. Moreover, agencies had little respect for what oth-ers were doing. The sum effect was "chaotic" (North 1931:13).

There also was a fair amount of debate about the purpose, identity, and appropriate societal role for services. Soon after coming into their own, formal helpers already were beginning to rethink their ambitions for themselves and their clients, in part because those ambitions were proving elusive. In the early- and mid-teens some caseworkers had warned that they might be so successful that they would work themselves out of a job (Kahn 1928). By the late 1920s the casework community was reflecting the "inwardness" (as Reynolds 1963:13 put it) that would become characteristic. Caseworkers were wondering if they were a genuine profession, and if so, of what sort. In a report on a staff discussion of relief and related issues at Cleveland Associated Charities, Boggs (1930:149) notes that "the group expressed also a feeling of restlessness and uncertainty arising from fast-changing theories and practices in casework."

One of the ironies in the historical development of supportive services is that the Great Depression began just as casework leaders, struggling to identify a theoretical foundation for casework practice, thought they had found a key missing piece in psychoanalytic theory. (I use the term here broadly, to encompass both orthodox Freudian theory and the theories of psychoanalytic thinkers who departed from orthodoxy, notably Otto Rank.) The complex and in many ways contradictory pull of these two developments—one a powerful set of ideas, the other a powerful social event—heightened tensions during the 1930s about how to interpret poverty, and peoples' responses to it, and therefore what to focus on in work with poor families. The presence of each event strongly affected the influence of the other on the development of supportive services.

The introduction of psychoanalytic theory and helping principles into everyday family casework practice was limited to a small handful of agencies with senior staff who had been analyzed, trained, or supervised by psychoanalysts, or in clinics run by psychoanalysts. (By 1929 only six of twenty-nine schools of social work around the country even offered training in "psychiatric social work"; Alexander 1972:522). But its attraction for the casework community was strong. Psychoanalytic theory offered a fuller and more coherent view of both human nature and the helping process than that provided in prevailing casework texts and training. At the same time its focus on internal psychological struggles, combined with a more general withdrawal in American society from public concerns and into private life during the 1920s, nudged the young casework field away from an already tentative focus on strengthening poor families' living conditions.

The Depression, beyond forcing social service providers to return their attention to poverty and its correlates, complicated their growing preoccupation with clients' emotional life as a source of their difficulties (see, e.g., Coyle 1935). It was simply implausible that mass economic insecurity, unemployment, hunger, and homelessness could be caused by millions of individual cases of emotional dependence, impulsivity, poor reality-testing, or other personality defects. Efforts by social service theorists to elaborate a psychologically oriented framework for understanding and helping poor families kept colliding with the apparent centrality of social and economic constraints on families' lives (as well as with procedural demands of the bureaucratic agencies in which services were provided, and with the kind of practical assistance demanded by the families' immediate difficulties).

## Emergent Roles, Tasks, and Organization

From the outset supportive social services were pulled in different directions. As I have described in chapter 2, their broadest "branch" was family casework, which explicitly required a generalist role, a role well-suited to work with poor families and their many, intertwined difficulties. The generalist role was adaptable to, and therefore created a casework role in a variety of agency and program contexts. (For instance, a report from the 1931 White House Conference on Children noted that family casework was at the "heart" of the day nursery experience; Cahan 1989:33). Yet an equally important attribute of effective helping was expertise within a particular domain. This tended to lead to specialization, with different practitioners each having their sphere and set of responsibilities. Many incipient caseworkers themselves wished to be trained and viewed as specialists. Further, many went to work for agencies, or worked in departments within agencies with specific missions—child protection, work with unmarried mothers, work with immigrants, overseeing material and financial assistance, and dealing with children's school or health problems.

Specialization was seen to have its costs, however. It contributed to a sense of social distance between helper and client, as well as to fragmentation within agencies and the helping community generally. Mary Richmond (1922:99) noted that "we could never get on without the specialists either in medicine or social work, but at times it is difficult to get on with them." She argued that specialists' activities were "disintegrated and disintegrating (p. 103)." Specialists viewed people through narrow lenses, rather than holistically. Rhoades (1925:20) noted that specialists see "the pathological symptom but not the offender, the intelligence quotient in place of the child, the tonsil but not the patient. . . . In becoming masters of the means we find that the means have mastered us."

To some extent expertise (such as it was) resided more in helping agencies themselves, their rules and procedures, than in individual staff. Casework leaders warned new caseworkers to follow the interviewing and record-keeping procedures taught in schools of social work or agency training sessions to the letter. The caseworker had to "align her individual [work] with the standards and procedures" of her agency, in order to minimize "friction, confusion, waste" (Lubove 1965:169).

In practice, regardless of the initial reason for contact with families, regardless of their own self-definition, caseworkers often got involved in many aspects of their clients' lives. Until the early to mid-1920s, much contact with families was through home visits, which could present a caseworker with a range of obvious problems requiring attention. Involvement in multiple domains also was stimulated by casework theory, which posited different areas of families' lives as interconnected, and family assessment protocols, which called for learning about all areas. By its very nature, work with families pushed caseworkers beyond the boundaries of a particular mission. A case that began as a child protection case could evolve to include domestic violence, unemployment, or lack of food or clothing. These in turn might require taking action on behalf of families, linking them to resources and mediating with other providers, landlords, or authorities.

Organizational developments nonetheless reinforced the trend toward specialization. Within a decade of their emergence, social services were already becoming centralized and hierarchical. (Settlements were an exception to this rule, maintaining a good deal of local independence.) Although bureaucratic organization ran counter to the general American preference for decentralization in social life, undermined the idea of services as rooted in their communities, and threatened caseworkers' autonomy and discretion, it met too many needs of the helping profession. Bureaucratic organizations provided a base for helping professionals to exert their influence on social problems (Larson 1977). They also provided an alternative to the prevailing inefficient, variable, and sometimes corrupt system of public administration that had been created by patronage democracy.

Early organizational developments in the social services were also influenced by the incorporation of business and engineering models. The boards of local social service agencies were often dominated by business interests, with contained few or no representatives of either labor or the communities served. These boards encouraged agency management to avoid involvement with contentious social issues. They pushed for the use of businesslike strategies of management, accountability, and direct service provision. They argued for greater efficiency and division of labor. (The former meant less home visiting and other kinds of time-consuming community work. The latter reinforced the trend toward specialization.) They promoted the engineer as the paradigmatic model for helping professionals. Berkowitz and McQuaid (1988) quote Gerard Swope, chief executive officer of the General Electric Corporation and a former resident of Hull House: "If the engineer can make contributions that will not only reduce human effort in production so that goods may be made at less cost and so be available to an ever increasing number of people, but can also cooperate with others, whether in the ranks of labor or the social service professions, who are applying the scientific method to the wider problems of society, he will come into his own.

At the systems level, organizational developments took the "loosely coupled" form that was to endure throughout the century. Religiously rooted federations continued to oversee their own networks of agencies. In addition, in each city a variety of intermediary, coordinating organizations emerged to direct and rationalize the efforts of individual agencies. These coordinating organizations captured corporate and philanthropic money and then tried to use this money to exert leverage over the policies and practices of direct service providers. Behind them was a vision of American society guided and managed by enlightened private groups, balancing business and civic interests (Cmiel 1995:66). What they did not reflect—nor try to—was the interests of poor families and communities.

Like specialization, bureaucratic organization had its early critics. "Over-centralization" was seen to lead agency administrators to lose the knowledge and feel of the neighborhoods in which their staff were dispersed. Numerous large bureaucratic agencies with local branches in a number of communities also contributed to what has been called fragmented centralization. Each organization watched and then imitated what the others developed and provided. (Skocpol 1992:90, calls this "analogous institution-building.") Each organization's local branch was both focused on its headquarters (to whom it was accountable) and inclined to view itself as the natural agency within its community for coordinating family services. In some local communities, a number of agencies—from the juvenile courts to settlements, societies for the protection of children, various private child and family welfare agencies, even day nurseries—provided similar services. Each agency often viewed itself as the logical coordinating agency, while at the same time attempting to ration increasingly limited resources and limit demand on its direct services. This was done by restricting eligibility (based on religious or ethnic group membership, moral criteria, residence, and other related factors), referral to other agencies, and periodic re-definition of the agency's mandate.

While professional helping agencies competed for resources and (ambivalently) for clients among themselves, they banded together against other community institutions. Polsky (1991:18–19) argues that early caseworkers combined the presumption of specialized knowledge with the strategy of bureaucratic organization, especially administrative centralization, to lessen the influence of lay helpers and the community in general. Churches, clubs, and other community groups were instructed by social work leaders that providing assistance to poor families was now the province of helping professionals (see Swift 1925). The growing role of helping professionals in determining the distribution of scarce resources to poor families through assessment and categorizing implicitly increased the power of agencies themselves.

Social service agencies' efforts to assert control over social problem solving had unintended as well as intended consequences. It contributed to decreased civic engagement, as community members converted their responsibility to the community to a yearly donation to the community chest that funded social services. As authority and funding increased for social service agencies, so did caseloads. (Caseloads may have been high all along. One study focusing on the period between 1900 and 1913 found caseload size in a Minneapolis family service agency to range from 80 to 225; Stadum 1990). Large caseloads made it difficult to achieve the ideal of working with families as much and as long as necessary. Due in part due to high caseloads and in part to the difficulty of persuading families to do what they did not think possible or made sense, caseworkers often ended up focusing on whatever "was most easily accomplished. Getting clothes for a child in rags was a much simpler task than getting the mother to agree to follow through on a doctor's appointment" (Stadum 1990:83).

*Shifts in Settlement Practice*

The 1920s brought a number of philosophical and practical challenges to the settlement movement. The settlement "process," particularly the focus on neighborhood-building, seemed out of step with the times. The utopian aspects of the movement (if not of all or even most individual settlements) were at odds with the businesslike climate of the era. Thus even as Jane Addams criticized caseworkers' "coldness of tone" and "excessive rationality," Mary Richmond criticized the settlement approach for relying too much on "the natural promptings of the heart" (Wenocur and Reisch 1989:50–51). Politically, the settlement movement also was out of step. Close involvement with the struggles and aspirations of poor and immigrant families had led even the more conservative settlements to support a Progressive reform agenda, one that was now not just repudiated but suspect.

Settlements struggled also at a very practical level to maintain a place in the emerging social service system now that they were no longer the sole provider of many services. Almost every innovation spawned and nurtured by settlements had led by the 1920s to an organization to take up, specialize in, and expand that innovation. Thus settlements now had to compete with boys and girls clubs, public recreation facilities, public health clinics and visiting nurse associations, public libraries, and evening classes for adults in the public schools (Crocker 1992:38). Since immigration had slowed dramatically, the "market" for some of these services—those focused most directly on one or another aspect of Americanization—was not growing.

Settlements also had to adapt to changing funding patterns. In order to secure a share of funding from local community chests and corporate funders, settlements felt compelled to mimic the organization, goals, and service strategies of casework agencies. Chambers (1963:119) notes that "in joining local community chests [out of financial necessity] local settlement leaders often felt obliged to stress their service functions and to restrict their social action programs." Settlements professionalized and departmentalized, and their work came more and more to resemble that of other family agencies. More of their staff had social work or related degrees. The group work that settlements had always done was reified as a distinct social work specialty and as settlements' own distinct contribution to social service practice.

Settlement leaders also sought a new niche in the emerging idea of prevention. They argued that settlements were uniquely suited to prevention, early detection of, and intervention in problems. Leah Taylor (1935:474) argued that "the informality of a settlement approach brings to light many minor problems where early service is essential to prevent the development of major problems." She went on to mention such examples as "incipient delinquency, the beginning of domestic trouble, health difficulties, landlord-tenant trouble, neighborhood sore spots, and homework exploitation." Polacheck (1991), a Hull House participant later tapped by Jane Addams to teach an English language class for adults, noted that as the class progressed, the formal activities of the class increasingly led to more informal conversation, debate, and sharing of problems; and that this was true of many of the structured activities at Hull House.

Although settlements made many adaptations to the climate of the 1920s, settlement leaders and staff resisted the notion that they were conventional service providers. Community-building remained an important mission of many settlements. Their staff refrained from viewing most children and families served as cases or clients. At least in rhetoric, if not always in daily interaction, settlements continued to emphasize the adaptive strengths of families. They continued to provide a wide array of basic services: during a typical month in 1927, among a range of other activities, the Northwestern University settlement in Chicago served 567 young children in kindergarten and other classroom programs; assisted 183 people in securing their citizenship papers; provided 1,708 glasses of milk to children; made 169 home visits; and helped 191 families who sought assistance with problems (Wukas 1991:45).

## The Evolution of a Helping Style and Focus in Casework Services

### *The Search for Theory in Casework Services*

From the beginning, social service providers had never been content to define themselves as simply providers of mundane help with practical things—finding jobs, helping with money for rent, helping get a sick child into the hospital, linking families to needed community resources. They viewed this work almost as an excuse for the more important tasks of helping clients become aware of their latent support needs, possibilities, and limitations and, more fundamentally, of reshaping clients' selves. One writer noted that underlying the mundane work of service provision was "a creative spirit working with the most precious thing . . . other human spirits" (Rhoades 1925:21–22).

Yet the grander rhetoric of casework (as with that of settlement work) was constantly undermined by experience. Already by the late 1920s service providers' optimism about their work, their sense of social service as a calling was diminishing. A chronic theme in the casework records and literature of the 1920s was clients' unresponsiveness to caseworkers' interpretations, suggestions, advice, and plans, and most of all to their values and preferences. Helping relationships felt unsatisfactory to frontline helpers. Caseworkers complained about not having enough time to work with families. "Aggregrate" analyses of case records showed a lower [rate] of success than had been anticipated (Garten and Otto 1964:32).

One line of response to such early analyses was to argue that the essence of casework processes and effects was not measurable (Brisley 1924). Another was to suggest that caseworkers had to be more selective about clients. Another was to seek more effective techniques. A 1925 article in *The Family* described an innovative effort to establish relationships in which clients felt free to discuss and critique the plans their caseworkers made for working with them. The author reports that clients reportedly became more invested in the helping relationship, took more active roles, and were more responsive to guidance (Rhoades 1925). Still another was to improve the quality of case records. One agency in Minneapolis changed its case record outline to include families' "assets," as well as problems or needs (Stadum 1992:129).

Another response by caseworkers to their frustrations over their effectiveness was to search for improved conceptual frameworks. Existing casework theory consisted of little more than a set of extremely vague precepts and a thorough outline of interview questions (designed to establish the facts of peoples' situation), complemented by a growing literature of case studies illustrating casework in practice. These did not provide an adequate framework for understanding clients' motives and behavior, the causes of their persistent difficulties, the reasons for their resistance to helping efforts, and what interventions might work to address any of these issues. Nor did existing theory and practice wisdom provide an adequate framework for defining appropriate expectations of and boundaries for personal helping efforts, especially under conditions of poverty.

The search for a distinct theory and method for casework services coincided with the gradual infiltration of psychoanalytic theory into psychiatry and child guidance work in the United States. At a broad level psychoanalytic theory complemented the public preoccupations and tensions of the times, particularly the conflict between the new public hedonism and longstanding values such as self-denial and moderation.

Early psychoanalytic theory embodied a view of human nature as a struggle between primitive, largely destructive drives and higher order mental structures that kept those drives in check. It viewed character as deeply rooted and behavior as at leastly partly shaped by unconscious mental processes. At the same time psychoanalytic theory seemed to deemphasize heredity as the shaper of peoples' behavior and, by implication, suggested that behavior was alterable through particular experiences. It suggested that most people had at least some "ego strengths," providing an implicit opening for formal helpers to look for and draw on clients' strengths and to acknowledge their complexity as human beings. It also suggested that most people, poor and nonpoor alike, were struggling (as best they could) to grow and develop.

Psychoanalytic theory's perspective on human nature placed what seemed so problematic about helping relationships with poor, immigrant families—resistance, denial, passivity, and seemingly self-destructive behavior; providers' confusion about their own own feelings; and the role of their own beliefs and values in helping—in a plausible and legitimizing explanatory framework. It suggested why individual change was so difficult, why it was not occurring even with adequate application of casework technique (Polsky 1991:113). Marcus (1935:134) warned that the idea that individuals' minds were "determined" early in their lives, and therefore were not easy to reform, would come hard to caseworkers, "who have so frequently been concerned to reform and rescue."

Psychoanalytic theory seemed to suggest that objective conditions were less important in shaping peoples' lives than the personal meaning people made of those conditions (Lubove 1965:113). It explained why clients' "irrationally" resisted caseworkers' suggestion that, regardless of the insecurity and hardship they experienced, their difficulties were at least partly due to personal issues that they were not acknowledging. Psychoanalytic theory relocated what caseworkers had felt to be struggles between themselves and their clients inside the mental apparatus of those clients. The helper's role was to support those parts of clients' selves that were struggling to choose the right actions, make the right decisions, and come to terms with their personal history and current reality.

Paralleling psychoanalytic theory's view of human nature, development, and change was a distinct theory about helping relationships. Beginning in the late 1920s a few casework theorists began to translate their own experience with psychoanalysis, as well as their familiarity with psychoanalytic literature, into terms that they thought useful for caseworkers. Caseworkers were urged to focus less on judgment and more on trying to "see things as they appeared to the client" (Leiby 1978:184). They were told that self-knowledge was critical to being useful as a helper and urged to try to be aware of their own feelings and reactions to clients, and their own contribution to the course of the helping relationship. They were told to worry less about technique per se: helping was not primarily a matter of "verbal acrobatics, or unassimilated methods" (Waite 1937).

A fundamental contribution of psychoanalytic theory was the idea that the helping relationship was itself a mechanism for bringing about change in clients. One casework theorist described the helping relationship "as a new environment which gives the client opportunity to work out his own problems" (Robinson 1930:184). The idea that the helping relationship was an important crucible for client change helped caseworkers rein in their sense of their rights over the client, which could now be seen as "limited to the control of what they gave of themselves as helping persons" (Garten and Otto 1964:60).

Psychoanalytic theory had implications for supervision that in many ways paralleled those for helping itself. Prevailing emphases on caseworkers' own "adjustment" to the demands of their particular agency were broadened to include attention to their reactions to clients and to their growth as professionals. The idea of a parallel process in the supervisory relationship and the helping relationship first began to appear in the casework literature, also influencing the practice of supervision.

In its emphasis on the subjective and intersubjective nature of helping, psychoanalytic theory questioned the prevailing casework ideal of the detached, disinterested helper. Casework technique, a reaction to the "spontaneous sentiment" and "undisciplined emotion" of earlier helping efforts of both charity workers and Progressive era reformers (Lubove 1965:122), would now be based on the disciplined use of emotions as a helping tool (i.e., on controlled subjectivity). This seemed to resolve some of the tensions in the helping professions about the relative importance of caring and technique. Questions nonetheless remained about the ends to which helpers were to put themselves in the service of clients: should they focus on self-knowledge or better coping? and should aims should be different for poor and nonpoor clients?

As numerous writers have pointed out (see, e.g., Germain 1970; Heineman 1980) psychoanalytic theory was not monolithic; different strands suggested different implications for casework. By the early 1930s theoretical competition was beginning to emerge between two schools in particular. One, known as the Functional School, led by Virginia Robinson and others at the University of Pennsylvania, subscribed to the ideas of Otto Rank. Different followers and subsequent historians emphasize different aspects of Rank's thought. One interpretation suggested that the helper's job was to create a context in which the client "tested his ability to ask for and use help," gradually becoming more able to do both (Germain 1970:17). In turn, through that process the client became better able to choose (wisely) and grow in his or her everyday life. Another suggested that the purpose of the helping process and relationship was to help the client become more aware of his or her own reactions and impulses, and how these shaped the attainment of goals (Tyson 1995). Rank's ideas reinforced the centrality of individual adjustment as a goal of casework, and the notion that individuals were responsible for coming to terms with reality. They also implied a relatively stronger focus on clients' present situation, as opposed to their personal history.

The other theoretical contender, known as the Diagnostic School, and

led by Gordon Hamilton from Columbia University, combined orthodox
Freudian theory with a measure of sensitivity to the importance of attending to the social contexts in which people lived. Functionalists tended to
contrast Rank's and Freud's thought by pointing out that while the former
assumed that human beings had the capacity to shape their own fate, the
latter really didn't believe in the possibility of growth. This was an exagger-
ation. While Rank's followers chose to interpret his thought in more optimistic terms, both his and Freud's theories were about limitations. As
Hamilton put it, the goal of casework was to help individuals live more constructively with their psychological disabilities as well as their objective life
situation (Hamilton 1940:24–25). By the late 1930s and early 1940s, ego psychology, with its emphasis on coping, adaptation, and reality-testing, would
emerge to form a bridge between the two.

In practice, psychoanalytic concepts found their way into everyday casework practice only slowly. If not always a personal analysis, the application
of psychoanalytic theory required years of training and supervision by someone who him or herself had had that same preparation. The limited impact
of psychoanalytic theory during the 1930s is illustrated by Heineman
(1980:492–493), using the example of the Children's Home and Aid Society
in Illinois, a respected child welfare agency. Throughout that period the society's case records contained almost no psychological terminology. As late
as 1938 the agency asked intake workers to "state whether a parent was
'morally defective.'" Heineman notes that throughout the period many practitioners continued to believe that most behavior was a matter of will, "and
hence amenable to punishment, inducement or reasoning."

Social service literature in the 1930s reflected contradictory views about
how quickly and in what ways psychoanalytic theory was influencing casework practice. Grace Marcus (1935:130) described the process as piecemeal
and gradual, but nonetheless profound. She called the introduction of psychoanalytic theory an important "inner-correction" within the field. In a response to Marcus's paper, Bertha Reynolds (1935:143) noted that only a tiny
percentage of caseworkers had mastered this new theory and asked whether
the rest, who lacked that preparation, should be said to not be practicing
casework at all, since they were not up to date? The principal impact of psychoanalytic theory, with its deemphasis on external reality, may have been to
remove practical assistance and advocacy further from the field of vision of
many casework theorists, if not of casework practitioners. Psychoanalytic
theory and practice principles also reinforced the inclination of caseworkers
not to accept the problems that clients brought to them at face value.

## Supportive Services and the Great Depression

*The Beginning of the Depression*

The 1920s was also supposed to be the decade in which poverty withered away in the wash of economic and technical progress. Economic growth did lift many workers into the middle class. But it left many others behind. The labor peace, civic-minded corporate welfare (e.g., generous contributions to community chests), and sense of optimism of the times were a thin veneer covering persistent, underlying problems (Freeman et al 1992:270). During the late 1920s demand for relief and assistance of all sorts began rising. By 1929 this rising tide was beginning to overwhelm local public relief offices and private family service agencies. At first, increasing demands for relief were attributed to poor peoples' growing sense of entitlement. Yet case-workers also remarked upon how few of the families coming to them for assistance had ever sought relief before (Reynolds 1931:26). By the early 1930s the United States economy had virtually collapsed. One in three wage earners was unemployed; millions more worked only part-time. Even those working full-time experienced significant pay cuts (Freeman et al 1992:319). Unskilled workers experienced the highest rates of unemployment, as companies tried to hold on to their skilled workers by giving them the unskilled workers' jobs. Ethnic minorities also found themselves the first to be let go by companies. Ill-health, malnutrition, and homelessness soared. Inadequate diet, compounded by overcrowding and other stressors, led to increases in dysentery, tuberculosis, pellagra, and typhoid (Freeman et al. 1992:320).

Social service providers, like others, were shocked by the fragility of the American ideology revealed by the Depression. Of what use was the belief in the value of hard work when so many willing workers were fired or could not find a job? How could the optimism that seemed to pervade American life in the 1920s have dissipated so quickly? Service providers were shocked as well by families' loss of security and confidence. One social worker's report described finding "fear; fear driving them into a state of semi-collapse; cracking nerves; and an overpowering terror of the future" (Patterson 1986:37). Reynolds (1931:38) quotes one mother, responding to a survey by a local family agency, examining how families who could find neither work nor relief coped: "I used to just sit wondering if the people next door would send in something after they had finished [supper]. Sometimes they would and other times they would have nothing left, and we just wouldn't eat. I'd tell the kids to drink lots of water and we'd wait for the next meal."

A new, and in some cases bitter rhetoric appeared in the social service literature. An announcement in the January 1929 newsletter of the Northwestern University settlement first asked readers to help locate jobs for the unemployed fathers coming to the settlement every day to seek help in finding work, and then asked: "Why shouldn't there be work? Thousands of automobiles go past the settlement every day. How can people afford to have them when their fellowmen have not enough to eat?" (Wukas 1991:49). One writer in a social work journal noted that the economic system was going through its periodic "disgorging of victims" (Silver 1932:58). This writer continued that American society must give up "the messianic economic romancing which characterized the pre-depression era, and all the apocalyptic dreams of miracle-working captains of industry" (p. 63).

The Depression led some in the social service community, especially the settlement community, to renew their social activism. It led others to struggle with whether to become activists for the first time in their lives. A handful of settlement and casework agency leaders led efforts to pressure local, state, and federal governments to increase public resources for relief. Yet increasing reliance on Community Chests for funding during the 1920s had made even the historically progressive settlements in many cities cautious about social action in concert with and on behalf of unemployed workers. Trolander (1987:23) points out that "it was settlements in the non-Chest cities of New York and Chicago that organized protest groups and engaged in demonstrations and other actions to get adequate relief programs." The most radical actions for most settlements were to assist individual families in desperate circumstances—for example, helping a family circumvent the gas company by turning its gas back on (Trolander 1975).

The Depression did not just challenge providers' (and many Americans') basic beliefs about their society. As the Depression continued into a second and then a third year, social service agency budgets, and public and private relief budgets were severely cut. During the 1930–1931 fiscal year the budget of the Philadelphia Family Society, a major family welfare agency, was cut by 42 percent. Budgetary cutbacks left some social service agencies "a shadow of their former selves" (Silver 1932:54). Family grants to those able to secure relief were often less than ten dollars a month.

Settlements, like other social services agencies, experienced budget cutbacks and struggled to meet urgent family needs for food, fuel, clothing, and shelter. For example, over time many switched from grocery orders to food boxes, which were cheaper but that upset families since they might contain food deemed unpalatable. An increasing proportion of settlement work, like that of other agencies, involved responding to emergencies. Trolander (1975:68) cites Lea Taylor, head worker at Chicago Commons, who noted that "the entire first floor was used for interviewing," much of it for families in crisis. Settlements used their networks to try to locate jobs, usually in vain, and drew on their historic creativity to develop make-work community projects for unemployed men. In other words, settlements used the opportunity afforded by a period of social upheaval to once again prove their worth—this time, in the words of one Minneapolis settlement leader, to "hold the fort, hoping against hope that reinforcements will soon arrive" (Karger 1987:82).

As relief budgets shrank and demands on those budgets increased, the differentiated responses to different family situations and the balance of responsibility for relief among public and private agencies that had just begun to be worked out, collapsed. New, often harsh, and in some cases bizarre rules for providing relief were created. Some local rules required social workers to wait until families were completely destitute before approving relief. In New York City, a rule called "Skip the Feed" required local offices of the Department of Welfare to skip every tenth family seeking relief (Hall 1971:12). Casework was also rationed. Agencies struggled constantly with whom to select for relief-related monitoring and follow-up. Some developed triage systems for deciding who could benefit most from supportive casework services—for instance, families at neither too high nor too low risk, with neither too many nor too few problems.

Local governments took their cue from business and political leaders, who, fearing massive social disorder, argued that "it was unwise if not actually unpatriotic" to admit the existence of the Depression, "or at least to talk about it openly" (Dunham 1938:16). Thus, municipal responses ranged from asking unemployed workers to sell apples on street corners, to asking workers who were not yet unemployed to share their work with those who were, to asking residents of each city block to care for the unemployed who lived on their block (Dunham 1938:16).

*Casework Identity and the Depression*

The Depression did not only cause fiscal shocks to the social service enterprise. There is a sense in the professional literature of the time that it severely complicated continuing identity struggles; in particular that it forced social casework off the track that it wanted to be on. Articles in the professional literature asked such questions as "What is unemployment doing to family social work?" (Queen 1932). Speaking in July 1931, Florence Waite noted that "no one would deny that for some senior caseworkers this year has meant a total relinquishment of what we commonly regard as casework" (Waite 1931:144). And Silver (1932:53) noted that the Depression had left social service providers "staggered and confused."

Even before the Depression turned the field upside down, there had been a growing awareness that casework needed to find a place between "pure therapy and public relief" (Lubove 1965:115). It was limited by the time available to serve clients, as well as by the financial resources and purposes of the agency for which the caseworker worked. Yet during the Depression many private family agencies were re-recruited to process relief applications and distribute relief. They were pulled back to the task of dealing squarely with poverty, just as they had been moving away from it. The Depression turned caseworkers who viewed themselves as skilled professionals back into "menial" relief-givers who did less interpersonal helping. Bertha Reynolds (1932:52) noted that "robots could almost do the handing out of the bare means of under-sustenance as well as we." The Depression led to impossibly large caseloads. These in turn forced social agencies into hiring thousands of untrained workers as case aides and interviewers, reminding professional caseworkers of the days of nonprofessional charity agents.

Throughout the 1930s the social services struggled to reconcile the common tragedy affecting millions of people with the strong belief that psychological factors are at the heart of human problems and with the contradictory belief that, as one writer (May 1936:143) put it, it is individuals' responsibility to adapt to the rules, institutions, and values of the culture in which they live. Many private family welfare agencies tried to hold on to established concepts and distinctions and continued to use morals tests. Meridel Le Suer, a poet and journalist of the time, noted that "charities take care of very few and only those that are called 'deserving.' The lone girl is under suspicion by the virgins who dispense charity" (cited in Freeman et al. 1992:327). Yet widespread and indiscriminate unemployment and hardship constantly challenged such practices.

Some caseworkers, finding that they had no answer to peoples' questions about what to do next or why they had lost everything in spite of playing by the rules their whole lives, assumed a passive stance. Reynolds (1963:139) argues that the passivity that was "in vogue in casework [during the 1930s] was probably compounded of many things, such as revolt against the advice-giving which had cursed our young profession . . . [and] application of the idea of emotional catharsis from the practice of psychoanalysis."

Casework theorists struggled to adapt their theories to what was happening inside service agencies. (Tyson 1995:55, citing Jesse Taft, ties the functionalists' emphasis on people having to come to terms with limitations "such as time and mortality" to the "severe limitations of agency-based services in the face of Depression-era needs.") And relief agencies rationalized their constant refrain that families must simply accept what was offered by referring to theory, especially such theory as emphasized the importance of people coming to terms with reality. Some theorists insisted that mass unemployment did not change the fact that there was a good deal of hidden mental illness in relief caseloads. Gordon Hamilton (1934:391) wrote that "in any relief population there will be be a percentage of persons with a marked trend to dependency and even parasitism." (Hamilton would not give up, either. In 1939, on the very heels of the Depression, she wrote that some social workers are "unable or unwilling to see poverty except as a purely economic event, without acknowledging the possible existence of childhood dependency wishes which, if they do not actually cause, may certainly prolong dependency"; cited in Ehrenreich 1985:74.)

Even for those who were psychologically healthy, the need to seek relief was seen to lead to feelings of "guilt or inferiority" and to the "psychological burden of failure" (Lubove 1965:110). Much effort was spent by the casework community trying to interpret peoples' despair. At a minimum the Depression was seen to create new problems in human relations. In analyzing the political activism that was one response to unemployment, a psychiatrist (Kardiner 1936:193) wrote that "[some] individuals vent their aggression in the form of hatred of the established order, fantasies or activities directed at the established order . . . such fantasies of change are based upon the threat of regressive attitudes initiated by their want."

In a different vein, the Depression was seen by some casework writers to "strip things bare," helping social service providers to see the essential common humanity of people, whether poor or not. Inadvertently, it helped service providers see the capacity of their clients, since some agencies hired clients to meet growing demands to interview aid applicants, process paperwork, and the like. Some of those who came in to family agencies to seek relief told staff that they did not like being treated as if there was something wrong with them (see Polsky 1991:141). This, and the reality of large volumes of people seeking relief, reminded helping professionals that not every contact with a poor family implied a need for casework.

A few casework leaders struggled to forge a new conceptual synthesis that encompassed both psychological and social realities and that balanced attention to peoples' needs and rights. Bruno (1933:7) argued that the mission of social workers should be to focus on the "complexities of human nature, wrenched out of all recognition by . . . an unjust social order." And a few theorists began to question the very foundations of the profession. Grace Marcus (1935:7; Ehrenreich:114) noted that "casework's fundamental purpose of adjusting the individual to himself, his human relationships, and his environment seems trivial and reactionary. . . . Casework is a sop to the underprivileged, obscures the issues of social justice, imposes on the individual the cruel burden of adapting himself to a psychotic society, and, insofar as it succeeds, constitutes a brake on social action."

The Depression temporarily gave a boost to generalist and community work. Workers in family agencies had to respond to and work with a variety of citizen organizations, some of them militant (e.g., the Unemployed Citizens League). They had to struggle with their own stereotypes about activists—for instance, that those who organized were communists and paid agitators. They had to respond to eviction riots and food riots.

Some social workers believed that the Depression, and the social service community's response to it, signalled a need for reform of services from within. One notable effort to do so was undertaken by the Rank and File Movement. Spano (1982) describes three main dimensions of this movement. One was an effort to strengthen social workers' identification with the working class. This included actively supporting various workers' organizations and their efforts to improve working conditions and social security, as well as pressing for better working conditions for both professional and paraprofessional frontline workers within the social services. A second dimension was repudiation of liberal assumptions about social change. These assumptions included the notion that social change was a "gradual process based on education and persuasion; the belief that individuals are good and will change . . . when they perceive their errors"; the reliance on facts to stimulate social change; the belief in a common good; and the denial that there are genuine conflicts of interest in society (Spano 1092:97).

The third element of the Rank and File Movement involved an effort to promote an alternative set of assumptions to guide interpersonal work with poor families. These included a focus on the rights of clients to self-definition and self-determination in helping relationships and an argument that helping professionals could not be (and should not view themselves as) objective, disinterested parties in helping relationships; rather, they should put themselves in the service of clients. The Rank and File Movement lasted barely a few years. Some members grew uncomfortable with the movement's connections to the Communist Party. Others heeded the warnings of more conservative agency leadership that they should desist if they wished to keep their jobs. (Such warnings were sometimes disguised as a criticism that members were "over-identifying" with the poor and unemployed; Spano 1982:87). The success of New Deal legislation also deflated the radical energy that had emerged during the Depression.

## The Passage of Aid to Dependent Children

Social service providers were not the only ones who struggled with the meaning of the Great Depression. Different segments of the American public took very different lessons from it. Those directly affected were personally changed forever. Yet the basic views of influential corporate and political leaders, and to an extent the general public, about poverty and dependency did not change. The denial that had led to unrealistic and futile responses during the early years of the Depression continued to characterize interpretations of its meaning. Many Americans continued to disapprove of both public aid and those who needed it. McElvaine (1993:179) notes that "for many Americans who avoided the ravages of the Depression, it became an article of faith that relief recipients irresponsibly had children for whom they could not provide. Some conservatives charged that relief women had babies in order to qualify for higher payments."

In spite of the continuing strain of skepticism over public aid, the depth and breadth of the Depression made it clear that local governments, complemented by private charity, were not capable of responding to national problems. Throughout the early years of the Depression the responses of local and state relief programs had been haphazard, chaotic, and insufficient. (Most state constitutions limited state borrowing power and thus the ability to respond to recession or depression.) At the same time the Depression did not lead to needed debate inside and outside of Congress about the nature of federal government responsibility for families. When Aid to Dependent Children (ADC) was first proposed and formulated, there was more discussion in Congress about financing formulas and administration than about social or political objectives.

One reason for the lack of substantive debate about the purpose of ADC was the assumption that it was meeting a temporary need that would dissipate with improving economic conditions. A second was the belief that a strengthened social insurance system for wage earners—the focus of the Social Security Act—would largely meet the needs of vulnerable women and children. In addition, many in Congress believed that defining the objectives of social welfare programs was a state prerogative (Leiby 1978:61–63). The way the original ADC legislation was passed "hidden among other, more palatable programs," also contributed to the absence of public debate about its purposes (Gittens 1986:86).

What debate there was about ADC illuminates how completely the arguments surrounding public aid have changed in sixty years. Within the Roosevelt administration there was some argument about whether ADC should involve cash or in-kind assistance. There was concern that cash assistance required more monitoring and record-keeping than in-kind. According to Austin (1988:118), Harry Hopkins insisted on cash rather than in-kind assistance, since he believed it "essential to maintaining individual independence and a sense of individual responsibility." There also was some debate about the relative merits of a categorical program for dependent children and their mothers, versus a pooled, general assistance program. Categorical relief was argued to "carry much less stigma than general relief," because aid to dependent children was viewed as "an investment in future citizenship," carried out in partnership with mothers and thus more acceptable to the public (Dunham 1938:37).

The social service community took what opportunities it had to argue for a role in any new federal programs. Speaking to the House Ways and Means Committee in 1935, Grace Abott noted that "mothers do not know, just because they are mothers, how to care for children in a scientific way, and if they get that supervision, they do know it" (cited in Mink 1995:30). Social service leaders argued also for the necessity of professionalism in the administration of new social welfare programs.

The continuing suspicion of government, and the lack of debate and thoughtful consideration contributed to a federal family support policy under ADC (and related child welfare programs) that left the conception of government purpose and responsibility for family well-being incomplete. The passage of ADC did force some reorganization—for the better—of state public relief programs. Nonetheless, the rationale, authorizing language, and funding of ADC (as well as new maternal and child health and child welfare programs) reflected a reluctance to define a government role in positive and normative, as opposed to residual, terms. The formal, legislated expansion of public responsibility for family well-being did not somehow replace the deeply rooted belief in local and private responsibility (see Grubb and Lazerson 1980). It simply added a layer of complexity to an already ambiguous situation.

The legacy of Mothers' Aid (and therefore of scientific charity before it) could be seen in many aspects of the ADC program. One dimension of that legacy was the exclusion of families in which the father was present in the family but unemployed. A second was inadequate grants. The maximum monthly grant per child under the original legislation was $18 for the first child, and $12 for each subsequent child. Another legacy of Mothers' Aid was a great deal of state discretion in program design. This would result in significant differences across states in eligibility and administrative standards, levels of participation, and grant size. Supervision of (and implicitly therefore the right to try to change) families receiving relief was also established from the outset as a key element of the program. Not least, the principle of using morals tests to determine elegibility for assistance was carried over. In the early years states could and did deny benefits to children born out of wedlock. These latter elements of ADC strongly qualified the entitlement basis of the program.

Gittens (1986) argues that the perverse design of ADC was self-evident from the outset. She mentions not only the exclusion of families with fathers still in the home but also the reduction of the base grant by the same amount as any money earned by recipients. Analyzing the emergent ADC program, Arthur Dunham, a respected figure in the public welfare field, noted that "our public poor relief system is the system of Elizabeth, made applicable by a few superficial changes to the new conditions" (Dunham 1938:12).

As formative decades for the elaboration of supportive social services, the 1920s and 1930s were difficult. The relatively rich theoretical framework for helping relationships provided by psychoanalytic theory (and psychology in general) implied that service providers no longer had to rely so much on faith in assuming that "sometime, somehow or somewhere" what they did would "result in social good" (Karger 1987:143). Conversely—and ironically—it also allowed service providers to acknowledge that the helping process was more complicated and harder to understand than had previously been assumed.

At the same time the historic social control function of supportive social services took on a new, therapeutic form. This new form was dangerous because it implied that the limits on poor peoples' freedom and opportunity were internal ones. It was dangerous because, as Polsky (1991) argues, the therapeutic approach to addressing social problems masks issues of power: over problem definition, over poor peoples' own self-definition, and, not least, over the role of the helper. Advances in theory and method did not resolve the tension between helpers' sense of expertise (and therefore prerogative) in recognizing and addressing poor peoples' needs and their clients' right to interpret and control their own lives. If such advances served primarily to increase success in gaining clients' cooperation with helpers' aims, then who benefited?

The establishment of a variety of emergency human service programs during the Depression contributed to the gradual burrowing of services deeper into the culture. Yet the Depression stimulated questions about the basic assumptions and intent of services from within the social service community itself, as well as from close observers. Although the great majority of services providers did what little they could to reduce peoples' hardship, that modest assistance often seemed grossly inadequate, even to providers themselves. More important, the Depression threatened the ideal of case-workers as dispassionate professionals looking into individual lives to discover the roots of problems, and more generally making sense of American society's complex social life.

At a broader level, the ambiguous and limited framework for family welfare established by the federal government in ADC and related programs—with its unclear purposes, limits on benefits, categorization, and partial coverage—would eventually increase the pressures on supportive social services, forcing them to cope with tasks for which they were ill-suited. Lack of clarity about whether ADC was intended primarily to support family well-being, protect children, or even strengthen parent-child relationships would not only buffet the ADC program itself for decades to come but would create policy vacuums into which supportive social services were pulled. The loose, ill-defined articulation between federal, state, and local programs, and between public and private institutional responsibilities, sowed the seeds for a lack of accountability in the human service system, with each program defending its prerogatives and, at the same time, viewing itself as only partly and temporarily responsible for family well-being.

Equally important, the creation of a set of programs targeted explicitly or implicitly at poor families laid the foundation for what would become a two-tiered social welfare system. The goals that emerged for services and policies for poor families were different than those for advantaged families: more corrective, less developmental. And when, as was the case almost every decade during the subsequent half century, the perceived need for universal (or at least non-categorical) services designed to support normal developmental tasks arose, there would be no obvious way to support such services with public funds.

CHAPTER FOUR

## The Quiet Before the Next Storm

The 1940s and 1950s were marked by optimism about the potential of helping services to address almost every imaginable social problem: from the generic anxiety and alienation associated with modern, industrial life, to the loss of confidence and self-doubt associated with cyclical unemployment, to the very specific help needed by modern parents in raising psychologically healthy yet economically competitive children. Funding for human services increased dramatically, contributing to the creation of large bureaucratic service organizations, and growing numbers of professionally trained providers.

Growth in helping services was first fueled by the tasks of relocating and readjusting veterans and their families. It derived later from an increasing preoccupation with mental health in popular culture. There was regular commentary in the media and academic literature on the emotional pressures of modern life. During the war years social theorists had become understandably preoccupied with the psychological roots of aggression and authoritarian behavior. This preoccupation carried over into the postwar period, and mental health professionals built on it to argue that professional guidance and, when necessary, therapeutic helping were critical tools for creating and maintaining a healthy society (see Graebner 1980; Lasch 1977). By the late 1950s some within the helping services believed their efforts were having a deep impact on American social life (Halmos 1970:4).

During this same historical period, however, there was a steady decline in supportive services for poor families, particularly noncategorical, neighborhood-based services. Private child and family service agencies were providing fewer basic services in poor neighborhoods, in some cases deliberately, in others not. There were new rationales, as well as growing opportunities and resources for work with middle-class families, and older urban neighborhoods were undergoing a change in the population of poor families, with fewer European immigrants and more racial and ethnic minorities. By the end of the 1950s some agencies had significantly reduced their historic, if ambivalent, mission of serving the poor. The remaining community-based providers—such as settlements—themselves struggled with changing neighborhoods and populations, loss of service roles, and identity issues.

The reluctance of some private agencies to serve poor, minority families contributed to a growing role for public agencies, notably child welfare and public aid departments (Bush 1988:32–34). This in turn meant that an increasing proportion of social services for poor families was provided in categorical programs, either by or on behalf of these public agencies. The more public agencies became involved in service provision to poor families, the more families (and types of families) they discovered who needed their supervision and services.

Even as some private social service providers were withdrawing from work with poor families, social service theorists continued the decades-old struggle to define a professional and yet useful role for work with such families. Their main historical argument, that supportive services were needed because the poor (particularly the new urban migrants from the South and Puerto Rico) were not capable of making decisions in their own long-term best interest, remained prevalent throughout the 1950s. This argument sat uneasily with that era's glorification of democracy and self-determination and its ambivalence about the power of the state. The solution to this dilemma, more often than not, was to take the position that the client's rights could best "be understood in terms of his psychological needs" (Keith-Lucas 1957:135). The helper's role was to suggest, to lead the client toward the right decision or action.

New elements in supportive services nonetheless emerged, and in specific local settings old ones reemerged. There was some effort to reconceptualize casework to make it more acceptable to poor families. This meant more focus on meeting immediate, pressing needs and on being actively supportive; efforts to be more sensitive to cultural differences in seeking and using help; an emphasis on withholding judgment; and, once again, a reliance on outreach and home visiting. There were a number of demonstration efforts designed to develop and test helping approaches responsive to the complex, intertwined difficulties of the most vulnerable families. Discrete innovations sustained a sense of progress in supportive helping services, in spite of the fact that research was beginning to raise fundamental questions about the effectiveness of such services.

## Changing Perspectives on Urban Poverty and a Changing Population of Poor Families

The 1940s brought a strong shift in perspective on the roots of most social problems, away from the social and economic system and back to individuals and families. The focus on an external enemy in World War II diminished attention to class and racial conflicts within American society. Renewed economic growth led to reinterpretation of the Great Depression, as both an aberration and a natural part of the business cycle. Economists argued that economic growth was the best antidote to poverty. As in the 1920s the notion that poverty would wither away of its own accord pervaded popular thought (Patterson 1986:85). Many who had earlier been concerned with economic inequality shifted their concern to the quality of life in American society as a whole.

The post–World War II period was marked both by a quest for normalcy and by a variety of political and social tensions. Underlying the return of peace was a continuing fear of disorder and conflict. The sense of social unity created by World War II dissipated quickly. Conservative politicians attacked those suspected of being sympathetic to socialist ideas. Union activists were labeled communist sympathizers by those they had worked beside for years (Reynolds 1963). Conservative newspapers attacked the poor, who were said to undermine society in their own way. In one incident a group of Aid to Dependent Children (ADC) families who had lost their housing due to fire, condemnation of buildings in which they lived, and other factors were put up briefly in inexpensive hotels. The *New York World-Telegram*, a conservative newspaper, learned of the arrangement and proceeded to write a series of editorials about ADC recipients staying in luxury hotels, "in mink coats . . . [with] maid service and laundry allowances to coddle the lazy" (Reynolds 1963:266).

African Americans and Hispanics found themselves the first to be laid off as war industries contracted. There was a rapid rise in joblessness again, especially among the young and minorities. This joblessness especially affected older youths and young adults in the inner-cities, "robbing [them] of their start in a working life" (Hall 1971:219). A severe postwar housing shortage would lead in the 1950s to massive urban renewal programs that destroyed the fabric of many inner-city neighborhoods, displaced hundreds of thousands of people, and contributed to the consolidation of minority ghettos.

Although job opportunity was diminishing, the massive migration of African Americans from the South to the north and Midwest that had begun with World War II continued into the postwar years. (Many migrants felt they had little choice. Rapid mechanization of agriculture was greatly reducing demand for agricultural labor in the South.) This migration, and the slow but steady erosion of jobs from urban to suburban areas, created growing stresses in many older inner-city neighborhoods. Some neighborhoods experienced almost complete racial turnover, with longstanding white residents leaving, and new African-American families trying to plant roots and adjust to new conditions. Community leaders and residents of of neighborhoods affected by racial change found that historical political agreements about the allocation of public resources no longer held. As a result schools, fire, and police protection, and sanitation deteriorated dramatically. High rates of unemployment and large numbers of dislocated people contributed to a breakdown in social organization and increases in a variety of social problems in traditionally minority neighborhoods.

Social service case reports from the 1950s began to reflect the injurious effects of these social and economic trends on poor families: declining job opportunities for males; a new kind of racial stigma—the stigma of marginalization—leading to a new kind of self-doubt; and among youth and young adults, growing skepticism of the validity of moral values imparted by parents and community elders (Nightingale 1994). Relief roles once again began rising, and as they did so, those forced to seek and rely on relief found themselves the source of public anger and skepticism.

The post–World War II years also brought a strong reiteration of the importance of the family as the institution that embodied society's highest ideals. Sound maternal care of children was once again postulated as a foundation of well-adjusted, productive adulthood and therefore of a healthy society. (This was an important theme in Benjamin Spock's "Baby and Child Care," first published in 1946; for a discussion of this book, see Graebner 1980:620). Women were urged to recommit themselves to social roles postponed or cast off during the war years. Kunzel (1993:163) argues that the family also became "a crucial site for fighting cold-war battles. . . . It was refuge, source of values, social order, protector of a way of life." It was even argued that a "vigilant" mother was the front line of defense against treason (Coontz 1992:33).

In spite of generally rising standards of living, poverty persisted for a quarter of all Americans, and a third of all children (Coontz 1992:29). Old perspectives on poverty mixed with new. There was, as always, much distinguishing between "accidental" poverty due to misfortune and chronic poverty due either to individual character or a subgroup's mores. Psychological perspectives on poverty that had first taken root in the 1920s, and become dormant during the 1930s, revived again. This time round they were mixed with analyses of the unique problems of African Americans in American society, notably the effects of racial prejudice on African Americans' identity and the ill-preparedness of African-American migrants for the demands of urban, industrial life. The notion of a culture of poverty gradually took shape, attached to African-American migrants and Hispanic immigrants to the inner cities. At the end of the decade a prominent social thinker would remark, almost casually, that "some cultures and subcultures breed poverty as surely as a waterfront breeds rats" (Boulding 1961:45).

In general the 1950s marked a shift in the locus of stigma in U.S. society from the generic deviance of immigrants, who simply needed time and assistance in assimilating, to the economic dependence, as well as the moral and behavioral deviance of racial and ethnic minorities. Along with this shift, a growing differentiation began to be made between white and black illegitimacy (Kunzel 1993). And women's dependency was gradually being redefined "from a norm to a pathology" (Mink 1990:179; by the late 1960s this would further undermine whatever tenuous political support remained for the ADC program).

There was an ever stronger differentiation of expert concerns about childrearing in nonpoor and poor families. For the former, concerns revolved around overprotectiveness, too much stimulation, and excessive nurturance (seen to lead to anxiety and related neuroses). For the latter, concerns revolved around the effects of too little of these activities. A profile of childrearing among families in poverty emerged, which would persist for four decades (see Geismar and Krisberg 1967:27–29). Poor families were viewed as adult- rather than child-centered, and poor parents as too burdened or otherwise preoccupied to attend to their children's needs. Although children were loved and accepted, poor parents were seen as authoritarian and restrictive toward them, showing little outward affection. As a result children had no models or experiences from which to learn empathy. Not least, poor parents were seen to place great, and at times undue, demands for mature behavior on their children, and to promote self-reliance at all costs.

As in the Progressive era, poor families in the late 1940s and 1950s were believed to have a restricted sense of community and of their social world, with little connection to mainstream values and institutions. They were particularly alienated from, and sometimes suspicious of, family service agencies. One two-year study of sixty-two low-income families from a New York City tenement district found that while they readily used health and recreation services for help with problems, they rarely used family social services, viewing them as stigmatizing or as inclined to interfere (Koos 1946). Service providers began to recognize that African-American and Hispanic migrants had brought their own helping traditions with them to the city. In the case of the Hispanic migrants, language barriers exacerbated the gap between families and agencies.

A new group of harder-to-reach and harder-to-serve poor was identified. Jones (1969:28) describes them as those who were "busily producing the delinquents who fought on Henry Street, in plain sight of its famous settlement house. Many were second-generation relief families. They kept away from the community centers, whose clientele was those of the low-income group who were on their way up and out."

## The Private Agencies Rethink Their Role

During the Depression years private, voluntary family service agencies had moved from providing a primary role in services to poor families to a partnership, or complementary relationship with public relief agencies. The creation of ADC had diminished their role in arranging (and ended their role in approving and supervising) financial assistance for poor families. Societal developments during the 1940s and 1950s nudged social service providers' concerns further away from poverty per se. The social service needs associated with World War II, as well as the return to prosperity as the United States economy shifted to a war footing brought caseworkers "abundant opportunities to serve clients in the social mainstream" (Polsky 1991:157). Serving such clients promised more prestige than serving the poor, especially the new minority poor. At the same time the seemingly new problems associated with migration of large numbers of minority families to, and their concentration in, the inner cities compelled a response of some sort from social service providers.

Private agencies adapted to changing external demands and opportunities by seeking a position that assured them both income and the continued ability to control their fate. This search led individual agencies in different directions. Many continued to provide casework services to poor families, but at a reduced level. Some chose to participate in the emerging field of supportive and therapeutic services for troubled families, soon to be called multiproblem families. Some agencies redefined their mission in such a way as to deemphasize both their historical, semipublic functions and their commitment to work with the poor. New mission statements included "service to all persons regardless of class," or "serving the community as a whole" (Bush 1988; Cloward and Epstein 1965). In its 1945 annual report, the Cleveland Family Service Association noted that "the idea that the family agency deals only with the misfits of society is out. There are times in the lives of most people when a caseworker could steer them through a troubled period" (Paradise 1948:29).

In addition to redefining their missions, family service agencies used a variety of strategies to maintain control over whom they served and how. They used intake to screen out families for one or another reason. They referred poor families to public agencies, and then "assumed" these other agencies were serving the families referred. They moved out of poor neighborhoods. They argued that they needed discretion in order to match their strengths—skilled, specialized casework focused on improving self-understanding—with clients who could benefit from those strengths. (In the process they neglected to acknowledge that they had a good deal of control over how and where they developed their strengths.)

Private agencies also mixed race-specific arguments with class-related ones to rationalize their decisions. One emerging position claimed that the meaning of African Americans' behavior was different from the meaning of the behavior of whites people and therefore required different responses. There was, for example, a view among some service providers that out-of-wedlock childbearing and childrearing were accepted within the African American community; that this community preferred taking care of its own; and that consequently, young African-American mothers who bore children out of wedlock did not need supportive services (see Morton 1993:100). Private agencies generally rationalized their unwillingness to serve African-American clients by arguing that problems that seemed to have individual causes for whites (whether psychological or situational) had cultural causes for African Americans.

Public sector helping services, linked to the Aid to Dependent Children program and to child welfare concerns, grew as privately sponsored services declined. This trend contributed to the growing elaboration of separate service systems for the poor and nonpoor and, by implication, for African Americans and whites. Yet, at the same time that private agencies wanted discretion in whom they would serve and how, they were reluctant to support a strong public service system. Polier (1989:8) describes the situation in New York City as follows:

Public services for dependent and neglected children were opposed in New York by voluntary agencies while hundreds of well babies were held in city hospitals waiting for foster care. . . . With sharply declining revenues, charitable agencies felt overwhelmed. Their way of meeting the situation was to limit intake of children while insisting on their traditional right to select those whom they choose to help.

## Settlements and Work in the Community

Settlements and other remaining community-based agencies had again to rethink their mission. The adjustment of immigrants was no longer an important societal task. A new one—addressing the consequences of racial turnover, changing neighborhoods and neighborhood populations—was emerging; at first, however, it was more felt than recognized clearly by many settlements. As longstanding residents left, they took some of the sense of community with them. Due to urban renewal, which proponents promised would end the existence of slums and urban poverty, a few settlements saw their neighborhoods literally disappear around them. Others experienced a complete turnover in the the ethnic composition of their neighborhoods, from second- and third-generation European immigrants to African-American migrants and Hispanic immigrants. The settlements also had to find a way to relate to public housing, another social reform tool, which proponents said would create powerful new community environments whose positive features would reshape the problematic norms and behavior of poor people. Not least, the settlements had to fight a continuing perception that they were superfluous.

As in the 1920s, some settlement leaders believed that settlements had no choice but to professionalize, to catch up with the private child and family agencies. Others focused on adapting the historic settlement mission and approaches to their changing neighborhoods. As in the Progressive era, a handful of settlement leaders remained politically active at the national and local level, trying to influence such issues as housing and urban renewal, primary health care, and welfare regulations and practices (Trolander 1987). Some settlements moved, seeking a new niche in a new neighborhood but in the process abandoning their history and ties to a particular place.

In some respects the rationales for the existence of settlements remained consistent. As neighborhood-based institutions, settlements saw themselves as well-positioned to do what more bureaucratic service agencies could or would not do. This included prevention and early intervention, outreach and follow-up: "It is important for someone to see the so-called 'closed' cases after they are closed, to see the child on his way to trouble, the family on its way to breaking up" (Hall 1971:xiv). It also included provision of noncategorical services, "bent to the pressures of [neighborhood residents'] needs, which defy all categories" (Hall 1971:xiv). Settlements continued to be important providers of after school and youth programs. They continued to serve as important problem-solving resources for families. In addition, they continued to do local surveys and neighborhood research, publicizing the effects of bad housing conditions or lack of health care.

Meanwhile, the task of community-organizing took on new meaning and renewed urgency, since the longstanding residents and families that had provided the critical mass of neighborhood involvement and leadership had moved out. The task of integrating newcomers into established neighborhoods arose. This contributed to interest in the social psychology of group relations and to the creation of such new institutions as "Councils Against Intolerance" (Hall 1971:224)

As Trolander (1987:137) points out, "the autonomy of the individual settlement house" remained both a liability and a strength. While settlements continued to struggle to secure social service funds, they were able to tailor programs to distinct neighborhood issues and needs. Some settlements, such as New York's Henry Street Settlement, accepted the new neighborhood realities, new populations, new housing patterns, and family vulnerabilities as their new reality as well. They responded and adjusted as issues surfaced. Henry Street developed programs such as Street Club Workers, to smooth conflict between gangs, and a predelinquent gang project, to work with incipient gang members and developing gangs. A number of settlements tried, with varying degrees of success, to establish a presence in public housing projects. They organized social services and community centers; they furnished model apartments, in which good housekeeping was taught (Trolander 1987:82). A few organized and supported tenant initiatives such as Henry Street's tenant council and cooperative nursery in La Guardia Homes on New York's Lower East Side.

## Casework Continues to Struggle with Its Identity

The field of social casework had always been characterized by two separate realities: the one found in the literature, as purveyed by casework leaders and teachers, and the one found at the frontline among practitioners with little formal professional preparation. This situation continued into the 1950s. As reflected in the literature, the casework field was so full of diverging opinions concerning assumptions, purpose, and practice that it was "difficult to know exactly what a social worker believes or really intends" (Keith-Lucas 1957:136). There was continuing debate about whether casework should strive to be more scientific or stay "clinical" (i.e., practical, inductive) in orientation. There were discussions about how best to work with poor families: whether to focus more on their rights or needs, on their adaptive abilities or self-understanding, or on an objective situation or feelings about that situation. There was debate about whether societal standards or situational realities was the more appropriate standard for evaluating clients' behavior.

There was also much discussion in the literature about the meaning of democracy as applied to helping relationships; poor peoples' right to self-determination; and the relationship between those concepts and the social work goal of promoting adjustment to reality and societal demands. Hamilton argued (1948:294) that social workers "do not impose upon the client their own goals or standards of behavior, their own solutions and morals. . . . They do not scold or moralize or threaten. Concrete services and practical assistance are non-contingent on conformity in behavior." Yet she went on to write in the same article that some families were not prepared to make their own choices, to use help wisely, or even to learn (p. 294). Another writer noted that while families had the right to choose their own paths, even self-destructive ones, that right ended at the point at which children's well-being was threatened (Lane 1952:66). On the other side of the argument, Bertha Reynolds asked in a 1952 talk how caseworkers could discuss "choices with people who have no choice [and how they could] treat anxiety in people who know nothing else in their daily lives" (Reynolds 1963:274).

At the frontline workers may well have struggled with the complicated causes of poor families' difficulties, as well as the nature of their own responsibilities. For the most part, practice was shaped, as always, by agency philosophy and history, time and resource constraints, and individual helpers' predispositions. And as always, caseworkers viewed families' situations and choices pragmatically.

New ideas about and approaches to casework with poor families nonetheless percolated, in both the literature and a small number of demonstration programs. There was an emphasis on the need for more attention to the social and economic pressures impinging on families. This meant first relieving the "pressure of need" before turning attention to the deeper, psychological roots of problems (Jones 1969:30). It was argued that being responsive to clients' presenting problems and preoccupations did not always create or exacerbate unhealthy dependency and in fact was crucial to building trust. (Related to the new emphasis on immediate, active responsiveness was an argument for less up-front assessment and diagnosis.) It was suggested that casework with poor families should be more informal and less impersonal. On the other hand a few writers, worried about the problem of false empathy, argued that caseworkers should not disavow the social control function of casework. As representatives of society, of its values and demands, caseworkers should seek an honest, constructive use of their power (Taylor 1958).

Discussions of the "strengths" perspective in helping, which would gain prominence three decades hence, began to appear in the literature, if not in widespread practice. Caseworkers were urged to pay more attention to individuals' and families' capacities and possibilities. Foster (1958:156–157) urged caseworkers working with poor families to focus less on the "chronology of all the trouble which a mother has gotten herself into" and more on the recognition of how she and the family were coping with the routine tasks of everyday life, "all those ordinary things which contribute to family life and which provide its strength."

A literature emerged focusing on casework with minority clients. It was argued by some that casework with African-American clients required different pathways to the same goal (Smith 1946). Since identifying with the client was seen as an important element of the helping relationship, caseworkers were urged to look past racial differences to find common human goals, worries, and preoccupations. At the same time the preoccupation with mental health in the general culture provided an opening for arguments that the psychological and social damage of prejudice and segregation had to be a core concern in casework with minority clients. Caseworkers were urged to be sensitive to African Americans' vulnerable physical self-image and conflicted (or damaged) identity. A number of articles urged caseworkers to monitor closely their own feelings toward minority clients. Reynolds (1963:216) describes a late-1940s meeting in a St. Louis social service agency, in which participants thought they had agreed on a proposal for a program of "block-by-block" counseling to strengthen childrearing practices in an African-American neighborhood. Then, an African American caseworker "brought out a few facts: that many mothers had to leave home at five in the morning to cook breakfast in suburban homes . . . that often mothers did not return from work until [late in the evening]."

## The Emergence of the Multi-Problem Family

Beginning in the late 1940s social service providers began identifying a group of poor families whose social functioning set them apart from the larger population. These families' problems were illuminated by the theoretical lenses of ego psychology and the "functional" school of social casework. Parents were seen to lack internal strengths, whether ego identity or a sense of direction and will (Wiltse 1958). Their behavior was characterized as immature, impulsive, disorganized, and neglectful. Their lives were characterized by dysfunctional relationships (inside and outside the family) and an inability to meet basic family needs. Difficulties and crises were perceived as having a demoralizing effect on these families, inducing a sense of hopelessness rather than serving to prepare and strengthen them. Together the psychological climate and interaction patterns in multiproblem families were regarded as operating to produce the central social problem of the era—juvenile delinquency.

The multiproblem family was seen to be chronically dependent on community services, and at the same time apathetic or resistant toward helping efforts. Its members also consumed a disproportionate share of public and private resources. A 1948 study of public assistance roles in St. Paul, Minnesota, found that 6 percent of families on public assistance were accounting for 50 percent of all public welfare expenditures: specifically, 77 percent of public aid expenditures, 51 percent of public health expenditures, and 56 percent of mental health and corrections expenditures (Buell 1952; Brown 1968:8). At the same time, services to multiproblem families were fragmented, focusing separately on individual members, with no common rationale or perspective.

This conceptual formulation of the "multiproblem" family served many purposes. In one respect it was simply an extension and intensification of the new profile of poor families emerging in the social service literature. In a study of a cross-section of families on ADC in San Mateo County, California, no more than 20 percent were found to be "able to solve the problems confronting them with only financial aid" (Wiltse 1954). In another respect, the multiproblem label provided a means of classing a whole set of social problems together so that they did not seem endless.

The identification of a new group of problematic families also provided an impetus and rationale for developing new intervention approaches;it was one expression of the broader impulse to rethink supportive services for the new urban populations. Starting with the "Family-Centered Project" in St. Paul, Minnesota (Geismar 1957; Overton and Tinker 1959), a number of demonstration projects elaborated an approach and set of principles for working with multiproblem families. These included: small caseloads (ten to twenty families), aggressive outreach to families, use of home visits to enter clients' own worlds, intensive casework, case conferences, and special "units" and teams (Kahn 1976). The key strategies for helping multiproblem families included patience to "ferret out ego strengths," "courage not to give up at signs of hostility," and an ability to work "creatively within limited goals" (Wiltse 1954:180; Garton and Otto 1964:113).

One well-known initiative of the era was the Neighborhood Improvement Project (NIP), begun in 1959 in the Farnham Courts housing development in New Haven, Connecticut (Geismar and Krisberg 1967). The NIP was a three-layered project. At its core was intensive, "family-centered" casework with thirty families whose social functioning and individual behaviors were determined to be particularly disorganized and dysfunctional. Surrounding that core was "open-door" casework to any family in the development who wished assistance. A caseworker was stationed in the project, available for walk-ins. Help could involve one contact, or evolve to include an ongoing relationship. The third element of the project was a variety of community organization activities, including the development of a cooperative nursery school. Together, the three sets of activities would "saturate" the neighborhood, getting at the varied roots of delinquency and family dependency.

Families were chosen for the intensive casework group based on the inability to perform basic family maintenance tasks; a "clear and present danger" of neglect or harm to children; an involvement with multiple human service agencies; and a past unwillingness or inability to accept and use help. Caseloads were small, approximately twelve families per caseworker. Casework was characterized by regular home visiting, persistent outreach, directness, and openness. Caseworkers were supposed to share their agendas and ask families' views on problems, follow a family's priorities, view and treat the family as a unit, and employ their own authority in a supportive manner. They could be "advisor, teacher, enabler, intervener, coordinator of treatment, expediter, supporter [or] confidante," as the situation called for (Geismar and Krisberg 1967:203).

One key strategy of the caseworkers was to "structure" the role performance and problem-solving behavior of families, identifying step-by-step behaviors and actions to be followed. The caseworkers also spent considerable time "correcting" and stabilizing relationships between the families served and other agencies: "acknowledging facts," "allowing and encouraging [sic] expression of negative feelings," "correcting the record," "distinguishing between past and present"—in effect, treating the staff of other agencies as if they too were clients (Geismar and Krisberg 1967:200)

The Neighborhood Improvement Project included a research component, which examined progress in family functioning and well-being along different dimensions. The intervention was found to have had measurable positive effects on families' health care practices and use of community resources, and more modest effects on basic parental dispositions and behaviors (e.g., impulsiveness, frantic worry about children, inability to focus on children's needs, immobility in addressing problems). Progress tended to be reflected in small achievements such as following through on appointments, acknowledging problems, or making food money last until the end of the month.

The researchers found that while intensive family casework helped families cope, it "left untouched a part of life that accounted for much" of families' difficulties (Geismar and Krisberg 1967:12). They noted a feeling among NIP project staff that they were only able to get a handle on part of the problem, that there were bigger issues, social forces that were out of their reach. Even in more psychologically vulnerable families, problems in functioning were interwoven with and inseparable from unemployment, poor schools, and inadequate basic services. In considering their work with the full range of community families (through the other project components), NIP staff concluded that there was no clear dividing line between multiproblem families and others. It was hard to predict up-front who would be able to cope with what demands and problems. In spite of the equivocal findings of the Neighborhood Improvement Project, Geismar and Krisberg (1967:386) argued that its experience, together with that of other demonstrations, suggested that better outcomes were "possible and perhaps within reach."

## Developments in Aid to Dependent Children

During the 1940s and 1950s the vagueness in the original legislative intent and language of the Aid to Dependent Children program began to create fissures in the implementation of the program. There was a good deal of argument within legislatures, public agencies, and the social service literature about the purpose and promise of the ADC program (see, e.g., Wiltse 1954; Keith-Lucas 1957). Was ADC intended primarily to promote overall family welfare, strengthen the parent-child relationship, or protect children? Did ADC promise poor families a basic right to assistance, or only a conditional right, based on deservingness or some other criterion? If the latter, then what should the measure of deservingness or other criterion be and who should decide? There was argument as well about the conditions of relief: Should it be more or less generous? Did receiving ADC imply a loss of civil rights? When a parent accepted ADC did it reduce her privacy rights regarding her children? Did it change her responsibilities toward them? Did it reduce her right to have relationships with men? Should receipt of aid be tied to or free from social control and supervision?

In the context of this basic confusion, the Aid to Dependent Children program evolved in haphazard fashion. States used the wide latitude they had been granted under federal guidelines to develop very different programs, with different rules and standards. States and localities used a variety of strategies to restrict eligibility and approval, undermining the apparent federal intent that ADC should serve as a modest safety net. They "denied aid to families with 'employable' mothers, dawdled in processing applications, established lengthy residence requirements (usually a year or more), and intimidated prospective applicants—sometimes by stationing police outside of relief offices" (Patterson 1984:87). So-called "suitable home" regulations were used to deny assistance to families in which children were born out of wedlock or that an able-bodied male was suspected to have deserted or be nearby.

Throughout the 1950s the great majority of poor families—as many as 80 percent in some states—did not participate in either ADC or general assistance (Patterson 1984:86). Grants to those who did remained well below levels needed to meet basic needs. The federal government paid only one third of relief costs, leaving the rest to states and localities. Local relief budgets had no political constituency and were sometimes cut during periods of budgetary strain. Moreover, ADC had been designed to be less attractive than the least attractive job (Goodin 1985). Not only were grants meager, but those who received relief were subject to a host of rules about how they could live, what they could eat and buy.

In spite of efforts to limit relief, enrollment levels increased steadily during this period. The harsh conditions of relief were not a deterrent to families that had no other option. And as ADC rolls grew, especially in urban areas, it did not take long for old worries about the costs and harmful social effects of public aid to resurface. Already by the 1940s families on ADC were seen as an economic burden on and social threat to society, the cause of rising taxes and of most social problems. A 1947 report by a business-funded civic group in Baltimore, the Commission on Governmental Efficiency and Economy, argued that local welfare policies and practices encouraged idleness, pauperism, illegitimacy, dishonesty, and irresponsibility. A news article about this report indicated that "Baltimore's Department of Welfare . . . was staffed by 'sincere' but 'impractical' people" (Posner 1995:201). Among other things, the Commission recommended an increase in day nurseries, presumably so that poor mothers could not use lack of child care as an excuse for not working.

Existing evidence suggested that poor families, particularly African-American families, turned to ADC as a last resort (Keith-Lucas 1957:10). Nonetheless, articles in the popular media throughout the late 1940s and 1950s created and continually reinforced the stereotype of ADC recipients as immoral and lazy, and as significant sources of drain on public budgets. Relief was accused of "sapping the will to work," and of "ruining families" (Patterson 1984:89–90). As with the Charity Organization Society agents in the 1890s, more economically secure citizens found it hard to believe that the large numbers of poor families in inner-city neighborhoods had few family or friends who could help out during times of need. Legislation was proposed in a small number of states, permitting the publication of names of relief recipients, with the aim of shaming them off the roles (Reynolds 1963).

In spite of continuing state efforts to restrict eligibility to the morally deserving, the changing profile of poor families as a whole made it increasingly difficult to withhold support from families with children born out of wedlock and those in which husbands were simply not around. These overlapping groups were becoming the majority of those seeking support, particularly in the inner cities where poor families were increasingly concentrated. Yet the need to respond to such families simply exacerbated the stigma attached to ADC and ADC recipients.

Public aid workers were in fact caught between public stereotypes and the more complex realities they observed every day (Posner 1995). Many of the families they worked with did seem to be unprepared for the demands of an urban economy and urban life. Some seemed overwhelmed; others simply were coping, doing what they had to do to survive. These were the same families that had survived generations of extreme hardship in the rural South or in largely rural Puerto Rico, through hard work, sharing, humor, a strong sense of community, and forbearance. Yet they now seemed in danger of long-term dependence on the state to meet even their most basic needs. Tasks such as the protection, nurturance, and supervision of children, once taken for granted, now seemed overwhelming for growing numbers of parents.

## A Shifting Casework Role in ADC

Casework in the ADC program eventually came to focus on three central undertakings. One was a continuation of the historic role in monitoring morality and seeking out fraud, reflected (and stereotyped) in the unannounced midnight home visits to catch out male visitors. The second was linking families with (or in some cases approving) resources necessary to meet their basic needs—housing, health, nutrition, clothing, fuel. The third, newer focus was on the prevention and alleviation of "dependency": addressing internal and situational obstacles to leaving welfare and preparing families for self-sufficiency. This was seen to require long-term casework, especially where families had lost the will to become self-sufficient.

Integrating these three roles was complicated, since it required that caseworkers walk a fine line between being supportive (and useful) and not making ADC recipients too comfortable. It was complicated also by the confusion about the basic purpose of the program I have already noted. There was constant tension between the mission of supporting families and that of assuring that children's needs were met. Were parents to be viewed as partners or as potential adversaries? Was the caseworker an agent of the state or a therapeutic agent trying to develop a trusting relationship? The ambiguity and variability in state and local policy regarding maternal employment in families receiving ADC further complicated the role of casework in the program. A few jurisdictions prohibited such employment, a few insisted on it, and most fell somewhere in between. Caseworkers often had a measure of discretion in the implicit social contract created with individual families, and evidence suggests that they themselves were ambivalent about maternal employment. Many ADC caseworkers believed that mothers on ADC should work, at least part-time, but they were also worried about the effects that going to work would have on maternal supervision of children.

For a time there was debate in the casework literature about the role of professional casework in the ADC program. Monitoring to assure adherence to rules and linkage to community resources theoretically could be accomplished by less well-trained caseworkers. Long-term casework to address psychological dependency and lack of skills was seen to require more skilled interventions. Charlotte Towle, in "Common Human Needs,' argued that public aid casework required psychological skill and sensitivity, because receiving aid was partly about taking help, something that was strongly stigmatized in American society (Towle 1973, reprint). Tied to this argument was the therapeutic assumption that once people realized that they could not meet their own needs "unaided," they were taking a significant step in assuming control of their lives. In other words, the caseworker's goal was to help people come to terms with their need for help (Keith-Lucas 1957:35).

The goal of developing a role for skilled casework in public aid was complicated by the lack of professional education of the vast majority of public aid caseworkers. As of the early 1950s fewer than one in ten had even one year of professional preparation. The large number of paraprofessionals in public assistance work provoked some critical observations about their lack of ability to "discipline" their reactions to and their inferences about poor people. Yet as one writer noted in rebuttal: "Every person who works in public welfare for some years before seeing the inside of a school of social work is not necessarily: (1) punitive, (2) resistant to learning, (3) prejudiced against people whose standards differ from their own" (Horne 1953:94).

A handful of local welfare offices used supervision and consultation to help develop the skills of nonprofessional caseworkers. The overwhelming majority of caseworkers continued to rely on predisposition, experience with prior clients, community norms, and common sense. The result was great variability in caseworkers' treatment of families within the same welfare office. While some caseworkers were very supportive, others could be very punitive, harshly criticizing parents, ordering them to stop certain behavior or end a particular relationship without considering the meaning of the behavior or relationship. One study found the practice of individual ADC caseworkers to contain contradictory elements: strongly disapproving certain behavior, combined with persisting in seeing that families got access to resources; being warm and supportive but conservative in approving services and resources; being paternalistic yet nonjudgmental (Keith-Lucas 1957:239–240).

By the late 1950s a new response to the lack of professional skills in public aid caseworkers was to seek to limit their discretion and standardize the role. This meant developing detailed procedural guides or manuals, and focusing training on familiarity with those manuals. The problem with this approach was that it failed to take into account that the meaning of particular client behaviors could only be evaluated by knowing the individual client. For example, a parent's failure to follow through on a request by a worker that she take a child to the doctor for a particular problem could be neglect or irresponsibility in one family, fear in another, misunderstanding in a third, and negative experience with health care providers in a fourth.

During the 1940s and 1950s the apparent retreat of poverty, and the range of psychological pressures associated with readjustment, cold war fears, and the renewed focus on family life led to a shift in emphasis in social services, away from a commitment to poverty-related concerns and toward a focus on individual adjustment. Yet by the mid-1950s it was increasingly clear that poverty remained an important feature of American society and, moreover, that its nature and correlates were changing. These changes exacerbated the retreat of private family service agencies from poverty-related work, creating a vacuum that would shape the strategy of the coming War on Poverty, pulling it even more toward social services than it was already inclined to go.

Beneath these broad developments, the historical struggle to find useful helping purposes and approaches in work with poor families continued. A distinct (although still psychodynamically rooted) approach to casework under conditions of poverty emerged in the literature. This approach found its way tentatively into public aid casework, and would contribute in the 1960s to the short-lived belief that it was possible to "casework" families out of poverty. It also contributed to the conceptualization of a new area of casework practice, with multiproblem families. This latter development created a trend in supportive services that would extend into the 1960s, and beyond, in work in intensive family preservation services.

Finally, during the 1950s historical concerns about class and culture in supportive services were gradually being converted to concerns about race and culture. A sense crystallized that the sources of poor African Americans' difficulties were different from those of poor whites; the solutions therefore also had to differ. Concern about urban poverty began to be converted to concern about the problems of African-American families. Since so many poor African-American families were concentrated in particular neighborhoods, poverty-related problem-solving would again turn to place-oriented strategies. A strategy that first emerged in the 1950s—"posing blacks as damaged to manipulate the therapeutic sensibilities of the middle class"—would come to define, and eventually to undermine the poverty-fighting efforts of the 1960s (Scott 1996:101).

# CHAPTER FIVE

# Service Reform as a War on Poverty

*It's not that we're against you. It's that we've got to do this thing for ourselves. It's the only way we'll ever feel our freedom.*
— an African-American Head Start worker to Polly Greenberg

The 1960s were a watershed in the evolution of supportive social services. The federal government, in its War on Poverty, stimulated the development or renewal of literally thousands of neighborhood-based programs in poor neighborhoods. This in turn led to a sizable increase in direct helping services to poor families. Innovation was spawned in heavily funded demonstration programs, such as Gray Areas and Mobilization for Youth (see Halpern 1995:89–105) and by committees of academics and other experts, commissioned by the federal government. A stream of federal legislation, beginning with the Economic Opportunity Act of 1964, provided funding and new organizational structures, such as community action agencies.

The innovative ferment led to new service emphases, such as early childhood intervention, preventive nutrition, and work preparation for youth, and new models, including Head Start and neighborhood health centers. New helping principles emerged to guide service design and delivery. It was argued that services should be shaped by family and community preferences; be conveniently located, informal, and friendly; avoid labeling and build on family and community strengths; and respect family and community culture. Service providers were urged to attend both to individual development and to the social forces impinging on and shaping the lives of individuals. They were urged, and frequently directed to involve community residents in defining, governing, and actually providing services.

The new helping principles were stated and restated in proposals, program guidelines, training sessions, and social service literature, eventually becoming part of the air that programs breathed. Because they were somewhat global, these principles provided only the most general guidance for everyday work with families, leaving often inexperienced practitioners to find their own way in defining and achieving the tasks of program implementation and interpersonal helping. The new principles were seen by proponents to represent the antithesis of prevailing practice in the human services, offering a critique of that practice that created implicit pressure for reform. Longstanding helping principles were either recast (as was the case with client self-determination), neglected (as was the case with "process" supervision), or rejected altogether (as was the belief in the importance of specialized knowledge and experience in helping very vulnerable families).

The 1960s brought extraordinary pressures to bear on old-line agencies and public service systems, who experienced increasing demand on their resources, mixed with rising distrust and constant pressure to reform. Among the private agencies still committed to serving poor families, a few responded defensively, particularly those that had either a conservative board and leadership, a strong identity in what they did, or both. A few agencies embraced change. Many others responded cautiously and reactively. The responses of local public assistance, education, housing, and to a lesser extent public health systems varied as well, depending on their history and leadership and on their opportunity to participate in the planning of reforms.

Supportive social services were influenced by the broad intellectual currents and became caught up in the larger societal trends and struggles of the 1960s. It was a time of both the narrowest views of human development and the broadest. Psychologists identified brief "critical periods" early in human development, on which peoples' whole lives were said to turn. At the same time some argued that human development and politics were "inseparable" (Greenberg 1990:15). Individual change was linked to community control of public resources and to greater political power for one's group.

Supportive services became an important vehicle for "assimilating" the new immigrants—the minority poor in growing urban ghettos—and for addressing the various social problems associated with inner-city life. Services became a repository for the inordinate promises and expectations of politicians, academic social engineers, and other "poverty warriors." They were a focus of the efforts of a new kind of social scientist, the program evaluator, who claimed to have the tools to measure the effectiveness of helping efforts. They became a platform from which minorities could express a new-found sense of both anger—over their historic oppression and exclusion—and empowerment; and they were a battleground on which the limits of that empowerment were defined. They were a locus for the clash of profoundly different analyses of poverty and images of poor people. Not least, they were the site where helpers and clients struggled to find a new, more egalitarian model for helping relationships.

By the end of the decade the historic optimism about the potential of services to improve poor peoples' lives had been converted to profound skepticism. Evaluation findings from key federal programs and scores of local ones suggested that helping services of all kinds had only the most modest effects. Efforts to fundamentally reform prevailing services had made little progress. The wisdom of involving the poor in service design, governance, and provision was questioned, as was what would later be called the permissive character of many programs of the era. At the same time the authority and credibility of helping professionals were severely weakened and would never fully recover. A few of the new models and approaches took root and would survive—Head Start, the Women's, Infants' and Children's' Food Program (WIC), community health centers, compensatory education programs. Yet even these would have to continue to fight for their lives for many years, and none would ever be funded at a level adequate to its purposes.

## Premises of the Era

Three clusters of ideas underlay much of the service renewal, innovation, and reform activity of the 1960s. The first had to do with the poor as unprepared for the economic and social demands of urban, industrial life. The second had to do with the poor as excluded, blocked from opportunity. The third focused on the unresponsiveness of the prevailing institutions that were serving the poor and the need to recast those institutions in a different mold. (The first two ideas created a nice paradox: improving opportunity would not work as a strategy without preparation, yet there would be no motive to become prepared without significantly greater opportunity.) Of these three sets of ideas, the first had a long history, the second was somewhat new, and the third was a genuinely new addition to poverty discourse. The idea of the poor as unprepared was really only a different way of stating the old view of poverty as rooted in the behavior and values of the poor themselves. That of the poor as excluded was a new way of conveying their lack of assimilation and civic participation. These old ideas nonetheless took on new meanings as they related to the social pressures of the era.

### Poor People as Unprepared for Industrial Society

Underlying the idea of the poor as unprepared was the notion of a distinct urban culture of poverty. This culture was characterized by a set of values and attitudes, ways of thinking, behaving, and even feeling, that certain groups of poor people were said to share. These included a fatalistic world view and a passive response to events; an inability to delay gratification and plan for the future; a sense of social and economic marginality; a distrust of mainstream institutions; and a lack of civic-mindedness, even with respect to one's own community. (For an overview of the literature on the culture of poverty see Valentine 1968; Leacock 1971). Related psychological characteristics included feelings of futility, inadequacy, and lack of self-worth. These latter attributes implied both why the poor needed help and at the same time why help was so hard to provide. Coles (1964:12) noted that "If strangers come, young and kindly people, white or black, to 'help' them, teach their children or feed or clothe them, or assist them in organizing or registering to vote, the first response, a measure of their sense of worthlessness, is to question why [these strangers] would want to do that."

The culture of poverty was seen to be the result of adaptations made by particular social groups over a period of generations to economic exploitation and hardship and social oppression. It was thought to be passed on from one generation to the next through childrearing patterns and local community norms and to be reinforced by the continuing need to cope with exclusion and hardship in the present. Lewis (1961:xxvi), for example, noted such characteristic poverty-related coping patterns as "the absence of food reserves in the home . . . the pawning of personal goods, borrowing from local money lenders at usurious rates of interest . . . the use of second-hand clothing and furniture." Proponents of the theory argued that "by adapting to poverty, the poor, besides being damaged, effectively closed the door on social mobility" (Scott 1996:87).

One central preoccupation of social scientists drawn to the culture of poverty thesis was the early family life of poor children. Psychologists turned their attention to home environments of young inner-city children, and found there a lack of books, toys, and sustained verbal interaction between children and adults. Inner-city parents were seen to provide little, or at most erratic, guidance, structure, praise, and limits-setting for their children. Daily routines were nonexistent. Both positive attention and punishment were provided inconsistently and ambivalently. The same child behavior might evoke pleasure one day, anger the next, and no response at all on another day.

Inadequate parenting was seen as both a major source of poor children's school difficulties and the critical mechanism for the intergenerational transmission of the values, attitudes, and behavior associated with the culture of poverty. Poor children did not acquire the host of skills and dispositions—in the areas of language, preliteracy, understanding of time, problem-solving, etc.—that provide the foundation for school success. They internalized their parents' lack of a sense of efficacy, and their doubt about the possibility of success, tending by an early age either toward "passivity and . . . resignation" or hostility and aggression (Greenberg 1990:99; Silverstein and Krate 1975). Equally important, they learned from early on that the larger world was a dangerous, unpredictable, and unforgiving place. Representatives of mainstream institutions, whether teachers or welfare workers or policemen, rarely had poor peoples' interests at heart. Playing by the rules of society would yield neither economic security nor societal respect.

Seeing it as a correlate of compromised parenting, social scientists also focused their attention on family structure, specifically the female-headed poor family. Female headship in poor families was a strongly urban phenomenon. In 1965 the percentage of poor rural white children in female-headed families was 3 percent, versus 35 percent for similarly situated urban children; for "nonwhites" the percentages were 14 and 54 percent respectively (Sheppard 1972:45). Female-headed families were viewed as inherently weak, lacking in positive role models for boys, and with little ability to shape children's development in positive ways.

In perhaps the most infamous words of what became an infamous policy paper, "The Negro Family: The Case for National Action," New York Senator Patrick Moynihan captured the sentiment of many social scientists of the era: "at the center of the tangle of pathology [in the Negro community] is the weakness of family structure. Once or twice removed, it will be found to be the principal source of most problems" (Moynihan 1965:30). Moynihan's principal interest was in promoting policies to strengthen the economic position of African-American men. He could have made many arguments to justify this goal, yet he chose to attack vulnerable families. Presumably he did so for strategic reasons. However, his benign motives would not matter in a few years when conservatives would use his (and others') language to dismiss as futile the very goal—federal leadership and investment in efforts to address poverty—that he was trying to promote.

The culture of poverty thesis certainly offered an explanation for the difficulties experienced by a growing proportion of poor urban families. Yet in most respects it was simply an updated expression of longstanding instincts. Its characterization of poor people as selfish evoked the pauper of the eighteenth and nineteenth centuries, people psychologically separated from work, moral sanctions, and caring about themselves or others. The culture of poverty thesis evoked the old idea of the poor as different from the nonpoor and raised once again the specter of poor people as a threat to society—to standards and mores, to social stability, and even to the economic system itself. It suggested that poverty was an attribute of poor people, rather than the result of economic and political arrangements (thus providing a rationale for keeping the focus of problem-solving attention on the poor themselves). It evoked again the idea that there were different kinds of poor people, deserving or undeserving, worthy or unworthy. As Glazer and Moynihan (1963:64) asked (with no irony intended) about the residents of inner-city neighborhoods: "And what after all are we to do with the large numbers of people emerging in modern society who are irresponsible and depraved? The worthy poor create no serious problem—nothing that money cannot solve. But the unworthy poor? No one has come up with the answers."

The motives of those who employed the culture of poverty concept varied. Its immediate antecedents could be found in the work of prominent African-American social scientists in the 1950s, notably Kenneth Clark and E. Franklin Frazier (Scott 1996:85). In the quest to promote civil rights and to end segregation in education and discrimination in jobs, they had argued that historical oppression and continuing racial prejudice and segregation had damaged African Americans in a host of ways. As the earlier discussion of Moynihan's policy paper illustrates, at least some people used the concept to try to compel federal government and public attention to and investment in the problems of the inner city (Scott 1996:95). Others appeared simply to find in it a convenient way to affirm their negative views of poor minorities and to reiterate the futility of investing resources in inner-city communities.

A number of social scientists of the time argued against the focus on a culture of poverty. Some critics implicitly acknowledged the existence of such a culture but critiqued the terms in which it was described. It was argued that "realistic attempts to deal with objective conditions" that vary form one social class to another cannot be construed as destructive or self-destructive (Leacock 1971:34). It should not, for example, be surprising that people who are deliberately excluded from housing and job markets should feel that following the rules of society is a waste of time and effort. The predominance of negative attributes in describing the culture of poverty was criticized, and a number of positive attributes of the poor, such as mutual support and a collective concern for children, highlighted. One critic argued that a more appropriate focus for researchers would be to ask how poor people "continue to function as human beings even under conditions of extreme adversity and deprivation" (Valentine 1971:209). The attributes defining the culture of poverty may have been "drawn from life" in inner-city communities, but they failed to capture the complexity of life in those communities (Herzog 1972).

Some critics denied the validity of the idea itself. The culture of poverty thesis was argued to be at best a form of more "learned and sophisticated stereotyping" (Valentine 1968:45) and at worst a dangerous new form of racism. It was argued to be no more than an abstraction, a generalization, of little use in understanding individuals and individual families. Not least, the need for, and harshness of, this thesis was seen to reflect more about its creators and subscribers than about its objects.

Whatever the arguments for and against the existence of a culture of poverty, the language and ideas on both sides set in motion an unhealthy dynamic in discussions of race and poverty, one that has existed ever since. The arguments for it did inevitably oversimplify the situation; they sometimes reflected fears and stereotypes that had nothing to do with the objects of the theorizing. Those against were often nothing more than an early version of political correctness and an effort to muzzle public debate about a crucial issue. The polarized quality of debate would lead in coming years to a loss of opportunity to discuss the issues involved honestly and openly.

*The Poor as Excluded*

A second idea underlying the service strategies of the 1960s, that of the poor as excluded, had a number of dimensions. By the early 1960s unemployment among urban minorities, particularly among African-American males, had become a serious problem. Skills mismatch accounted for only a portion of this unemployment. Job discrimination and the movement of jobs to the suburbs also played important roles. For the first time in history, there appeared a group of Americans who were more or less outside the national economy. General economic growth in society was seen as likely to have little impact on unemployment in the inner-city (Katz 1989:91).

Another critical dimension of exclusion was residential: the growing concentration of poor, largely minority, families in neighborhoods geographically and socially isolated from their larger urban environs. Residential exclusion was caused by a mix of factors. These included the historical residential segregation of urban African Americans, beginning in the first decades of the century; the deliberate cutting off of minority neighborhoods from surrounding areas through highway programs and other urban renewal strategies (such as razing housing to create a buffer zone); and the location of public housing in the heart of ghetto neighborhoods (Halpern 1995; Massey and Denton 1993). A third dimension of exclusion was political. Lacking representation, the poor and minorities had little ability to influence government priorities and policies and the public and private sector practices—in employment, housing, education, and other human services—which had such powerful influences on their lives.

These first three sources of exclusion created a fourth, which was psychological. In the 1950s a line of argument about juvenile delinquency had emerged, which viewed delinquency as a result of some youths' exclusion from the opportunity to use socially approved means (education, part-time jobs) to achieve socially approved goals (i.e., stable work; Cloward and Ohlin 1960). This line of argument was extended in the 1960s to the poor as a whole. Perceiving no place for themselves in society, more and more poor people were "defaulting [sic] on the system" (Beck 1967). Echoing the Progressive era, it was argued that a social chasm had opened up between poor minorities and the larger society, which contributed to mutual mistrust. There was fear (prophetic as it turned out) that exclusion was a kind of "social dynamite." The anger it caused would eventually be transformed to violence.

Addressing the various dimensions of exclusion became the focus of an increasingly active civil rights movement in the northern and midwestern ghettos during the 1960s. The African-American and Hispanic communities struggled continuously to find a constructive response, shifting their emphasis from integration to self-reliance, the development of autonomous local institutions and economies ("separate development"), and community control of public institutions. This shift profoundly affected the development of the new supportive service models, and relationships between helpers and clients.

*Prevailing Services and Social Institutions as Unresponsive*

The third idea underlying the service strategies and reforms of the 1960s held that prevailing social institutions, including child and family service agencies, schools, and welfare authorities, were unresponsive to the distinct support needs and newly articulated rights of poor families. At first, the critique of prevailing services came primarily from foundations, academics, and government officials. They viewed themselves as trying to return public institutions to their ideal of service and their role of mitigating the harshness of the marketplace (Marris and Rein 1973:52). For conservative foundation officials, critiquing mainstream service institutions was a safe and acceptable way of acknowledging the issue of racism and racial discrimination (see Ylvisaker 1973:20). As various rights groups who claimed to represent the poor gained a voice during the decade, they joined in the criticism. Their critique of prevailing service institutions was deeper, for it involved a fundamental questioning of traditional authority relationships in American society, and of the motives of those who held power and authority.

The specific critiques of prevailing services to the poor made a good deal of sense. As I have noted in chapter 4, many agencies had all but abandoned inner-city neighborhoods. A 1964 survey conducted in Boston's Roxbury neighborhood, home to eighty thousand people, found only four voluntary family service agencies remaining. The survey concluded that the community was "grossly underserved by social welfare agencies" (Perlman 1975:9). Prevailing public services were said to be impersonal, bureaucratic, and often dehumanizing. Their tendency to give staff narrow and specialized roles did not fit the interconnected support needs of poor families. Prevailing services were seen to make little effort to reach out to poor families to overcome "estrangement, suspicion, ethnic differences and language barriers" (Jones 1969:28). They were accused of inadvertently, or even deliberately, undermining families' efforts to cope with and escape from poverty.

The public service systems, notably public aid and, to a lesser extent, child welfare and the juvenile courts, were the target of the most criticism, due to their legal and policy mandates and their sometimes harsh treatment of families. Yet even such institutions as settlements became targets. Trolander (1987) notes that settlements were accused of wanting to change the poor rather than support them in their own self-determined efforts. Their philosophy of consensus-building was seen as cover for support of the status quo. Their failure to identify themselves as advocates for the poor by default put them against the poor, on the side of the power-holders. Settlements were also accused of not having enough minorities on their boards and staff.

As a whole the prevailing service system was incoherent, with its components often working at cross-purposes. Each inhabited its own world and viewed families differently. While frontline providers from different public and private agencies sometimes worked informally with each other, administrators had little or no contact. Few providers viewed the communities in which they had branches and programs as important referents for their work, nor did they see community residents as a potential resource to help carry out their mission.

By the mid-1960s the critique of prevailing services would expand to in-clude professionals and professional helping generally. It was assumed that professionals' willingness to reflect critically on the services they provided was limited by "careerism, political interests, and the public relations needs of [their] agencies" (Dubey 1972:230). At best, professionals were seen to have a kind of lopsided expertise, with great skill in assessment and diag-nosis but much less ability to use information about a poor client to forge a useful helping relationship (Jones and Weissman 1969:95).

The sources of criticism of prevailing services shifted during the decade, with various rights groups playing a growing role. As this occurred, the cri-tique of services became caught up in something larger: a fundamental questioning of societal institutions, rather than an interest in reforming them. The claim of service providers "to be acting benevolently . . . in the best interest of others" was rejected (Gaylin, Glass, Marcus, and Rothman 1978:x). Rights groups asked who had the "moral, intellectual, political or any other type of authority to teach, much less enforce, codes of collective behavior" (Heclo 1996:47). They asked what gave professionals the right, let alone the wisdom, to counsel and advise people from different groups than their own? What gave professionals the right to stand between poor citi-zens and their entitlement to basic supports from society? Why should pro-fessionals be trusted at all? By the late 1960s some leaders of rights organi-zations were arguing that existing service institutions were too corrupted to be reformed, and thus had to be replaced. If, in the short run, that hurt peo-ple who depended on those institutions, it was a price worth paying.

Service institutions and professionals became a target of the anger of var-ious rights groups, in part because they played a disproportionate role in, and seemed to have a good deal of power over, poor peoples' lives. They also hap-pened to be visible and definable, unlike the amorphous power structures of politics, business, and real estate interests. Such criticism was not invalid. Services and helping professionals were paying the price for problems that had been neglected and denied for half a century. In particular, it was the his-torical stance of wise, protective parent and the historical claim of benevo-lent intentions that most infuriated some in the minority community.

## Service Reform as a War on Poverty

### Goals and Basic Approach

Each of the the three ideas described above played in role in shaping the broad goals and strategies of the federal government's War on Poverty.

The goals were to increase opportunity, to increase children's and adults' capacity to take advantage of new opportunity, and to turn social and educational services toward these two purposes. Increasing opportunity implied improving access to the labor market, as well as to those experiences and institutions that naturally prepare people for success at work. It also implied reforming key institutions that mediated access to opportunity, particularly schools, making them more responsive. Less clearly, it implied organizing and empowering the poor, so they would be better able to define their situation and priorities, meet their own needs, and make collective demands.

Increasing the capacity to take advantage of opportunity implied the direct provision of enriched, "compensatory" experiences for children, complemented by efforts to strengthen their parents' ability to nurture and rear them appropriately. For youth and adults, it implied the provision of experiences that addressed the psychological and social roots of dependence and alienation and at the same time prepared youth and adults for work. The need to make prevailing helping institutions more responsive implied finding new principles for service provision and a new basis for helping relationships. If the helping principles of prevailing services and the knowledge and experience that professionals brought to helping relationships were not only not unique but were irrelevant, then something had to be substituted for those, and someone had to be the source of new ideas.

In spite of the broad implications of its three underlying premises, the War on Poverty was waged primarily through neighborhood-based social and educational services. In spite of the acknowledged need for more employment opportunities, a job creation strategy was seen as too costly and too difficult to achieve politically. In spite of the acknowledged historical and continuing damage done by residential segregation, there was no intention or plan to address this politically sensitive problem. In spite of the recognition that prevailing social (and economic) institutions—situated outside poor neighborhoods—were unresponsive to poor families, the War on Poverty took place largely within the boundaries of those neighborhoods. Indeed, revitalizing poor neighborhoods themselves became an important goal of federal investments. It was argued that the key to ameliorating poverty was to address "the individual problems that are faced by the poor in their own communities" (Kravitz and Kolodner 1969:33). As Greenberg (1990:66) put it, drawing the threads together, "uncrippling crippled communities, and unparalyzing paralyzed adults, would help children grow up uncrippled and unparalyzed."

*Sources of Innovation Within Services*

The service reform tasks of the War on Poverty required a simultaneous focus on inventing new service approaches and principles and on influencing prevailing services. Historically new service ideas and approaches had come from within the professional service community, as a response to theoretical developments and to new populations, situations, and service needs. Leaders of one or another professional community would use professional journals and their graduate seminars to present new practice principles. Leaders of historically innovative agencies would introduce a new service or element of practice, which would be picked up gradually by similar agencies. These two groups played less of a role in generating innovation in the 1960s. This was partly a matter of choice. (The professional human service community was accused by planners in the federal government's Office of Economic Opportunity (OEO) of remaining aloof from efforts to rethink services; see, e.g., Pumphrey 1964, citing the comments of OEO's Sanford Kravitz). It was due also to the times. Professionals—whether educators, administrators, or frontline providers—were seen as the source of the problems needing to be addressed within services. In their place, three groups assumed a greater role: academics, foundations, and the members of poor communities themselves.

Balogh (1996:15) notes that in the 1960s academics found "a unique perch at the confluence of bureaucratic, ideological and heuristic power." They played two very different roles. A small group worked within the civil rights movement. The majority devoted their energy to reintroducing the Progressive era idea of attacking poverty scientifically. Like their Progressive forebears, they believed—wrongly as it turned out—that social science knowledge could be converted directly to intervention methods. Thus knowledge of how environmental factors shaped early cognitive development could be used to create carefully designed programs of cognitive and verbal stimulation, which would boost poor children's IQ and aid in their later school success. Poor parents could be taught specific techniques to support the practices of preschools, shedding deeply rooted norms and beliefs for the good of their children's future. The demonstration program, an approach that had emerged in the 1950s, took on greater importance as a vehicle for reform. It was linked to the new field of program evaluation. Alternative policies and practices would be tested against each other. Social science methods would separate what worked from what did not, and the latter would be discarded.

Foundations initially provided seed money for much key demonstration activity. The Ford Foundation's Gray Areas program was probably the single most important source of ideas for new program models and approaches (see Halpern 1995:89–101). The Gray Areas program supported innovative efforts in five cities, each somewhat different. The Ford official responsible for Gray Areas believed that simply providing money and ideas for these prevailing services to reform themselves would not suffice (Ylvisaker 1973). What was needed was to take a low-income community, identify and pull in all the institutions working in that community, and cajole them into participating in a coordinated attack on poverty, intervening at a number of points and in a number of ways simultaneously. The central focus was on programs for children and youth, including preschool, youth development, summer employment, enriched elementary school programs (remedial reading, tutoring), and primary health care. Service institutions would join together in a common effort, and community residents would have a voice in planning and providing services.

A few reformers—notably the religious and political leaders of minority communities—had a very different, if more amorphous, vision of what was needed to improve services. They argued that more respect needed to be given to the perspective of poor people on their own lives, and their experiences with human services. This vision would be translated into the principle of participation of community residents in service planning, design, and administration. Such participation would sometimes complement and support and sometimes clash with the priorities of academics and professionals. Thus, for example, although both academics and poor people viewed early childhood education as an important priority in new services, they often differed on what children needed to get out of those services.

*New Wine, and Old Wine in New Bottles*

Under the umbrella of the community action program, or through direct funding from Washington, scores of new community-based human service programs were put together and began operations between 1964 and 1966. These included Head Start and other "compensatory" education programs, neighborhood health centers, day care, after school and summer programs for school-age children and older youth, adult basic education, and neighborhood service centers. They included family planning programs, legal services clinics, and homemaker aide programs. Many of these programs also included individual or group casework and family counseling among their services.

A new institution, the Community Action Agency (CAA), was created by the Office of Economic Opportunity to be the stimulator and co-ordinator of local War on Poverty efforts. This new institution was given a variety of mandates, including mobilizing the community to solve its own problems and initiating, and sometimes managing the new services created by the federal government. It was also seen by some as the logical institution to lead an effort to create a coherent and comprehensive service system at the community level. This idea—ubiquitous now, but new at the time—was borrowed from the Gray Areas program, with its focus on concentrating resources in particular neighborhoods, on comprehensive local planning, and on the creation of local governance entities to guide reform.

Community action agencies focused varying amounts of energy on encouraging existing service agencies in their communities to work together in planning and providing services. The principal venue for joint planning was the CAA board, which was supposed to reflect different constituencies within local communities: as one participant put it, "the local principal, the minister, the settlement house director, the head of the tenant's union, the articulate welfare mother, the bright ex-convict who is a neighborhood leader" (Wofford 1969:101). Many CAA boards had a rocky start. There was little effort to prepare board members with no experience in the human services for their planning and governance responsibilities. CAAs and their boards also had little leverage in the way of authority, resources, or credibility to apply to local system reform. To more than a few local service providers, the CAA board was primarily a new source of patronage. During the course of the 1960s the federal government was increasingly likely to by-pass the CAA governance mechanism and work directly with individual grant programs. Not least, the weight of the federal strategy was to add dozens of new programs to local service environments, which if anything added to local fragmentation.

While community organizing and institutional reform received the most attention (and criticism) at the time, direct services were the major focus of most community action agencies. One study of fifty-one community action agencies found that Head Start was the most frequently provided program or activity (in forty-one agencies), followed by compensatory enrichment programs, health services, youth services, and other kinds of direct services. Only a handful of agencies in this sample did any kind of community organizing (Clark and Hopkins 1968:64).

Although the new programs sponsored by the War on Poverty varied in specific objectives and target population, they embodied a number of common principles: the targeting of whole communities of poor families, rather than selected "cases"; relatedly, an orientation toward serving whole families, even when formally charged with serving a particular family member; involvement of community members in program design and governance, as well as direct service provision; provision of an array of services in the same program; outreach to families; advocacy activities, including attempts to pressure large public bureaucracies to reform; and attempts to embed the program physically, socially, and temporally in community life (Halpern 1995:172).

Surrounding all of these principles was the idea of conceptualizing, targeting, and organizing services geographically. This included the notions of defining a neighborhood or community and concentrating service dollars in it, and of community ownership of services. It included the old settlement idea of using neighborhood-based services as a platform for rebuilding community and recreating natural social support structures. At the same time community action and the various neighborhood-based agencies it spawned in some ways turned the settlement idea on its head. Neighborhood residents took over and converted the socialization and acculturation mission into one focused on political empowerment. They claimed that neighborhood improvement required not improved people but political power and control over resources.

Although there were more or less autonomous programs for different purposes—primary health care, early childhood education, family counseling, work preparation—there was a tendency for frontline staff in different programs to be flexible in their sense of role and role boundaries (sometimes because neither were very well defined). Indeed, collectively the various program models of the era stimulated the renewal of generalist helping, or what one provider called "community practice" (Taylor and Randolph 1975). Generalist helping in the 1960s embodied most of the traditional elements—referral to and mediation with other service providers, "kitchen table" therapy, crisis assistance. It meant meeting needs not met by traditional agencies, as well as responding to whatever was brought before one. There was an increased emphasis on flexibility in where and how one entered the life of a family, the boundaries of one's role, and in when and how one was available to help. The director of one program noted that "Your job is to grab hold where you can and do what you can, and not waste time with silly questions about professional turf" (Taylor and Randolph 1975:10). In the context of the intense interplay of psychological and sociological theories during the 1960s, generalist helping was also defined by proponents as viewing peoples' poverty-related difficulties as multiply determined, caused by the interaction of broad economic and social trends, community factors, and individual vulnerabilities.

### *The Participation of the Poor in Service Design and Delivery*

The theme of community participation was central to the service strategies of the 1960s. Participation was both a powerful and an ill-defined idea. It was intended to strengthen poor peoples' sense of attachment to the larger society, reverse their fatalism and apathy, improve their sense of competence and efficacy, and give them a voice all at once. Participation would reconstruct traditional, informal means of dealing with communal problems in smaller communities. It would reorganize what were viewed as disorganized communities, resulting both in new bodies to act on common concerns and in more coherent, better integrated local service systems. Participation would also create a more equitable balance of power between mainstream institutions and their clients. It would provide an avenue for poor people to share their perspectives and priorities with those institutions, and when necessary put pressure on them. It was seen also as therapeutic; it would rechannel and reverse dysfunctional coping. An activated and organized poor might even "become therapists for society, uncovering paralyzing internal conflicts and releasing society from them" (Gottlieb 1974:55, quoting Warren Haggstrom).

Participation was ubiquitous in the new OEO programs, more variable and circumscribed in existing agencies and programs. In the former, community residents played a role in program design and policy-setting, as well as direct service provision. In both old and new programs, clients played a greater role in defining the terms of the helping relationships in which they were involved. A more controversial expression of participation was in poor peoples' newfound sense of entitlement in evaluating professionals and their work. Suddenly, historical platitudes within the social service community about clients' rights to self-determination took on real life. Clients were demanding to determine their own fate, and at times the fate of their helpers as well.

Paradigmatic of the emphasis on participation in the programs of the 1960s was the use of community members in helping roles. The indigenous helper was argued to have greater potential than the professional both to understand and be accepted by poor clients and to know how to communicate effectively with them. Shared life experiences made the indigenous helper more familiar with and accepting of families' childrearing, coping, and problem-solving traditions. It was assumed that indigenous helpers cared more than professionals about their clients and felt a greater responsibility to the community in which they and their clients lived. They would therefore make themselves more available at any time and place and devote more energy to addressing communitywide problems. As one advocate of indigenous helpers noted: "To solve problems for his clients is as important to him as having his own problems solved" (Normanda 1972:327).

In established agencies, schools, and public aid offices, indigenous helpers tended to perform "auxiliary" tasks, such as cleaning up, filing and record-keeping, greeting and initial "intake," outreach, and helping to transport people to appointments. This was sometimes criticized as a new form of exploitation. As one commentator put it, "aides are really maids" (Goldberg 1969:15). In the new OEO programs, paraprofessionals were more likely to be service providers in their own right. They assumed responsibility for tasks that professionals had previously claimed, such as case management, supportive casework (provision of guidance, advice, and encouragement), and crisis intervention; they also performed tasks that professionals had been reluctant to undertake, such as client advocacy and community organizing.

In the early 1960s there was some effort to differentiate between professional and paraprofessional helping, in part to neutralize professional opposition. As the decade wore on, such effort, like professionals themselves, came under increasingly harsh attack. Professionals found that everything that distinguished them—carefully distanced helping relationships, specialized knowledge and language—now disqualified them to work with poor families (Grosser, Henry, and Kelly 1969). They found their historical prerogatives and their very role usurped by untrained helpers with no credentials, helpers who saw few boundaries in their helping roles. Professionals were not even to be trusted as supervisors of paraprofessionals. It was argued that it was their responsibility to earn the trust of frontline workers (Normanda 1972).

## Two Programs, Two Fates

The War on Poverty yielded genuinely innovative service models, full of both strengths and vulnerabilities. Some would prove enduring; others never found a niche, perhaps being more a product of the times. Each had its own story—for instance, the struggle of the neighborhood health centers with the medical establishment and with their own mission in relation to health; and the struggle of legal aid with entrenched interests in real estate, public housing, and public aid. I have chosen two very different initia-

tives to describe briefly, which shed light on very different aspects of War
on Poverty service reform.

### Neighborhood Service Centers

The Neighborhood Service Center (NSC) program was the exception to
the tendency for most service development and reform to occur within specific content areas. Neighborhood centers were intended to serve all residents within geographically defined catchment areas, ideally with no more
than fifty thousand or so residents. They were the most generic of the
OEO. program models, envisioned as a link and mediator between community residents and other services and institutions (including the new
OEO. programs) and as the center of gravity of their community. They
were intended as a locus for generalist helping, providing varying mixtures
of outreach (or "casefinding") information and referral, help with applications and paperwork, advocacy, informal or formal case management, and,
not least, community organizing and "social action." Many provided at least
some direct services, such as counseling for personal or family problems,
work preparation classes and job banks, and/or child care.

Neighborhood service centers were also supposed to make some effort
to coordinate services within their catchment areas. This could range from
serving as a centralized intake source to collecting other services and service
functions under one roof to trying to shape policies and practices of other
agencies so as to create a coherent, integrated local system.

Some neighborhood centers operated as one program within an existing
service facility or agency, whether a settlement or CAA office. Others were
created from scratch, using a vacant storefront or office. A few NSCs, envisioned as multiservice centers, took over and, as necessary, "built out"
large, vacant facilities. Convenience, visibility, and physical accessibility
were seen as important criteria for choosing a location.

Principles of service included an "open-door" policy, which translated
into accepting walk-ins, trying to maintain long working hours, and keeping staff available; giving as much time to an inquiry or problem as was
needed to untangle it; and "unbiased case channeling," which meant evaluating a person's needs from a perspective free of a particular discipline
(Kahn 1966:119). The idea was to respond immediately, concretely, and un-
critically to peoples' requests. Zurcher (1969), who studied the development
of Neighborhood House in Topeka, Kansas, noted that the first question
asked by those community members who ventured in the front door was
"What can it do for me?" Residents tested its concrete usefulness in ad-

dressing their various poverty-related difficulties—housing, food, clothing, health problems, legal problems.

Neighborhood centers developed their philosophy and approach partly by taking the most criticized features of traditional services and doing the opposite. The Stanton Street Neighborhood Center, part of the Mobilization for Youth program on New York's lower east side, reflected this strategy. Its first principle was informality. One rule of Stanton House was that "appointments are not required here. When a client arrives, he is asked only his name" (Jones 1969:33; originally people were not even going to have to give their names, but many new clients objected). Frontline workers were instructed to be "available to all" and, to the extent possible, on demand. The help provided was to be flexible, client-driven, and open-ended. An initial contact could lead to anything from simple information and referral to long-term casework.

Frontline staff at Stanton Street quickly became overwhelmed. Lack of time, of role clarity and boundaries, and of clear expectations ground them down. Staff reported feeling like their clients, hemmed in by large, indifferent bureaucracies and endless needs and crises (Jones 1969). Eventually, case aides were hired and roles became more differentiated. Long-term counseling was dropped, due to lack of time (Jones 1969:40). Time pressures nonetheless continued to plague workers. These pressures led the center to limit intake; staff began to jump in and solve problems, rather than helping clients learn to do so themselves. Time pressures, combined with the unresponsiveness of welfare, housing, and other public systems to client problems, led workers to overidentify with clients, or blame them, or sometimes both. One caseworker wrote in her journal that her clients' perception of the world as "hostile, withholding, powerful, [and] aggressive" was basically accurate, but that their self-protective coping mechanisms "may be largely self-defeating" (cited in Jones 1969:42).

Staff of the Stanton Street Neighborhood Center kept records of the types of assistance people requested initially and the kinds of services provided over time (Jones 1969:53). The great majority of people coming in (70 percent) had a problem related to AFDC, either of eligibility or of unmet needs such as clothing, food, or a financial emergency. Smaller percentages (30 to 40 percent) had problems with housing, health, schools, or the courts; substance abuse; child welfare issues; emotional illness; or child care and/or unemployment. Given the preponderance of community residents' concerns and problems, good working relationships with the staff of public bureaucracies and the ability to develop sustained helping relationships were both important to Stanton Street staff. Their reluctance and to some extent inability to develop either kind of relationships limited their effectiveness as problem-solvers.

Other neighborhood service centers, though differing in philosophy from Stanton Street, experienced similar developmental patterns. The Roxbury Multi-Service Center (RMSC) in Boston was forced, within a few years of its inception, to become more selective in accepting clients and referrals (Perlman 1975). Staff began to shut down psychologically, labeling and categorizing clients, passing difficult cases back to referring agencies. Like those at Stanton Street, Roxbury staff took to "telling other agencies more forcefully to perform the service for which those agencies were responsible" (Perlman 1975:77). Although such practices had a basis in reality, staff were also projecting their frustrations onto clients and other helping agencies.

Evidence from evaluations of NSCs on the whole failed to find much in the way of positive effects. Residents of poor communities liked having the centers in their communities. Staff of direct service agencies and public bureaucracies did refer individuals and families to some NSCs. Yet the centers served only a tiny percentage of residents in their catchment areas; were at best modestly effective in helping with employment, housing, family, and other basic problems; and failed to improve tangible or intangible aspects of community life, including the supply or quality of such basic services as child care and health care (O'Donnell and Sullivan 1972:295; Kahn 1969:42; Perlman 1975:ch. 5).

The limited effectiveness of NSCs was due to a combination of lack of good community resources to refer people to, lack of follow-up after referrals were made, and the time-limited support roles chosen by or forced upon NSC staff. It was due also to a mismatch between the centers' own limited resources and the potentially unlimited demands made upon them, especially when, as was usually the case, they did not set clear priorities and limits for themselves. Funding for the centers never materialized at anywhere near the level originally envisioned in Washington. Positions identified in center plans remained unfilled. The mismatch between resources and demands tended to be paralyzing and sometimes demoralizing for staff.

Neighborhood service centers were also unsuccessful in achieving their broad service coordination mission. They were not able to rationalize the flow of people to different agencies and programs. As I have noted earlier, their staff did not develop strong relationships with those of other agencies (O'Donnell and Sullivan 1972). At best, other agencies, including other

OEO programs, might agree to let a local NSC do preliminary intake, but they would rarely give up their own intake procedures. Some agencies, including local welfare departments or nursing services, experimented with placing staff at NSCs, but few relocated in a significant way. Most NSCs never got beyond signing interagency agreements outlining referral criteria and procedures and doing a modest amount of case coordination.

### Head Start: Paradigm of an Era

Head Start was in many respects the paradigmatic program model of the era. Its early history captures clearly both the aspirations and tensions underlying the service reform efforts of the 1960s. The idea of addressing poverty through a preschool program for poor children was not new in 1964. It had been tried in nineteenth-century infant schools, in settlement nursery programs of the Progressive era, and later in kindergartens. As Grubb and Lazerson (1980) argue, poor children, particularly younger ones, have always been the "bearers of the American dream" of social mobility. Yet the idea of early childhood intervention still had to be rediscovered and clothed in the particular assumptions, preoccupations, and goals of the time, particularly the idea of community participation.

This rediscovery was helped by a number of fortuitous events. One was the Kennedy family's long interest in mental retardation (one of the Kennedy daughters was retarded). The Kennedys had a foundation that funded the work of Susan Gray's Early Training Project in Nashville, a preschool program designed to prevent "progressive retardation" (i.e., boost IQ) and foster school readiness in poor, African-American children. Gray's approach is illustrated in this anecdote cited by Zigler and Muenchow (1992:5): "the children loved to ride tricycles, but were only allowed to do so if they asked for them properly and identified the particular tricycle they wised to ride." Teachers in Gray's program also "read to children several times a day." Gray reported that her summer program, supplemented by home visits during the year for joint work with children and mothers, raised children's IQ by ten points. Sargent Shriver, head of OEO, learned of the project and was impressed.

Susan Gray's work was not singular. Her approach was echoed in a number of "experimental" preschool programs around the country, as well as those being run by the Ford Foundation's Gray Areas programs. The former usually included home visiting components, in which home visitors strove to "teach" poor mothers how to be better teachers of their young children and in some cases worked directly with those children (some of whom were still infants) to stimulate cognitive and language development (see Beller 1979). The Gray Areas preschool programs provided models of what a Head Start program might look like in a poor urban community.

Underlying the interest in preschool education was the findings from culture of poverty researchers on the deficits in poor children's family lives. There was also a growing body of basic research in psychology that suggested that early experience had a powerful influence on later ability; that there were certain critical periods in development; and, somewhat contradictorily, that intelligence was not fixed, as was commonly assumed but, rather, was malleable. Not least, Sargent Shriver was an astutely political person. He sensed that a program for preschool children would be attractive even to the most conservative constituencies.

In early 1965 the Office of Economic Opportunity assembled a panel of social scientists and charged them with outlining a model early childhood program. The result was a comprehensive program: a salad of health services (including screening and immunization), nutrition, family social services, and community development activities, as well as preschool education for three- and four-year-old children. Parents were to have a significant role in the program, not just as objects of parent education but as partners with professionals. The advisers recommended a small pilot program, serving at most some hundreds of children, but politics demanded a much more dramatic gesture, and Head Start was launched as an eight-week summer program for some half million children. (Within two years it would become a ten-month-a-year program.)

Hundreds of poor communities had to be encouraged to apply for Head Start grants, and some forty thousand teachers had to be trained in a matter of a few months. This somehow was done, although, unhappily for OEO, most of the initial applicants were school districts, and none of the proposals sent in envisioned hiring and nurturing the development of paraprofessionals. As Greenberg (1990:6) notes, poor communities themselves were mostly silent. Gradually, with assistance and prodding from OEO staff, more community-based organizations, especially the new community action agencies, prepared applications to sponsor Head Start programs. Most local sponsoring organizations started from scratch, bringing community representatives together either during or after the application process to elaborate a local program. This new freedom to create programs—combined with the actual need to do so—was both exhilarating and, as often as not, paralyzing. Greenberg (1990:45), who observed and participated in the process in numerous local programs, notes that there was too little working through of broad statements; the poor were not able to "outline the procedures, propose the schemes, and make the comprehensive schedules" underlying well-implemented programs. Despite this inability, community people were often strongly resistant to accepting assistance from early childhood professionals. This could be very painful to the latter group, who believed that they knew good early childhood programs in their bones; they felt forced to observe what seemed like needless struggle to invent and refine that which already had been invented and refined in model programs, with well-developed philosophy, curricula, and teacher training approaches.

Professionals, usually in the role of resource people, nonetheless had much to learn themselves. At program planning meetings they had to learn to let their questions to community people about program design or curriculum issues "seep and soak through several hundred years of never having been asked" (Greenberg 1990:96). Head Start was in some ways profoundly different from the professionally run programs with which they were familiar. It was designed as much to be a vehicle for adult development and community mobilization as for child development. Most early childhood professionals had little experience in these areas. Head Start was intended to be an institution that drew its life and energy from the community. That put professionals who were not from the community in an ambiguous position.

Tensions about quality pervaded the early years of Head Start (and remain to the present day). Its rapid early growth, primarily for political reasons, made it impossible to build the program carefully. Visitors in the early years more often than not found either rote, mechanical drilling going on or aimless play with too little structure and purpose. Teachers had little or no repertoire of learning games and activities to draw on to strengthen children's language and vocabulary or their discrimination, problem-solving, and other skills. There were no materials for science, math, or art activities. Administrative activities such as program planning, staff supervision, and financial management were also performed erratically. Some programs experienced chronic conflict with the public schools into which they were supposed to be feeding children.

Underlying concerns about quality was the question of which of the many purposes of the program was most important: the best possible preschool classroom experience for children, parent education, the employment and empowerment of parents and other community members, or the organization of the community? These questions related in one way or another to the purpose of parent involvement and the role of parents in the program. At one extreme was the view that the whole purpose of Head

Start was to create alternative environments for poor children, different from those of family and community. In the middle were those who thought it futile to try to counter the children's larger social ecology—parents, home, community—with a program that served them a few hours a day, a few days a week. Rather, efforts had to try to take into account and to strengthen that ecology. Those efforts must include parent education about childrearing and related matters, and support for parents' own efforts to grow and develop. At the other extreme were those who believed that the most important thing Head Start could do, the only thing that would make it effective, was to empower parents politically. The thing that would most help poor children would be to see their parents (who after all were their primary role models) as decision-makers, organizing and acting collectively to address community problems and meet needs.

A variation of the latter two views held that it was critical for parents to be involved in Head Start, but primarily in their children's education. Children would thereby see and feel their parents' commitment to education, and parents in turn would see their children and their children's actions in a new light (Zigler and Muenchow 1992:101). A parent might observe a teacher praise a child's artwork, and thus see both that artwork and her child differently and how positively her child responded to praise.

Beyond the problems of classroom and management quality, and of tensions about purpose, Head Start was developing numerous strengths. It was a national program, with goals and standards set outside local communities, which nonetheless managed to meet the needs of those communities. It was informal and open to, indeed not differentiated from, its surrounding community. It provided the beginning steps of a career pathway to some parents. Head Start programs provided badly needed health services and nutrition and helped families with a variety of concrete problems. Head Start programs also served as a center for community discussion of important childrearing issues. Parents got together to discuss and argue about what their Head Start center should try to accomplish; who their children were, after all; what their ideals for those children ought to be; and the implications for their own roles as parents. Head Start was a lively institution, that added life to communities. And it did all these things with chronically inadequate funding. Staff salaries were so low that they rarely lifted those staff who were poor out of poverty. (Amazingly, that continues to be the case twenty-five years later.)

Local Head Start programs, like other OEO programs, sometimes ran into invisible walls, defining the boundaries of empowerment. These walls were not only invisible, but moved, depending on the whims of OEO officials. The Office of Economic Opportunity was in a tenuous position itself and was mistrusted on all sides—by Congress, other federal agencies, mayors, and the poor themselves. Within two or three years the Bureau of the Budget had established a measure of control over the OEO approval process, and people with little substantive knowledge of specific program areas were making crucial decisions about which proposed ideas lived and died. Thus, in Head Start proposals, "what was cut [more often than not] was carefully worked in educational 'frills' like psychological services and teacher development work" (Greenberg 1990:40).

By 1965–1966 growing pressure from Congress led the Office of Economic Opportunity to evaluate the effects of Head Start on children. A series of local studies were funded, mostly of high quality programs, which focused on the effects on the children's IQs. Some showed short-term gains, which subsequently (though not surprisingly given the stability of IQ) disappeared (see Zigler and Muenchow 1992, ch. 3). In 1968 a major national study was launched, using a raft of child measures, which seemed to find that little if any positive effects of Head Start were carried into the early elementary school years (Cicirelli 1969). The study had numerous sampling and methodological flaws—for example, 70 percent of children sampled had participated only in summer programs, though by then Head Start was a ten-month program; the comparison group was more advantaged; the study ignored many important components and purposes of Head Start; and so forth. In retrospect it was absurd to make inferences about Head Start as a whole, given the diversity in local programs; it was also absurd to seek a definitive judgment so early in Head Start's life as a program.

Nonetheless, proponents of Head Start were in a delicate position. In an increasingly conservative and war-weary political climate, any vulnerability in a program was an excuse to decrease funding. Head Start would survive. Its Washington managers used the equivocal findings of the early research to argue that Head Start had to become a national laboratory for new approaches to helping poor children and families. Perhaps, they reasoned, three or four years of age was too late to help poor children. Perhaps interventions that did not alter children's family environments were destined to be too weak. These lines of thinking suggested the need to develop and test new approaches focused on the earliest years and on parents themselves. Head Start leadership initiated what would prove eventually to be two decades of research and development on parenting and family support demonstrations; at the time this provided the scientific cover needed to keep the larger preschool program alive. (For reviews of that research see Halpern 1988 1990).

Head Start survived also because its rapid early growth created a constituency in hundreds of poor communities that could be mobilized at times of jeopardy. As Skerry (1983) has pointed out, its many components allowed it to seem different things to people with different interests. When it could not argue for its beneficial child effects, it could argue for its role as a health care and nutrition provider, or as an employer of poor people, or as a national laboratory for research into effective early childhood programs for the poor. Head Start leaders could and did argue that it was not an expensive program—although its low costs were carried on the back of poorly paid staff.

Yet in its limitations, just as much as in its strengths, Head Start raised basic questions about truly neighborhood-based programs in poor, isolated neighborhoods. It reflected the generic limitations of a poverty-fighting strategy rooted in, and reliant on rebuilding the social infrastructure of poor neighborhoods. One key to poor children's educational success is ethnic and economic diversity in their schools and classrooms. Yet Head Start classrooms were not ethnically and economically diverse; in fact, they were just the opposite. Because the neighborhoods in which Head Start programs were embedded were isolated from the larger economy and labor market, jobs in Head Start rarely led to jobs outside the community. The Head Start culture was ambivalent about parents' working, especially in minimum-wage, dead-end jobs outside Head Start itself. Also, there was no one in the centers who viewed it as their role (or had the knowledge and experience) to help less resourceful parents keep moving steadily from less to more demanding experiences.

## The War on Poverty Assessed

The effects of the assumptions and service strategies of the War on Poverty have been debated for almost three decades: Did they bring greater social citizenship or contribute to greater social marginalization of the urban poor (Rochefort 1984)? Did they slow or speed up the worsening condition of poor families? The depth and breadth of poverty lessened during the 1960s, yet it was impossible to determine how much of this was due to general economic growth and how much to new social welfare programs and increased social welfare spending on the poor. Some poverty-related social indicators, including dependence on welfare and illegitimacy rates, continued to worsen. Minorities made employment gains during the 1960s and early 1970s, but the majority of these were in the public sector (Mead 1986:41). Urban residential segregation and migration of jobs to the suburbs, important causes of inner-city residents' employment difficulties, did not lessen, and probably worsened.

The initial answers to the broad questions about the War on Poverty were distorted by undue expectations and inappropriate evaluations. The effects of specific programs on children and families were found to range from modestly positive to nil, at least according to the methods and measures chosen by the first generation of program evaluators. It would take some years for the program evaluation community to acknowledge that it had prematurely evaluated new programs struggling to find their footing; had overstated the power and sensitivity of its methods; and had perhaps done more harm than good to the many programs, such as Head Start, with which it became involved. A number of the innovative programs of the era—neighborhood health centers (which became community health centers), the Women Infant and Children's Feeding program (WIC), even Head Start after a fashion—would eventually prove themselves. But even the most useful programs were crippled by the public doubts fostered in early evaluations.

Evaluators were not the only ones at fault. The federal government's time frames for bringing new program approaches to maturity were unrealistic; there was too much premature judgment, second-guessing, and scapegoating. The Office of Economic Opportunity was constantly hedging its bets on community action. (As time went on less and less funding for services went through the community action program.) It also pulled the rug out from under programs. Thus Office of Economic Opportunity planner Sanford Kravitz noted not more than two or three years after the Neighborhood Service Center program was initiated—by his own agency—that "Building . . . new neighborhood centers amid slum squalor is immoral" (cited in O'Donnell and Sullivan 1972:288). And Head Start administrators concluded, inaccurately, that reaching children when they were three or four years old was too late; this in spite of the fact that they knew the program was still plagued both by quality problems and lack of clarity about priorities and mission.

Lost among the giant evaluation studies were continuing, modest efforts to find relevant and effective helping strategies under conditions of poverty. For instance, a small group of practitioners working in neighborhood-based programs struggled, once more, to find a relevant and effective casework. Their basic strategy was to integrate the clinical principles worked out in the multiproblem family demonstrations of the 1950s with the more constructive of the new principles of community-based family support emerging in the OEO programs. One caseworker, attached to a preschool in a housing project on Chicago's west side, identified a number of hard-won principles for providing parenting support and guidance: a "down-to-earth" approach; use of familiar words and terms; some flexibility in timing and location of meetings, balanced with an effort to establish regularity; rephrasing and enlarging on mothers' own words; pointing out areas of competence; and helping mothers learn to put themselves in their children's place (Bowles 1972:392–396).

Not more than three or four years after the War on Poverty programs were initiated, a search began for the reasons for their apparent failure. It was argued that implementation was weak; that the assumptions, particularly regarding participation, were faulty; or even that the services provided were worsening the problems they were designed to address (what Hirschman 1991, would later call the "perversity thesis"). It was hypothesized that the poor themselves were resistant to the strategies developed; either that the "cultural deficits of poor people [were] just too intractable" or that the poor deliberately resisted helping efforts (Valentine 1971:212).

There had been warnings even before the decade's events transpired. In 1961 Kenneth Boulding noted that society "seemed [sic] to spend a good deal of effort [to improve the well-being and prospects of the poor] through schools, police and social work, churches and various social agencies . . . and with remarkably little success" (Boulding 1961:53). In the same volume, the anthropologist Thomas Gladwin noted that the likelihood of breaking the intergenerational cycle of poverty by intervening primarily with children was low. Such a strategy, he noted, had never worked in the past (Gladwin 1961:74). And the present generation of urban poor were now even more isolated and unprepared than those in the past. Yet the inability of the service-oriented strategy of the War on Poverty to improve the well-being and prospects of poor urban families seemed inevitable only in retrospect. No one could have predicted the impact of the Vietnam war and the mid-decade urban riots on the political will and mood of Congress and the public. The riots provided conservatives an opening to take control of image-making about the poor, with devastating consequences for poor minorities (see Scott 1996:98). The conceptualizations of poverty and poor people, originally intended to spur action on their behalf, ended up being used once again to blame and marginalize them.

To some extent, difficulties could have been predicted simply by lining up the various rationales and elements of the War on Poverty service strategy next to each other. It proved difficult, as Greenberg (1990:66) noted, speaking of Head Start, to combine "the wisdom of psychology and the [freedom] movement." It proved hard to reconcile the task of preparing "unprepared" people with that of empowering them. The image of the poor as unprepared, even damaged, clashed with the call for professionals to have more confidence in the poor, to trust their judgment and their perspective on improving services. The pattern of simultaneously denying the legitimacy of professionals and using them as trainers and resources in new programs, was confusing and debilitating. Because the new OEO programs were politically vulnerable, their leaders and staff were reluctant to acknowledge and try to work through internal conflicts in mission and priorities.

### Participation and the Attacks on Professionals

Of all the strategies associated with the service reforms of the 1960s, the principle of community participation in policy-setting, program design, and service provision received the most criticism. It was a strong idea, consonant with American ideals. But it was oversold, rushed into existence, and became entangled in civil rights and growing minority militancy. It also was supported only ambivalently by the federal government. There was never a sense of boundaries or limits; there was no recognition that some kinds of participation made more sense than others and that participation was only one among many elements needed to improve services.

There was too little attention to the reality that people needed extensive support and specific knowledge in assuming new responsibilities. Teachers of young children needed to know something, beyond their personal experience, about the developmental tasks and issues that young children were wrestling with, about how to respond to a shy child or a to a child with specific fears. Those who were counseling adults needed to know something about the psychology and developmental course of helping relationships. Self-knowledge, a critical prerequisite to helping others effectively and constructively, was also disparaged, as an artifact of white, European culture.

The various justifications offered for indigenous paraprofessionals' "unprofessional" practices—failure to keep appointments or to keep accurate records, resistance to supervision—kept those paraprofessionals from learning to be competent helpers. (With respect to records, one advocate noted that "Being with people and working with them . . . cannot be conveyed in words." Speaking of supervision, the same advocate argued that "The indigenous worker knows that it is a great achievement to get his client's trust and that most of what it said is confidential. Why, he feels, should he share it with someone else?" Normanda 1972:328–329).

On the other side, the almost unremitting attacks on professionals did more harm than good. Professionals became increasingly defensive as the decade wore on. In a kind of mirror image of what the poor had experienced historically, professionals resented their loss of individuality in the eyes of both outside observers and their clients, as well as the loss of the presumption that they were trying to help. (This latter was parallel to helpers' own historical presumption that the poor were not doing all they could to help themselves.) Professionals argued (somewhat disingenuously) that they were not the ones who had made the "essential diagnoses" of poor people historically; rather society as a whole had made it (Gottlieb 1974:95). Although, not surprisingly, most felt hurt and angry, some struggled to figure out what it meant to be more responsive. (Often professionals' efforts in this regard were themselves attacked as demonstrating their insensitivity and lack of understanding.) Some tried to put their knowledge, discipline, and experience at the service of community members involved in social action, offering to help articulate or clarify demands on local welfare offices or housing authorities. However, such offers also seemed to do more harm than good.

In general, the attacks on professionals created a climate that reduced the likelihood that they would acknowledge their own feelings of vulnerability and uncertainty; they also lessened their commitment to work together with poor people to figure out what it meant to provide responsive helping services under conditions of poverty and social exclusion. In many specific instances when poor people tried to take responsibility for defining and addressing their own concerns, professional helpers failed to support them. They could not swallow the idea of paraprofessionals performing the work of professionals. Polsky (1991:189) argues that professionals survived the attacks of the 1960s by "acknowledg[ing] a number of criticisms without abandoning their underlying faith in normalizing intervention through personal therapies." It is more accurate to argue that professionals both knew at some level that they were not reaching some people and yet genuinely believed that, as Beck (1972:190) put it, it was "absurd" to strive for equality in helping relationships. If the client does not "grant" to the helper "special abilities to assist in the problem-solving at hand," than she and the helper are left with no basis for a helping relationship.

*Neighborhood-Based Services as an Engine for Service Reform*

The use of neighborhood-based services as the engine for reform of the broader human service system—through the demonstration of new helping principles and approaches, pressure on prevailing service institutions, and efforts to assume a leadership or coordinating function—was only modestly successful. For one thing, it placed too many expectations on new programs and muddied their mission. As the Neighborhood Service Center experience illustrated, staff in neighborhood-based programs only had so much energy; it could be expended either on helping community residents or on community organizing and social action, but not on both at once.

The new OEO programs were also ill-suited to overall leadership roles in local service systems. Lacking financial authority or the resepct that comes with a history of good services, they had little leverage over existing service providers. They also never figured out how they wanted to relate to established helping agencies. They wavered between total avoidance and wholescale attacks, with periodic ambivalent efforts at cooperation. The strategy of dealing with the unresponsiveness of prevailing institutions by by-passing them and/or repudiating them, had questionable effects. These institutions were still serving poor families, indeed ever more vulnerable ones. Yet they often were painted as so completely hurtful to poor children and their families that little opportunity was left for seeking out common ground. The core work in helping, found in individual helping relationships, was hard to influence in a positive, constructive way through political means.

The disavowal by many OEO programs of a half-century of experience and assumptions about helping left a large void that remained unfilled, and left a lot of inexperienced frontline providers with little to go on. Looking back, one participant in the service experiments of the era noted that they had been "long on polemics and ideology, short on specifics and soundly based practice" (Taylor and Randolph 1975:xi). In retrospect it was possible to see that such traditional helping competencies as self-awareness, attention to boundaries, knowledge of developmental issues, and understanding of the development of helping relationships were neither useless nor irrelevant. It was possible to see that poor people had the same kinds of personal and family difficulties as their more economically advantaged peers. Discussing the casework experience at the Stanton Street Neighborhood Center, Jones and Weissman (1969:101) note that although workers were "specifically directed not to give long-term psychological help," community residents often came in to discuss problems in adult relationships, parent-child relationships, feelings of anger, sadness, depression—in other words matters that seemed to require such help.

At a broader level, the focus of most service reform effort within the boundaries of poor communities inadvertently contributed to the isolation of neighborhoods that were already becoming increasingly isolated. At its best, local participation was only able to compensate slightly for poor peoples' fundamental sense of exclusion. The small percentage of community residents who became active in neighborhood programs did gain jobs and work experience, information and connections that could be used to improve their family's well-being and perhaps their social standing in the community (Dubey 1972). Proponents assumed that poor urban neighborhoods were full of untapped resources that could be mobilized and fed into the service enterprise. Yet those resources were rapidly thinning out under the pressure of too many vulnerable families in too small a geographic space. Moreover, the resilience and adaptive coping that had characterized life in African-American communities in the South had not survived well when it had been torn from its historical context.

Heclo (1996:44) argues that the style and approach that marked service (and other, broader) reform efforts in the 1960s led not to a sense of progress in addressing social problems but to greater divisiveness, "public distress and cultural confusion." Minorities' emphasis on group pride and celebration of group strengths undoubtedly was the forerunner of the "strengths" perspective in supportive services for poor families. Yet the principle that there was no change without struggle or without conflict carried high costs. The anger, resentment, and sense of entitlement that some poor people brought to programs could sabotage the good things that were going on in those programs. One participant in the service reforms of the era characterized the experience as a "struggle between our destructive parts (evil) and our capabilities for greatness (good)" (Greenberg 1990:295–296). The inability—in the end—to reconcile the tensions that infused reform efforts during the era left a shaky foundation for the future. The loss of trust and belief in the helping services, and the loss of a sense of identity and purpose among providers, would complicate future efforts to construct a positive vision for supportive services.

# CHAPTER SIX

# Developments in Aid to Families with Dependent Children

*Helping those who are not doing their best to help themselves poses*
*extraordinarily difficult moral and political problems.*

—Christopher Jencks, 1985

During the 1960s the Aid to Dependent Children (AFDC) program continued to be buffeted by the contradictory impulses and unanswered questions that had shaped it from its beginning. Yet as with other public service systems, inherent tensions in AFDC were exacerbated by the turbulence of the era. Local welfare offices had to cope not just with shifting policies and legislative priorities but also with pressure from the new Office of Economic Opportunity (OEO) programs, from a new welfare rights movement, and from growing and changing caseloads. By the end of the 1960s the AFDC program had become the repository—part symbol, part lightning rod—for all the anxiety, anger, divisions, and sense of betrayal created by the events of that decade. It would remain such a repository thereafter, making constructive reform all but impossible and resulting, finally, in its demise in late 1996.

The number of families on AFDC, which had doubled during the 1950s, doubled again during the 1960s (Lampman 1971:ix). The unyielding growth in welfare rolls during two decades of prosperity and economic growth was due to a mixture of factors. Deteriorating job prospects in or near inner cities contributed to growing numbers of poor, single mothers with children and thus a greater need for AFDC and, indirectly, to lengthening stays on welfare for those families in the program. There was an increase in the number of young, unmarried women who decided to keep their babies and a greater willingness among poor families to seek and accept benefits. In addition, as a result of the pressures of welfare rights litigation, fewer denials of eligibility were made. Many families were referred to local welfare offices and helped through the application process by the various OEO programs, especially the neighborhood service centers and the new legal aid agencies. After 1965 AFDC became an important doorway to the new Medicaid program, an additional incentive first to apply and then remain on AFDC.

Piven and Cloward (1972:415) mention another little-noted reason for rising welfare rolls: the fallout of the urban renewal measures of the 1950s and early 1960s. That fallout included the forced break-up of extended families, increasing rental costs for substitute housing (which pushed some families into the welfare system), and the use of public aid as a response by local housing relocation agencies. And Patterson (1986:181) points out that the Bureau of Public Assistance, the federal agency that administered AFDC, also contributed in numerous, subtle ways to the growth in the welfare rolls; for example, by issuing directives against state and local practices that denied aid to families with children born out of wedlock.

Responses to the rising rolls and lengthening stays on welfare shifted during the course of the 1960s. Between 1962 and 1967 there was an increased reliance on casework intended to "rehabilitate" AFDC recipients and address obstacles to self-sufficiency. There was some effort, from within academia and liberal circles, to normalize (or destigmatize) the receipt of AFDC, or at least to focus on its protective functions, so that rising rolls would not be seen as purely problematic. A central question was how to create "a more constructive tension" between the rights of welfare recipients to a measure of dignity and the risk of long-term dependency created by a sense of entitlement and long spells on welfare (Lampman 1971:xii). Later in the decade a shifting political climate and the apparent failure of efforts to rehabilitate AFDC recipients through casework, led to an interest in more direct strategies for pulling and pushing AFDC recipients into the labor force, through work incentives and requirements, and work preparation programs. Work replaced casework as the magic bullet that would not just reduce welfare rolls but obliterate the culture of poverty and strengthen inner-city communities.

As the 1960s wore on, there was growing attention to administrative reform as a means of reducing welfare expenditures. This translated into an intensified effort to reduce overpayment and fraud through increased scrutiny of and pressure on local welfare offices, including sanctions on frontline workers for mistakes in approving requests for assistance (Handler and Hasenfeld 1991:120). There were efforts to create detailed rules and procedures for every eventuality and situation, as well as a detailed paper trail for every frontline worker action.

While it was growing rapidly, and trying to cope with changing policies, the AFDC program was under almost constant attack from different quarters—politicians, the media, the civil rights community, and, for the first time, welfare recipients themselves. Conservative media and politicians found that attacking welfare was a safe way of attacking poor minorities. The ubiquitous rights movements of the era found welfare a tangible and convenient target for fueling their organizing activities. For the poor themselves, expressing anger at welfare officials was one modest way to get back at a system that in the past had seemed to go out of its way to deny benefits and inflict humiliation.

The shifting, sometimes contradictory strategies of AFDC reform during the 1960s reflected Americans' historic ambivalence about poor people and the tendency to view poverty through the tricky lens of morality. The old questions—who deserved support; what those deemed deserving were deserving of (Lampman 1971:xiii); who ought to be excused from work expectations—just would not get answered. Three new elements intensified this historical ambivalence. One was lengthening spells on welfare. Although fear of creating dependency was as old as relief itself, never had so many families been perceived as genuinely dependent. Thus the causes, meaning, and effects, and the best way to respond to dependency became a defining concern. The second element was the (new) argument that the poor, like other special groups, were entitled to special treatment and support from society. The third new element was race. The growth in the welfare rolls was disproportionately concentrated in the inner cities, binding American ambivalence about welfare more closely to white Americans' feelings about race.

Further complicating attitudes toward poor people and poverty were the first signs of growing economic pressure on working-class families. The women's movement was psychologically freeing more advantaged mothers to enter the labor force, and economic realities were forcing working-class mothers in. The idea that poor women should receive support so that they could care for their children in their homes began to crumble. Childrearing was losing its status as an activity that strengthened communities and society and served the national interest.

## "Caseworking" People Out of Poverty

The interest in casework services for AFDC recipients had been present throughout the program's history. It intensified in the late 1950s when it became apparent that the need for the AFDC program was not going to "wither away," as had been hoped and predicted (Handler and Hollingsworth 1971:103). Amendments to the Social Security Act in 1962 strengthened the incentive to provide social casework in the program, providing for federal reimbursement of 75 percent of the cost of casework services (versus the standard 50 percent for the cost of administration). In order to qualify, states had to reduce caseloads and develop individual service plans for every child and family on the rolls, based on a wide-ranging assessment (Polsky 1991:163). There were also supposed to be services for families not yet on welfare but at imminent risk of dependency (somewhat akin to today's Intensive Family Preservation Servies in child welfare). In addition, some funding was authorized for the training and professional development of caseworkers.

Casework services under the 1962 amendments had a number of purposes, most somewhat vague. In the 1950s the casework community had been able to justify its work with AFDC families in relatively modest terms. It was providing instruction in home management, making sure that children received health care and went to school, and making sure grants were used efficiently and to meet basic needs. The new objectives reflected some continuity in purpose. Casework was supposed to help poor families mobilize their capacities and "make the best of their situation" (Handler and Hollingsworth 1971:105; Leiby 1978:304). It was supposed to help strengthen family life. There was still a strong element of child protection. The specific foci of many state and local programs included children's physical and emotional well-being (and for older children, school progress), childrearing and family relationships, and parents' personal problems. A new, albeit more tentative, objective was to address obstacles to what would later come to be called job readiness.

In other words, although inspired by growing AFDC rolls, the new casework program was not intended simply to reduce those rolls. Caseworkers were given flexibility to shape their work with particular families as they thought appropriate. The goal for some recipients would be to help them leave welfare; for others, to help them attain a "higher degree of self-confidence and independence" (Handler and Hollingsworth 1971:104). In practice, linking recipients to experiences that would directly prepare them for work was not emphasized; even less, linking recipients directly to work. Work was not seen by caseworkers as something that would automatically improve family life or children's well-being, especially in families with young children. In addition to their ambivalence about the appropriateness of work, most caseworkers had little knowledge of the labor market and few contacts with employers.

In practice, casework emerged as a serious activity only in selected local offices. The frontline staff who were supposed to do casework still had to collect information and investigate and process people for approval (and recertification) of AFDC grants. Caseloads continued to be too high—sometimes well over 100—to allow regular contact with families. There were never enough trained caseworkers. Fully a third of caseworkers did not have a college degree. Only a handful had any social work training. There was only one graduate level caseworker for every 23,000 relief recipients (May 1964:104–105). The original vision of the legislation had been for casework capacity to be built up gradually over a period of years, but Congress never approved the training and personnel preparation funds to support capacity-building. It also proved difficult to recruit professionals into public assistance casework, as well as to retain those recruited (Polsky 1991:178–179).

Frontline and supervisory staff turnover, which reached 40 percent per year in some jurisdictions, compounded the problem of the lack of skills among caseworkers. Although time in the casework role could lead to burnout and emotional withdrawal, it also was critical to the gradual acquisition of those evaluative skills and a repertoire of responses that could be gained only through experience. More experienced workers were often less bureaucratic in their work than new ones. They knew better how to work with and around rules and procedures (Blau 1965:658). Turnover also severely reduced continuity in helping relationships. One study found that "the larger case records were biographies of dependency but written like an anthology. Literally dozens of persons contributed a page, two, or three" (May 1964:109).

In a study of casework services in Wisconsin, Handler and Hollingsworth (1971:106–107) found that caseworkers focused primarily on helping families cope with concrete, discrete problems in their day-to-day lives. Most discussion and problem-solving focused on children and children's issues and health concerns; little on the mothers' own lives and futures. Caseworkers tried to "avoid topics which (a) might lead to complaints and requests and (b) would result in the caseworker finding it difficult to make delivery or be of help" (p. 107). They might occasionally help arrange a skills assessment or mention a training program, but there was little follow-up. There seemed to be a preoccupation with avoiding conflict. Caseworkers provided little advice about behavior or feedback about decisions, and they tended to ignore or simply not confront recipients with transgressions of AFDC rules.

Welfare recipients in the Wisconsin study in turn rarely reached out to caseworkers for assistance, except when there were grant-related problems.

They reported feeling neither compelled to follow advice nor bothered by what advice and feedback was given. They reported not minding the intrusion of caseworkers into their lives, including unannounced home visits, and they felt caseworkers were generally fair and trustworthy. In other words, they had low expectations of what caseworkers could or should do to help them (Handler and Hollingsworth 1971:108). The limited role and impact of casework in this study was due in part to the mismatch between the preoccupations of the caseworkers and the poor families they served. It was due also to the infrequency of contact, typically a forty- to fifty-minute home visit every two to three months.

Gottlieb (1974) found that frontline workers in welfare agencies were under a variety of pressures that made constructive helping almost impossible. High caseloads, high staff turnover, endless paperwork, a priority on avoiding mistakes all contributed to a sense of getting nowhere, of going around in circles. Workers frequently did not have time to process the paperwork that would release resources for their clients. Often it was easier simply to not respond to clients, to not mention resources to which a client was entitled or help that the worker could provide with a problem. Workers were "constantly [called on] to justify their actions" to supervisors, based on rules. They seemed to lose their commitment through a thousand small acts by supervisors: "A worker came to a supervisor for approval of a client's request for a bed. She had made a home visit and presented almost passionately the client's dire need of the bed. Citing an administrative ruling, the supervisor denied the request" (Gottlieb 1974:32).

Casework services also were affected in different ways by caseworkers' continuing responsibility to determine eligibility and monitor and adjust grants. This role, with its implied dependence of client on case worker, as well as the potential for coercion, added one more complication to helping relationships that were already complicated by cultural differences, lack of clarity about expectations and goals, and sometimes mistrust. Caseworker discretion in this area would become a target of administrative reformers during the 1960s, creating still another set of constraints. In their efforts to assert greater control over AFDC budgets, federal and state officials added a constant stream of regulations, rules, guidelines, and reporting requirements (Polsky 1991:179). These occupied more and more of caseworkers' time, further reducing their capacity to provide helping services. The increasing bureaucracy affected supervisors as well. Handler and Hollingsworth (1971:44) report that directors of local welfare departments seemed worried about the right things: "securing adequate quarters and resources for workers . . . trying to ensure for workers the feeling that [they] had support, that they could take risks or present problems." Yet those directors also had to worry about the increasing number of federal audits.

## Casework Evaluated

The struggles of public aid caseworkers to find and sustain a helpful role were compounded by the behavior of the social work community as a whole. That community was reluctant or unable to define what effectiveness meant in the context of the AFDC program, making it difficult to evaluate casework efforts. This in turn contributed to growing skepticism in Washington and in academia toward the social work community's argument about the importance of highly skilled workers in the AFDC casework roles. Further, a growing body of evidence failed to support this contention.

During the 1960s a number of evaluations of professional casework in the AFDC program were undertaken. Most of these evaluations compared AFDC casework to the garden-variety casework provided in typical urban welfare offices. Most studies found few or modest positive effects of professional casework—perhaps slightly reduced reliance on AFDC, slightly better family functioning, or greater use of community resources. One review of seventeen studies of "high quality" casework with poor and vulnerable families, most undertaken during the 1960s, concluded that "In none of the studies was there clear evidence that professional casework produced results superior to no treatment at all, or in any way better than the minimal services provided by non-professionals" (Fischer 1976:137). Typical of the studies was one evaluating the effects on 83 indicators of enriched social casework on families newly enrolled in AFDC—family functioning, housing, health, use of community resources, and so forth (Mullen, Chazin, and Feldstein 1972). The investigators found virtually no effects, with the explanations including poor implementation, better than expected casework by public aid caseworkers assigned to control families, and the apparent fact that "individualized counseling" was perhaps a low priority among the families served.

Another study took place in Chemung County, New York (Brown 1968). A group of 195 "multiproblem" families on AFDC was randomly assigned to either enriched, skilled casework (by caseworkers with masters degrees) or to more typical public assistance monitoring. Families in the enriched treatment group had weekly to biweekly contact with their caseworker over a two-year period. Researchers measured services received by both groups and the effects on a host of domains, including family relationships, parenting, budget management, use of community resources, children's school progress, and contact with child welfare authorities. They found that the treatment group had received a great deal more help, but that there were no positive effects from enriched casework. In fact, families with the most contact with caseworkers over the two-year period made the least progress. Both the caseworkers and the local welfare department director felt that "a great deal of good was done in some cases" (Brown 1968:126). Yet the findings led the researchers to state—and this was in the mid-1960s—that "there is great confusion in the field about what casework can or cannot do and what casework is or is not" (p. 19).

Not every study confirmed the ineffectiveness or inappropriateness of professional expertise. Weiss (1973) studied the help-seeking behavior of a sample of AFDC recipients over a six-month period. Some received assistance from professionally trained caseworkers, some from nonprofessionals. The latter were generally new hires who came in through one or another War on Poverty "new careers" initiative. (Polsky 1991:179, describes the increasing reliance on nonprofessionals in public aid casework as "expedience . . . elevated to a mission.") During the six-month period, the women in the study sought help for a wide variety of problems, some their own, some of other family members, some the family's as a whole. He divided these into two broad categories: help with gaining access to resources and other services (health care, housing, admission of a child to a camp or preschool program, etc.), and support and guidance ("help in imposing structure on a confusing situation, in choosing some line of action, and in maintaining the confidence to act" [p. 320]).

In general, women in the sample were not suspicious of professional helpers; in fact they preferred them to nonprofessionals because they were generally more decisive and authoritative, and better at moving the women toward action on a problem. The women wanted a helper who they believed posessed special strengths that could be "lent" to them, put in their service. Weiss (1973:321) reports that "a number of respondents complained to us that they could not discuss their problems with the young women the public assistance agency was increasingly hiring as social workers." At the same time professionals were perceived much more positively in providing support and guidance than in helping with access to monetary or in-kind resources. There were frequent disagreements with professionals about the latter.

Studies such as this nonetheless could not counter the weight of negative findings from experimental studies. With each equivocal or negative finding, it became more more difficult for professional casework advocates to argue that the measurement of outcomes failed to capture important or subtle effects; that lessons were learned that would strengthen the field; that families appreciated the services. At best the evidence pointed to a "lack of any basic therapeutic meeting ground between recipient and worker" (Gottlieb 1974:96). At worst, it raised questions about whose interests the casework community had at heart.

## Attacks from North, South, East, and West

From the perspective of the social work community, the lack of evidence for the effectiveness of professional casework came at a bad time. During the 1960s, as in previous decades, AFDC recipients and the AFDC program itself were attacked in the media and in Congress; the former for all the reasons poor people had always been attacked, the latter for promoting dependency and weakening poor families. With each succeeding decade, the language of attacks on welfare recipients had become harsher. In the 1960s the conservative print media made almost constant references to welfare chiselers, freeloaders, and parasites, who were preying on the generosity and forbearance of productive citizens (Gottlieb 1974:18). Welfare increasingly was seen as rewarding immoral behavior, destroying families, and even encouraging people to stay poor (Spalter-Roth and Hartmann, undated:10).

In the 1960s, for the first time, poor people and their advocates joined the attacks on welfare. Poor people rejected the right, as well as the capacity of welfare workers and others to define and label them, to place them in dependent positions, to claim to be able to understand and evaluate their lives. Public interest lawyers, legal aid clinics, organized groups of welfare recipients, civil rights activists, and academics writing critically about welfare joined to create a welfare rights movement. This movement focused on four issues: assuring basic constitutional rights, especially due process, to welfare applicants and recipients; reducing the discretion of local welfare offices and frontline practitioners; assuring that welfare recipients received the financial and material assistance to which they were entitled; and removing personal morality and behavior of welfare recipients as a legitimate concern of the welfare system.

The effort to assure due process rights for welfare applicants and recipients was undertaken in the courts (and led periodically to the Supreme Court). For the most part the federal courts affirmed those rights and struck down a number of discriminatory practices. In 1970 the Supreme Court declared that welfare benefits were not a promise of charity but a matter of statutory entitlement for qualified families. The attack on the discretion of local welfare offices came in three forms: educating recipients about their rights; legal action; and direct action, through protests and sit-ins. (It was argued by some welfare rights advocates that "dependence" on the good will and discretion of welfare authorities was more psychologically damaging even than dependence on the welfare check itself.)

Local discretion—in interpreting eligibility and the amount of eligible families—had historically set AFDC apart from other categorical cash entitlement programs (Handler and Hollingsworth 1971). Applications for assistance were simply turned down, and grants were reduced or terminated, for vague, arbitrary, or trivial reasons (Piven and Cloward 1971:156). The most subtle, subjective, and immeasurable dimensions of peoples' lives—personal and family relationships, childrearing—were evaluated by invisible yardsticks and declared suitable or unsuitable. The discretion in the AFDC program was due in part to the strong states' rights philosophy of southern Congressmen whose seniority gave them authority over the AFDC program. More generally, it was due to the public's historical ambivalence about poor peoples' claim to support. This ambivalence led to vague statutory language regarding purpose and eligibility (e.g., whether and how moral criteria were to be used), which in turn left the fateful and sometimes difficult decisions to local public aid caseworkers and their supervisors. Some frontline workers identified more closely with poor families, others viewed themselves as the final guardians of the public purse, still others saw themselves in a parentlike role, and tried to balance nurturance and control.

One approach to combating discretion was to help welfare recipients learn the minutiae of welfare law, so they could use to their benefit the same arbitrary and petty rules that had been used against them for so long. For instance, recipients were made aware of their right to request "special needs" grants providing for household necessities, such as bedding and winter clothes. This approach sometimes involved local campaigns that made a public issue of recipients' rights to be informed about things for which they were eligible. Legal questions about these campaigns sometimes found their way to the courts along with more traditional due process questions.

A more subtle dimension of the welfare rights movement was the rejection of the right of "others"—the public, politicians, academics, social workers—to label and categorize welfare recipients. Related to this was the rejection of the client role and of the rights of caseworkers to try to change welfare recipients' behavior. This latter was not about efforts to pressure welfare recipients to work. As Piven and Cloward (1971:171–172) point out, welfare recipients continued to buy into the "work ethos"; they believed in and valued work. It was—ironically, given welfare rules—primarily about out-of-wedlock childbearing.

Welfare rights activists in all these areas received intellectual support from a small group of welfare "theorists," who developed several differing critiques of welfare. Gottlieb (1974:17–18)) describes a number of these. It was argued, for example, that it was unjust to impose on welfare recipients "standards of morality which are a matter of free choice for other citizens." Relatedly, it was unjust to apply core American myths to people who were socially and economically excluded—particularly the myth that "the accepted way of life works well for everyone," that if one played by the rules he or she would be rewarded with a decent job in a decent neighborhood. It was argued that poor people, like others, wished to reciprocate for the support given them but were put in a position by society that made it impossible to do so. They were demeaned, stigmatized, put under the stress of chronic material hardship, and given no place in the social system. They were not to blame when they "defaulted on the system."

Local welfare departments tried varied responses to the pressures of welfare rights activists. A few listened and adjusted. Some made gestures that appeared responsive: increasing budgets for emergency or clothing allowances; establishing a community services division, or starting a small prevention program; establishing formal mechanisms for recipients to offer advice and feedback on procedures and practices. More typically, welfare bureaucracies drew on their bureaucratic skills to contain reform, or to turn it inside out. The campaign to raise consciousness about special grants, discussed earlier, was made irrelevant in some states and localities by simply eliminating the special grants program altogether (Davis 1996:152). In response to the campaign to limit discretion and standardize practice, welfare departments created detailed regulations and procedures for everything, dramatically increasing the complexity and bureaucracy of welfare programs.

For better, and sometimes for worse, individual discretion had been a tool used by workers to frame their helping efforts. As discretion was replaced by detailed regulations and procedures, frontline workers' time was increasingly consumed by paperwork. As always, frontline welfare workers took the brunt of the anger and resentment stimulated in welfare recipients by their advocates. Individual welfare recipients became more assertive toward their caseworkers. They made a variety of requests for additional support, citing rules and regulations that the frontline workers may or may not have been familiar with. Since frontline workers felt they were doing the best they could under difficult circumstances, they viewed welfare recipients' new assertiveness as an affront or as ingratitude: "I know there is not enough in the grant, but they should not make demands on us" . . . "They start yelling before I have a chance to help" (Gottlieb 1974:60). The frontline welfare workers of the 1960s were in the wrong place at the wrong time. They happened to be there when poor people finally turned the tables, treating those in authority with the same lack of individuality with which they themselves had been treated for so long.

### The Emergence of Work Incentives, Work Requirements, and Work Preparation

By the late 1960s the growth in the welfare rolls, the activism and occasional militancy of the poor, and the personal behavior of welfare recipients were becoming irritants to Congress (and less directly to the American public). Casework was having no apparent effects on either the size of welfare rolls or the behavior of welfare recipients. Many were also concerned about the weakening attachment of inner-city residents to the labor force. In 1967, therefore, new amendments to the Social Security Act shifted the rhetoric and to a modest degree the course of AFDC once again. Work—the one thing that Americans had always believed could solve problems and shape people up—replaced casework as the means of rehabilitating welfare recipients and reducing welfare dependence.

The 1967 amendments created the Work Incentive Program (WIN), which strengthened work incentives by allowing welfare recipients to keep some earned income without a reduction in their grant; it also allowed states to require some welfare recipients to participate in work preparation activities or work. (The original legislation included a freeze in the amount of federal matching funds available "for AFDC cases caused by illegitimacy or desertion"; this was repealed a year later; Patterson 1986:174). The 1967 amendments incorporated the casework strategy, but gave it more focus (on family planning, among other issues). Yet they also separated income support functions from social services, reversing the assumption that the two were inherently intertwined. One result was a gradual weakening of whatever supportive casework services had been providing, since discussion of income maintenance issues had always provided an opening for discussion of other issues.

Different supporters of the new emphasis on work saw different dimensions of WIN as critical. Those committed to work incentives argued that the poor were no different than anyone else and simply lacked financial incentives to work. Those preoccupied with work requirements suspected that the poor were different from everyone else—or had become different due to the corrupting effect of welfare—and would not work or prepare for work unless required to. (This seemed to imply the need for continued supervision of poor people after they left welfare and until they internalized the values of the nonpoor.) The latter group also argued that people on welfare should be obligated to do something in exchange for receiving a check. Those who viewed work preparation as the critical element of WIN believed it to be a sounder approach to rehabilitation than casework. Work preparation was premised on the idea that some welfare recipients were not ready to work because they lacked the skills and dispositions to do so. These skills and dispositions, which most people acquire naturally and incrementally in the course of growing up, going to school, observing adults, participating in community activities, and so forth, were identified, packaged, and organized into modules to be taught in classes.

Under the WIN program local welfare departments referred two classes of recipients—mandated and optional—to state employment agencies. There they would be assessed (for work history, aptitude, barriers, etc.) and then referral to vocational education, on the job training, or work. Those mandated to participate included unemployed fathers, children over sixteen, and anyone else at the state's discretion. Optional participants typically were mothers with school-age children. Theoretically, recipients mandated to participate in WIN could have the adult portion of their grants reduced if they refused a placement recommendation without good cause (Handler and Hollingsworth 1971:153). Optional participants could not be sanctioned.

The strategies that emerged to form the work preparation approach for welfare recipients derived from the employment and training programs developed by the Department of Labor for the War on Poverty. These programs, gathered under Title V of the Economic Opportunity Act of 1964, funded training for actual and potential welfare recipients, with a bias toward fathers in the AFDC-U program. Their antecedents included the labor bureaus of the charity organization societies and the settlements, and the public works and public service service employment programs of the New Deal. As usual, the findings from those earlier programs were viewed selectively. For example, while there was some evidence that workers who had lost jobs felt better about themselves when they worked for a relief check, there was equal, if not more compelling evidence that makework jobs yielded little psychological or actual benefit to people.

Under WIN, welfare recipients were referred to local employment offices by welfare caseworkers. Those offices were supposed to create teams consisting of a counselor, job developer, coach, and work-training specialist. The idea was to create a coherent service package. Recipients were supposed to be assessed and placed in a component, such as a job readiness class, community work experience "slot," or a job. Once placed they were supposed to be followed by a team member, usually the counselor. State welfare agencies were required to make arrangements for adequate child care for mothers wishing to work. They also were supposed to provide "follow-up" services to families who returned to welfare after an "unsatisfactory" work experience (Handler and Hollingsworth 1971)

The first few years of the WIN program revealed many of the dynamics that would define and shape welfare to work programs in the years to come. The language of the federal statute was vague and at points contradictory, making the intent hard to decipher. This pushed a variety of issues down to the states to resolve in their own way. Among these were whether placement in work, work preparation, or "rehabilitation" was the highest priority; who should be expected to work or engage in work preparation; and how and when sanctions should be applied. The states in turn handed these issues down to local welfare offices.

The federal government also failed to provide the resources to implement WIN, with the not surprising result that most states took very narrow positions on mandatory participation. Much of the practical responsibility to make WIN work rested with state employment agencies, who were ambivalent about their new role and mission and whose staff had little experience working with welfare recipients. Staff of local employment offices sometimes had the same stereotypical views of welfare recipients as others who did not know them first-hand. For instance, they viewed welfare income as no more legitimate than income from illegal activity (Gordon 1978:62).

During the first two years of the WIN program 1.6 million of the 2 million families on AFDC were "assessed" for WIN. The great majority of welfare recipients were exempted from the program, primarily because they had young children. (AFDC caseworkers had the discretion to exempt any family from the program for whom participation might be "inimical to the family's welfare"; Mink 1978:118.) Some 20 percent of recipients were deemed appropriate for referral to the program, and of these, 77 percent were actually referred. Of those referred, about half were eventually enrolled in the WIN program. This represented about 5 percent of the total AFDC population. Most of this 5 percent were men, mothers of older children, and older youth.

The experience of those enrolled in WIN set a pattern that would characterize much welfare to work practice in the following decades (see Herr, Wagner, and Halpern 1996). The majority of enrollees spent a good deal of time in limbo, waiting to be placed (or re-placed, if they had dropped out of an activity), or on waiting lists for a particular training program or class. More than a few were referred back to AFDC as inappropriate referrals. The most common placements were basic education and vocational education, which each served about 20 percent of participants. Rates of passage of the GED exam were very low; completion of vocational education programs somewhat higher (Gordon 1978:36–37). People liked vocational education, but some complained about pressure to accept available slots in areas of little interest to them (Garvin 1978:ch. 5). Another sizable group of participants primarily received counseling (Lescohier 1978:175).

The least utilized component was on-the-job training, which served less than 1 percent of enrollees, but nonetheless was responsible for 6 percent of successful WIN job placements. Job development (i.e., locating jobs for people) and placement were found to be ill-developed components of WIN. The dominant practice was simply to fill job orders as they came in to the employment office, "regardless of the degree of match between job seeker and job requirements" (Gordon 1978:52). Three quarters of its participants left WIN without completing any class or program. Less than 10 percent of those who terminated WIN did so with a job, and "of these, it is unclear how many actually received jobs because of WIN" (Mink 1978:113). Most of the few mothers on welfare who found jobs through WIN returned to the welfare rolls within months of their foray into the labor force (Smith 1978:197). There was no recognition that people placed in jobs might lose or leave them, and thus no effort to help them stay employed.

Criticisms of WIN by participants centered around four issues. One was the frustration and disappointment that accompanied long waits for (or between) placement in activities or components. A second, which particularly affected those who entered the program because they wished to go right to work, was the torturous path people had to take to get to the point of assistance with job search and placement. (To cite just one small example, physical examinations were required in many local offices, which could takes weeks to schedule and complete.) A third complaint was about the rigidity of the program structure. As one participant noted, "no matter what you said [to program staff], you had to go along with how they set up the program." A fourth, and related, complaint was lack of choice in selecting activities (Garvin 1978:105; Lescohier 1978:176). As with the earlier casework strategy within AFDC, WIN participants' disappointment was tempered in some instances by modest expectations. For others, though, the WIN experience dampened whatever tentative feelings they might have had about trying to find a place in the labor force.

WIN was succeeded by WIN II, established by the so-called "Talmadge" amendments to the Social Security Act in 1971. This new program brought a shift from an emphasis on work preparation to an emphasis on job search and job placement; theoretically, it expanded the mandated population to AFDC recipients with children six years old and over (Handler and Hasenfeld 1991). On the job training and community work experience were to receive greater priority; educational activities and counseling less. The time allowed between placements was reduced to two weeks per placement and two months per year (Mink 1978:117).

WIN II was intended to communicate clearer expectations and create clearer obligations and sanctions. It did lead to an increase in the number of welfare recipients who registered for WIN. Its instinct to let people start with some work experiences, rather than forcing them to struggle to complete basic education, was sound. (People with histories marked by frustration and failure in educational settings were often unable and unwilling to stick with the drill and related classroom work characteristic of adult basic education. Forcing them to begin the journey out of welfare with adult basic education simply resulted in one more experience of failure with school-like activity.) At the same time the orientation toward employment-related activities led to a good deal of "creaming"—selection of the most job-ready for participation in the program. There also remained under WIN II a fundamental sense of ambivalence about appropriate expectations of the great majority of welfare recipients with young children. And there was still little conception of how to create constructive pathways toward work—types and sequences of activities—and appropriate types of interpersonal support for those recipients who proved to be far from job-ready. Both of these basic issues—but particularly the latter—would plague the work preparation field for the remainder of the century (see Her and Halpern 1991; Herr, Wagner, and Halpern 1996).

## Conclusions

During the 1960s poor families on welfare continued to be buffeted not only by economic insecurity and hardship but also by ideological cross-currents. The goal of supporting deserving women and children gave way to the goal of rehabilitation and the legal requirement to support all poor women and children (regardless of personal behavior). These goals in turn gave way to the goals of reducing the welfare rolls, preparing people for work, and getting them into the workforce. None of the earlier goals left the stage of the welfare reform morality play as they were supplanted by others.

At least some of the shifting about during the 1960s was due to the struggle against the reality of a growing caseload in a program that originally had been intended as temporary, not as an integral part of Social Security. Like the hypothesized culture of poverty, a culture of welfare seemed to be emerging, characterized by entrenched dependency. Like poverty itself, the use of welfare was coming to be seen to be seen as something self-perpetuating, a set of values and behaviors that children inherited from their parents rather than a particular type of family support program.

*The Beginning of the End for Public Aid Casework*

Public aid casework would never recover from the blows it suffered in the 1960s. Some of those blows were self-inflicted, others were not. With respect to improving families' lives, the social work community had overpromised what casework could deliver. Casework reached too few welfare recipients too erratically. And the casework community was too ambivalent about its goals. Was the surest path to strengthening family life and children's well-being to get parents into the labor force? To make sure mothers fulfilled basic parental responsibilities and devoted their energy to protecting and advocating for their children? To improve the mental health of women? The majority of caseworkers were at best ambivalent about whether pushing recipients quickly into the labor force was a good thing.

Caseworkers' preoccupation with the barriers to work faced by welfare recipients—whether mental health problems, substance abuse, or family difficulties—put them on the wrong side of political if not public sentiment. Caseworkers had not been able to demonstrate that their helping methods ameliorated personal problems. Moreover, while personal problems posed barriers for some welfare recipients, for others work occasionally helped reduce their personal problems. (The challenge was, and remains, that it is impossible to predict who will fall into which group; thus the argument for letting people sort themselves through experience; Herr, Wagner, and Halpern 1996:6). By the late 1960s politicians and the public at large had less patience with the idea that individual situations and problems constituted a reason for nonwork, as well as less patience with social workers' approach to helping. When policy priorities shifted toward work preparation in the later 1960s, caseworkers had neither the experience nor connections to the labor market to carve out a useful role.

Beyond the limitations that came with an ambivalent mandate and an impatient public, AFDC caseworkers during the 1960s were increasingly hemmed in by rules and regulations. The loss of discretion for frontline workers was a particularly damaging legacy of the era. For all its potential for abuse, discretion was not abused by the great majority of caseworkers. Caseworkers were constrained and disheartened by the climate of distrust created by the rules under which they now had to operate. They were caught between politicians demanding reduced costs and poor families struggling to get by on what already was too little.

There is evidence that the dynamics found in the 1960s studies of constraints upon casework in AFDC persist. In a recent study of public aid caseworkers in Chicago, Edin (1993) found that the caseworkers not only deliberately avoided asking questions that might lead to knowledge of recipient transgression of AFDC rules, they also ignored or did not act upon what they did learn incidentally. They did so because they knew assistance levels were too low to support families and because they lacked time to deal with the paperwork and other demands that would ensue. One caseworker told the interviewer that "you're busy enough with the stuff that inundates you" (Edin 1993:90). The workers in this study also reported that confronting clients with transgressions could lead to conflict and arguments, and it was just easier to avoid the emotional toll involved. For their part, AFDC recipients were acutely aware of the corrupting effects of this pattern. As one told Edin (1993:109), "Public aid is an agency that I believe can teach a person how to lie. If you tell them the truth you won't get any help. But if you go down there and tell them a lie you get help."

*Broader Problems*

There were three broader problems with AFDC debate during the 1960s, problems that would continue through the coming decades and ultimately prove fatal to the AFDC program. The first was the tendency to confuse the provision of a safety net with the design of interventions to move families toward self-sufficiency. A second, and related problem was the tendency to confuse the task of figuring out how to support growth and development in people (a growing number of whom had difficult histories) with the desire to create and enforce social obligations for welfare recipients. The third problem was the tendency to view different domains in poor women's lives—particularly childrearing and economic support—in isolation from each other, complicating their efforts to balance and manage different responsibilities, particularly childrearing and economic support.

Why was it not possible to imagine a welfare program that balanced different goals—assuring poor families decent financial support; attending to the often blocked personal development of parents; and conveying social expectations in a clear, but not punitive way? Why was it not possible to imagine a welfare program that simultaneously supported poor mothers' efforts to care for and provide for their children? It was not possible because those debating and formulating policy either distrusted their own (and society's) compassion, or distrusted poor adults, or both. It was not possible because those formulating policy focused only on the attributes of the least motivated, least well-functioning welfare recipients and used those as a basis for designing policies and programs. It was not possible because the two principal motives behind welfare policy—one being to provide welfare recipients opportunity for growth and independence, the other to teach them respect for discipline and hierarchy—were hardly reconcilable.

The result was that the welfare system did not do a good job with any of its objectives. It went part-way toward relieving the hardship experienced by vulnerable children and families, and then no further. By the late 1960s the average welfare grant for nonfarm families of four remained at half the amount needed to lift a family above the official poverty line (Patterson 1984:163). Welfare even exacerbated distress by needlessly viewing and treating vulnerable families as deviant. The motivation and capacity to meet parental responsibilities was undermined by the implicit message that being on AFDC made one an inadequate parent almost by definition.

When the goal of moving welfare recipients toward work was introduced, it was done so not just tentatively but ambivalently. Vague statutory language, massive exemptions, and inadequate funding attested to continuing reluctance to let go completely of the notion that AFDC was first and foremost an income support program for vulnerable families. Why was WIN, like its successors WIN II and the Family Support Act of 1988, never funded adequately? Some have argued that there was never an intention to do so. Handler and Hasenfeld (1991:41) argue that WIN—like those subsequent programs—was intended primarily as a symbolic gesture, not a genuine effort to wrestle with the difficulties experienced by welfare recipients, whether of their own making or not. The proclamation of work requirements for welfare recipients was intended to reassure the public that those recipients were being held to the same standards as everyone else. It was intended to reinforce the centrality of work as the criterion for judging peoples' worth in American society, even as working conditions worsened for millions of Americans.

At the same time the welfare system was not designed or suited for moving people toward stable employment, which for many welfare recipients was a gradual process, and for all an unpredictable one. In the first place, no one knew how to recreate artificially, in a limited time frame, the thousands of small, subtle experiences that most Americans have growing up that prepare them for work. Job readiness classes, in which people were lectured about and simulated searching and applying for jobs and dealing with typical job-related difficulties, proved of limited utility (Gordon 1978:ch. 3). Most frontline workers had little experience with this task. Welfare recipients who expressed interest in work were deflected into rigid bureaucratic programs that frustrated them. Those mandated to work experienced a system that constantly conveyed ambivalent messages about that mandate.

Perhaps it was not appropriate to expect the same government program to aide and guide "both the people expected to work and those not expected to work" (Garfinkel and McLanahan 1986:178). Yet at an even more basic level the problem was—and continues to be—to design a policy that accepted individual differences in priorities, capacity, and situation among families on welfare but was simultaneously fair to all involved and satisfied the American public's expectation that welfare recipients try their best. Most welfare recipients, like other Americans, viewed caring and providing for their children as the highest priorities in their lives. Nonetheless, welfare recipients, like other Americans, varied in temperament, capacity, and preferred paths to meeting responsibilities and should have been given some options. Under conditions of poverty, both caring for and providing for children are enormous tasks and should be appreciated and supported as such.

Allowing welfare recipients a measure of choice in priorities was complicated by a trend that had little to do with welfare policy and practice per se. This was the beginning of a long-term increase in job-holding among married women with children, across social class and including women with young children. In future decades many voters would see "little reason to excuse single women from the obligation of work solely because they are responsible for rearing children" (Burtless 1995:73).

More generally, both liberals and conservatives missed the forest for the trees. Liberals, preoccupied with protecting children, could not see how encouraging or even requiring parents to work could be in children's best interest. They could not see that social expectations, when appropriate and realistic, are good for people. Expectations reflect a belief in those of whom expectations are held. Conservatives refused to see the possibility that there were any other ways for welfare recipients to demonstrate good faith—that one was making one's best effort—than low-paying, dead-end work. Such conservatives discounted the value of meeting parental responsibilities and making a contribution to one's community. They could not see that rather than coercing the poor to function, it was more fruitful to recognize and build on the functioning they were already doing. A compliance orientation would yield at best a pro forma response.

The argument that all work, no matter how meaningless or demeaning, was of greater value to families and to society than nurturing children, simply did not hold up; it was also repugnant to those whose ancestors had experienced slavery. In debate concerning his ill-fated Family Assistance Plan, President Nixon argued that "scrubbing floors or emptying bedpans is not enjoyable work, but a lot of people do it—and there is as much dignity in that as there is in any other work to be done in this country—including my own." To which welfare rights activist George Wiley answered, "You don't promote family life by forcing women out of their homes to empty bedpans." The work-test, he argued, was "nothing more than forcing mothers into a kind of servitude" (Mead 1986:109).

At any rate, the circle had closed: once stigmatized for working and neglecting their children, poor mothers were now harshly criticized for not working and preferring to care of their children. Welfare, recently attacked by welfare rights advocates and the poor as needlessly punitive and stigmatizing, and only recently barely turned into an entitlement, was now attacked as too permissive in character, too entitlement-like. Reflecting on developments in welfare policy and practice in the 1960s and early 1970s, Mead (1986:47) asked why "work and family difficulties actually got worse among the poor just when the nation mobilized to help them?" But the nation hardly mobilized to help poor families during the 1960s; and work difficulties had begun worsening well before the half-hearted and ambivalent efforts of that era. The permissiveness that some saw creeping into welfare, as well as other social programs, and the related decline in authority, reflected the pressure service providers experienced to set to rights historical imbalances in the power to label and define, and in poor peoples' ability to shape their own lives.

If one continues to follow the shifting currents of welfare reform into the 1970s, and even the 1980s, one sees the same patterns repeated over and over: the proclamation of a crisis, that welfare's permissiveness was undermining families and that no alternative could be worse than the prevailing system; the announcement of a totally new approach that would change the culture of welfare; the failure to fund that approach adequately, combined with half-hearted implementation by states and localities. Each failure to meet expectations—WIN, WIN II, the WIN demonstrations in the 1980s, and finally the Family Support Act—seemed to put Aid to Families with Dependent Children deeper into a hole from which supporters of the program could not extricate it. Ultimately, it proved easier to bury the program than to find a way to save its life.

# CHAPTER SEVEN

# The 1970s: Struggle for Renewal in a Shifting Environment

*The crisscrossing patterns of organized help fail to support some people,*
*and the boundaries of that failure coincide, to a large degree, with the*
*boundaries of economic class.*

—Malcolm Bush

The 1970s were a complicated period in the development of supportive services for poor families. The patchwork of old and new agencies and programs struggled to maintain at least a measure of continuity, as well as to discern and respond to emerging trends. There were forces pushing toward what Kahn (1976) and Meyer (1976) described as a broad, active, developmental vision of services, and toward greater coherence within and among service systems; there were equally strong forces pulling in the opposite direction. A model of a community-based, preventively oriented, family-centered service system, led by generalists, emerged in a number of reform proposals. But funding trends, policy developments, and the continuing formation of problem-specific constituencies contributed to more and more specialization and fragmentation. The ideals of a coherent continuum of locally based services would haunt as much as animate services in the next decades.

By the early 1970s many in the social service community were exhausted both with reform and the upheaval that had accompanied it. They were weary of poverty as a social problem. The War on Poverty initiatives had placed the basic tensions underlying helping efforts in a new light. They had pointed up a deeply rooted anxiety about issues of power and authority, and trust and discretion in services. They had raised questions about service providers' right to define poor peoples' problems, their capacity to understand poor peoples' lives, and about the relevance of professional knowledge and experience. Yet the social service community as a whole was not ready to consider and respond to such issues directly.

There were nonetheless many catalysts and pressures for new reform efforts. In the first place, the War on Poverty service reforms had first subsumed and then failed to address systemic problems in child and family services that were already present and known about in the early 1960s. Participants in a 1962 seminar that brought together academics and government officials described services to poor families as fragmented, misaligned, and reactive (Land 1964). It was noted that "agencies that deal with [vulnerable] families in the first instance do not act—in fact they are not expected to act—as agents or representatives of any kind of integrated community system" (Kahn 1964:9). Each agency or program assumed that another was taking responsibility for the vulnerable families that passed through its doors. Responses to families usually took the form of isolated, momentary reactions to an immediate situation—for instance, a mother failing to make an appointment for her child; they were not part of a longer relationship (Kahn 1964:11).

The service reforms of the 1960s had not only failed to deal with these systemic problems, they had exacerbated them, creating new a host of new service types and sites and leaving an even more chaotic and fragmented service environment. Moreover, when the War on Poverty ended, the worsening systemic problems in child and family services were allowed to rise to the surface and become issues in their own right. Within the mental health field there was a sense that the historical models of care and treatment had failed, both for the chronically mentally ill and for poor children and adults with acute problems. Within child welfare pressures were growing due to the emergence of child abuse and neglect as a national problem, the growing demand for child protection mechanisms, and a rapidly growing foster care population. These pressures were exacerbated by the child welfare system's still unclear mission and by the decline in supportive helping provided by public aid departments, due to the separation of income maintenance and social service functions. (Services to poor families were like a shirt that is too small; every time the wearer tugged it in one direction, an opening appeared somewhere else.) Other newly discovered or rediscovered problems also emerged during this period, which stimulated service reform and led to new service approaches. These problems included adolescent pregnancy, substance abuse, school difficulties, nonwork, and homelessness.

At a broader level the crisis in the authority and perceived legitimacy of the human services, stimulated by the events of the 1960s, continued. Arti-

cles and books proliferated on the role of social services in perpetuating social and economic inequality (see, e.g., Gil 1976); on the dilemmas and contradictions of helping poor families; and on the perverse effects of formal
helping institutions on traditional means of meeting needs and solving
problems (Lasch 1977). One observer pointed out that the benevolent intentions of social services masked the enormous damage service providers
did to clients' liberty, rights, and sense of autonomy (Glasser 1978). Another noted that "the social services function to encourage people to redefine
their needs and their views of what a solution to their problems entails"
(Galper 1975:67).

In addition to being compelled by crises and stimulated by the emergence of new problems, reform during the 1970s was motivated, as always,
by new ideas and service concepts. Some of these drew on the innovations
of the 1960s. For all the turmoil of that period, it generated premises and
approaches that proved durable. Providers who worked with poor families
continued the struggle to find a new ground for helping relationships,
somewhere between their own perspective and experience and that of their
clients (see Van Galen 1993:8). Public and private agencies continued to experiment, selectively, with such principles as community participation in
planning and the use of paraprofessionals. In spite of the apparent limitations of such strategies, they were seen to contribute to more informed
helping efforts, and compensated in some small measure for poor peoples'
sense of social exclusion (Mayer 1976). New initiatives at the agency and
community levels promoted the role of generalist family workers. The continuing, or growing, need for generalists, especially for case managers, was
due in large measure to the ever greater fragmentation of the social service
system (Sosin 1990:620). In addition the notion that service systems are
best conceptualized and organized, if not governed, at the local community level continued to influence service reforms.

The newer concepts of the era included early childhood (birth to three
years old) intervention, family-oriented services, and network interventions
(e.g., creating and strengthening social networks, identifying and supporting the work of "natural" caregivers). In the mental health field the concept
of "primary prevention"—working with children and families at risk before
problems have surfaced—was deemed a revolutionary advance (Albee
1980). It was argued that actively supporting and strengthening families was
the surest road to enhancing child and adult well-being; and that families
had to be reached and supported before problems became critical and perhaps intractable (see, e.g., Joint Commission on the Mental Health of Children 1970:13).

The focus on renewing the role of generalist family workers, and on intervening with young families before problems became serious, was consistent with family service agencies' historical mission of shoring up poor families and helping them cope. These were the services that nurses, home economists, case workers, and child development specialists had always offered. But in its new forms prevention was no longer so general and diffuse. Some new prevention programs defined their target population by medical factors (e.g., low birth weight), others by parental psychological vulnerabilities or family income or age of parent. Likewise, different programs focused on different bad outcomes to be avoided. The varied conceptions and emphases led to an extraordinarily heterogeneous network of new models, initiatives, and approaches, residing mostly at the margins of the major service systems.

Some at the time saw the emerging crises in public social services, especially child welfare and the new service concepts discussed above, as an opportunity to rethink the whole system of public child and family services. Yet the same categorical funding patterns and narrow mandates that were creating the need for generalists and for community-based parent support programs for young families were making it harder to fund them. Moreover, by the late 1970s a tension was already emerging in urban social services between the ideal of a preventively oriented, community-based service system and the realities of a system driven by child protection and foster care; growing numbers of poor families with multiple, serious problems; and the continuing erosion of local discretion in service provision (see Kamerman and Kahn 1989:ch. 1).

When it did happen, reform could be very disorienting. Established service agencies tried to stay attuned to events, picking up on new approaches, target populations, and problems, balancing categorical programs with more flexible ones. New purposes and initiatives often undermined existing ones, drawing away funding and management attention, leaving the older ones suspended in place. Sometimes agencies that responded to new approaches and moved in a new direction found themselves alone, with their funder having decided to try something else.

New federal mandates, new state programs, and new self-declared priorities led to constant turmoil in some settings. For instance, federal efforts to combine the family casework services provided by public aid and child welfare authorities, were sometimes combined with changing state priorities and local administrative reorganization. The result was that local welfare and child welfare offices in some states were reorganized two or three times over the course of a few years (Oliphant 1974:282). The director of a county Department of Family and Children's Services in Georgia, commenting on his department's reorganization, noted that "morale is incredibly low, error rates have sky-rocked, and I believe services to clients have decreased. . . . We destroyed the old structure before we had a replacement" (Mikulecky 1974:21).

More fundamentally, developments during this period did not release significant new resources for supportive social services. Although federal funding for social services increased dramatically during the early 1970s, primarily through new federal matching and revenue sharing programs, states and localities used the increase to substitute for other sources (Wickenden 1978). Beginning in the mid-1970s, federal funding leveled off and began a long decline (exacerbated by inflation). At the same time the situation of poor families and low-income neighborhoods was deteriorating at a growing pace.

## A Shifting Federal Role

The federal government's efforts to find an appropriate role in meeting social needs and dealing with social distress continued during the 1970s, albeit at a much more moderate pace than in the 1960s. One focus was reducing the complexity and fragmentation of the service system itself, or, to put it differently, enhancing the coherence and responsiveness of services. Behind these objectives was the shadow of an idea that would later come to dominate services; that of cost containment. In his January 24, 1972 message to Congress, President Nixon noted that:

> Today it often seems that our service programs are unresponsive to the recipients' needs and wasteful of the taxpayers' money. A major reason is their extreme fragmentation. . . . We need a new approach to the delivery of social services—one which is built around people and not around programs. We need an approach which treats a person as a whole and which treats the family as a unit. We need to break through rigid categorical walls, to open up narrow bureaucratic compartments, to consolidate and coordinate related programs in a comprehensive approach to related problems. ("Notes And Comments," 1972, pp. 263–64)

During President Nixon's first term his administration tried various strategies to address the fragmentation produced by scores of categorical federal (and corresponding state) programs. The most of ambitious of these was an effort to get decategorization legislation through Congress. This effort was resisted by congressional committees, whose members feared the loss of jurisdiction and oversight power that was tied to specific categorical programs. Beginning in 1972 the Nixon administration (and later those of presidents Ford and Carter) funded demonstrations in specific states and localities in specific areas: service integration; state-level reorganization of services, especially the creation of service clusters that could be managed in a unified manner; improvement of information management systems; more systematic planning; and fostering local systems that afforded greater continuity of care. Some demonstrations focused on getting local agencies in different systems (e.g., schools, community mental health, and community health centers) to work together more closely; others on improving the capacity to track clients across programs and systems; others on reinvigorating case management; still others on joint planning and goal-setting to create cross-system priorities.

These demonstrations were not focused specifically on services to poor families or to services in low-income neighborhoods. They did, however, yield lessons that would be relevant to the renewed wave of service reform in poor communities in the 1990s (lessons, unfortunately, that would be largely overrun in the interest of action). The costs of trying to coordinate and collaborate more effectively proved to be high in both money and time, especially in relation to the modest returns in improved service. While it was often possible to generate collaborative agreements, it was almost impossible to get agencies to share funding and information on clients, to give up control of intake, to alter eligibility or service boundaries, or, most critically, to agree on underlying goals. Looked at as a whole, the service system presented a conundrum for reformers, since it was both loosely coupled and interdependent. Joint planning, agreements, and coordination at one level or in one corner of the system did not influence practice at other levels or in other corners. Yet lack of change at those other levels or in other parts of the system strongly constrained discrete reform efforts. Not least, service integration strategies seemed only distantly related to the core difficulties frontline providers experienced in their day-to-day work. Thus, not surprisingly, those difficulties remain untouched.

The Nixon administration's commitment to creating more coherent services may have been genuine. But it competed with an equally strong interest in devolving social service priority-setting and policy-making to states and communities, which naturally would reduce the federal government's power to impose order on the social services. (President Nixon's philosophical commitment to reducing federal control over social services to poor families did not extend to welfare, which he believed to be a federal responsibility.) Devolution was motivated by a genuine, and seemingly logical belief that the closer service planning, design, and management was to the 40,000 or so local units of government in the United States, the more responsive services would be to local priorities and conditions.

In 1974 Nixon's commitment to devolution found expression in the passage of block grant legislation in a few discrete areas. These included employment and training (The Comprehensive Employment and Training Act), community development (The Community Development Block Grants) and social services (Title XX of the Social Security Act). The purpose of Title XX, and later the Social Services Block Grants, was to decentralize decision-making about how and where to use service resources, and thereby make the use of funds more responsive to local concerns (Sosin 1990). There also was some thought that decentralization would provide the foundation for more coherent local service systems. Under Title XX state and local advisory boards were mandated to make sure different interests were represented in decisions about how to use funds. Many such boards started out with energy and purpose, but within a few years most were inactive. Some local political jurisdictions responded creatively to the flexibility afforded by federal block grants; many others did not respond at all.

More established providers and politically influential individuals and groups tended to control disbursement of Title XX funds (Sosin 1990), which went mostly to foster care, child day care, and services for the elderly. Since poor urban neighborhoods were not formal political or government units, they usually were not given power to plan their own services, let alone claim resources. A few community groups had joined the planning and governance process, but as they received no funds, they became less active over time. The net effect for residents and neighborhood-based service providers in poor communities was no increase in control of how funds were used and little change in resources, especially for noncategorical programs. Critics argued that all things considered, the federal government had proven better able and more motivated than states and localities to assure that service resources went to the most vulnerable families and communities, if not always in the most coherent fashion. But they were arguing against the grain. The Nixon administration's devolution efforts were only the first in what would be repeated assaults during the next two decades on federal power, leadership, and responsibility for social welfare. Ultimately, these assaults would prove successful.

A third component of federally stimulated service reform during the early 1970s was an effort simultaneously to separate income maintenance concerns from family service issues and to rationalize casework services to poor families by combining the separate helping services provided to poor families under AFDC and child welfare. The "investigative" mandate of AFDC workers was narrowed to income eligibility, theoretically in order to avoid confusion between judgment of economic need and deservingness for support based on functioning and behavior (Kamerman and Kahn 1989:42). The historical, increasingly tenuous link between the receipt of AFDC and the acceptance of casework supervision was broken. In theory, family services to AFDC recipients would be provided by new family service workers in public child welfare departments (Oliphant 1974:281). In the event, such services never materialized, due to lack of funding, administrative inertia, and the already overwhelming responsibilities of child welfare family service staff. Moreover, the splitting of income maintenance and social services weakened, and in many instances severed, the remaining tie between public aid departments and private family service agencies, causing the latter to turn to the public child welfare agencies for funding. (I return to these issues at a later point.)

By the mid-1970s both service integration and decentralization efforts began to be affected by the federal government's growing preoccupation with reining in ballooning federal spending on social services. The 1967 public welfare amendments to the Social Security Act had contained clauses that increased the federal match for social services to families on AFDC (the federal government would pay three dollars for every one dollar spent by states); allowed states to purchase and be reimbursed for services from voluntary agencies (dramatically increasing the pool of service providers); and allowed states to be reimbursed for services to past or potential AFDC recipients, as well as to whole low-income communities (e.g., for a day care center in a poor neighborhood). Both states and cities jumped at this opportunity, and between 1969 and 1972 federal expenditures on public assistance-related social services rose from $354 million to $1.3 billion (Notes and Comments 1973:99). Almost all this money was used to replace rather than supplement state and local funding. (In the case of older, industrial cities especially, it was replacing declining tax revenues.)

The explosion in federal spending on social services in the early 1970s led in the late 1970s and 1980s to persistent efforts to cap and reduce spending on a range of programs—from social services in AFDC to most remaining Office of Economic Opportunity programs, public service jobs, and day care programs. Social services were criticized again as wasteful and unaccountable. State and local governments and service providers, who had rapidly become dependent on this new federal largesse, protested. When threatened with funding cuts, they acknowledged the limitations of services, their incoherence, inefficiency and wastefulness. What was needed, they said, was reform not cutbacks. Thomas (1994:53) argues that when the era of sheer growth in social services ended, the service community substituted "growth by specialization" and argued for the need for a continuum of care.

Redefining or inventing new problems, populations, and service elements did lead to some new funding streams: for instance, services for the prevention and treatment of child abuse and neglect, and services for teen parents. But any new funding was more than offset by the long-term damage done by state opportunism in using this brief opening to subsidize all kinds of services (many of which did not go to poor or vulnerable families). That opportunism was the beginning of the end for federal social service spending. It created a permanent, negative perception in the minds of Congress and the public, of large, unacccountable, and defensive service bureaucracies wasting billions of dollars to no good purpose. Because the large amount of new federal social service funding that had flowed to the states during the late 1960s and early 1970s had been used largely to replace existing state and local funding, the effects of federal government cutbacks were exacerbated (Wickenden 1978).

The new authority given to the states to involve private, voluntary agencies in federal matching programs also led those agencies to become increasingly reliant on categorical funding. For many (e.g., settlements) this appeared to solve the chronic problem of having to raise their whole budget anew year after year, a problem that had intensified (in part because older board members were not as committed to the new, minority populations served). Those agencies that historically had provided a good deal of noncategorical services talked themselves into believing that they would continue to provide the same friendly, flexible services that they always had. Some agencies simultaneously sought to stabilize their budgets with new federal categorical funds and started new departments whose mission was to develop noncategorical, neighborhood-based programs. Yet over time the increasing reliance on categorical funding would profoundly alter the sense of mission of many remaining neighborhood-based agencies; in particular, it would weaken their sense of belonging to their local communities.

### Old and New Concepts Shaping Services

Below the cross-currents of shifting federal priorities, much of the reform and developments in supportive services during the 1970s and 1980s was stimulated by discrete concerns: either a delimited problem or population, or a specific new idea, or a concern rooted in a single local institution or setting. Discrete new approaches or local initiatives usually derived from the broader ideas and ideologies in the air and as a result often took the same direction. Yet separate reform impulses rarely came together. In retrospect, one can look back and see a lot of initiatives that should have connected but never did. Perhaps the cross-currents of federal and state priorities kept discrete reforms from conglomerating. Also, at the time there was little conscious attention to the problem of taking promising new ideas to scale, of insinuating them into large public bureaucracies.

Part of what was occurring during that time was simply the continuing efforts of specific agencies to solve their own problems and to be more responsive or coherent within their purview. (This dimension of service reform has long been ignored in the service literature.) For instance, New York City's Department of Social Services attempted to address the difficulties poor families were having in gaining access to needed resources and appropriate services, and in negotiating the system as a whole, by creating neighborhood social service centers, and deploying paraprofessionals as intermediaries (Cohen 1976:28). One group of paraprofessionals worked in the new service centers as "neighborhood aides"; another worked as administrative aides, helping with intake and eligibility determination; still another as "case aides," linked to professional staff.

In 1971 the board of the Community Service Society (CSS), one of New York City's largest and oldest social service agencies, concluded that the prevailing focus of its work (primarily office-based individual and family casework, which tended to reach and serve working-class families) was no longer appropriate. The agency needed to concentrate its resources on the "severe social problems" of poor families (Goldberg 1980:202). It convened a committee that, with the help of its research arm, prepared a report outlining a new direction. The society would choose particular "strategic" areas for intervention, primarily neighborhoods but also specific populations; identify key neighborhood institutions and groups; help them organize and mobilize resources—help bring people together, form policy committees, do strategic planning, identify information on innovative service approaches, and secure funding; and do comprehensive community data collection to feed into planning and measure community change. It would also close some existing family service centers and redeploy its professional casework staff as community plans and priorities dictated ("Notes and Comments, SSR 1972a).

In its rationale for rethinking its approach to work with poor families, and for focusing on strengthening poor communities, the Community Service Society noted that individuals' well-being was a function of their community's well-being. It noted that "an approach that focuses primarily on individuals may help some people but will not really alleviate the problem of a sick community. . . . Communities must become the client" (Notes and Comments, SSR 1972a:208.) This report provoked a mixed reaction in the family service community. Some saw the CSS's self-reform effort as courageous. Others noted that after the experiences of the 1960s it should have been clear that an outside institution could not simply go into poor communities uninvited and offer to help them solve their problems. Still others noted (in perhaps an overinterpretation of the proposals) that there was a danger in asking good, solid caseworkers to become community organizers. Moreover, there was known to be a shortage of experienced caseworkers for vulnerable families in New York City. Why exacerbate that problem?

The implementation of the new direction proved rocky for CSS (Goldberg 1980). The professional casework leadership and staff within the agency had largely been excluded from the deliberations leading to a new mission and approach that would profoundly affect them. The fact that some were offered roles in the implementation of the new approach could not compensate for this lack of consultation. Furthermore, professional caseworkers were being asked to implement an approach—community action—whose values were substantially different from those of casework and whose defining activities and procedures were notably more ill-defined. And they were being asked to do so with little preparation (Goldberg 1980:207). Their years of experience and rich casework knowledge seemed useless to the new tasks. Compounding these constraints were budgetary problems that resulted in the firing of a large number of caseworkers. In 1973 a new executive director, Alvin Schorr, took charge of implementation. (He recalls observing that the "CSS was embarking on War on Poverty strategies just as the nation was leaving them behind"; Schorr 1997:138). The turmoil in the agency boded ill for the success of the new approach. The CSS board was deeply divided. In addition to professional staff who had been dismissed, many others had quit. The agency had encouraged scores of community organizations to submit proposals, and then ended up funding none of them. Little traditional casework was being provided, and the agency seemed to be adrift (Schorr 1997:139).

Given these factors, it is not surprising that what could have been a major experiment in rethinking services in poor neighborhoods never took hold. Specific programs were tried in specific local communities—in one neighborhood a program designed to advocate for families who had been improperly denied welfare; in another a family support center for single parents, which provided day care and social support; in a third a center intended to establish more integrated services. A technical assistance division was created, which employed community residents from poor neighborhoods to mobilize community groups for problem-solving. But the broader idea of turning a social service agency into a resource for local communities' own efforts to address poverty-related problems was never implemented.

### The Focus on Prevention and Early Intervention

While existing service institutions like CSS were struggling to reinterpret their historic missions in order to stay relevant, be more effective, or find a niche, a shifting ideological and intellectual climate also was creating new service directions. Reform and problem-solving rhetoric shifted away from a concern with poverty to a focus on discrete problems and risk factors. These included teen childbearing and childrearing, single parenthood, low birth weight and infant mortality, child abuse and neglect, family violence, specific mental health problems (e.g., maternal depression), and substance abuse.

By their nature these new problems (or high risk populations) directed the attention of interventionists to families with young children, with the goal either of preventing a particular problem, ameliorating its effects, or both. At a conference on "Crises of Family Disorganization," Pavensted and Bernard (1971) asked: "Are we building resources at the bottom of the hill to catch children after they fall, instead of building fences at the top of the hill so children won't fall in the first place?" Yet the useful effect of these new concerns in directing attention to the potential value of early intervention was offset by their tendency to further fragment service responses to families.

As each problem was "discovered" by its associated discipline or professional community, it led to new legislation, government bureaus, and government and foundation initiatives, as well as to a new community of semi-specialized providers. For instance, in 1973 the National Center on Child Abuse and Neglect was formed, to be part of the U.S. Children's Bureau, and in 1974 the Child Abuse Prevention and Treatment Act was passed. In 1978 an Adolescent Pregnancy Act was passed and an Office of Adolescent Pregnancy Programs (OAPP) created. Further, existing state and federal agencies developed their own programs for new problem constituencies. (To complicate matters even more, the specialized prevention programs developed in each area drew on many existing state and federal programs for their substantive services; e.g., OAPP programs drew on Medicaid, Title I in education, family planning services in maternal and child health.) If one had lined up the various problem-specific initiatives, one could have seen that they were simply serving overlapping populations from different perspectives. There was, however, little incentive to emphasize this view. In the midst of the period Kahn (1976) described the continuing multiplication of concerns and accompanying new approaches as mutually-in-the-dark interventions into families' lives. He argued that, in spite of the prevention rhetoric often attached to problem-specific initiatives, they affirmed a narrow, instrumental conception of the purpose and role of services.

A very different dimension of the shift away from poverty as the locus of problem-solving and reform was a call for fostering child development, particularly early childhood development. The rhetoric here did not focus on poor children and their families; rather, it remained diffuse and abstract, arguing the need for American society to create new social institutions to promote child development. For instance, the Joint Commission on the Mental Health of Children (1970) called for the creation of local child development councils that would register, monitor, and, as necessary, arrange services for and create new programs to serve all children under their jurisdiction. Local councils would be overseen by Child Development Authorities composed of the executives of major public service agencies, elected officials, and community leaders.

Prevention of and early intervention for specific problems, and the broad interest in deliberately promoting child development intersected contributed to, and in some respects were subsumed into a third idea: that of early childhood (birth to three years old) intervention. This new service concept was focused loosely on poor children and families as a group. It reflected the contraction of poverty-related concerns back into the homes of poor families. It also indicated a return to the historical focus on family functioning (rather than on inadequacies in the social structure or on relations between the poor and the non-poor) in societal efforts to address the causes and consequences of poverty (Schlossman 1978).

The emergence of early childhood intervention (ECI) was fueled directly by several factors. One, alluded to in chapter five, was the weak findings of the first Head Start evaluations, which seemed to imply either or both that Head Start was intervening too late or that interventions that did not change home environments of poor children were destined to be too ineffective. Another was a virtual explosion of research and clinical attention to infancy, primarily in psychology and psychiatry. This research and clinical work demonstrated the enormous amount and range of developmental activity occurring during infancy, including not only cognitive but socioemotional development, development of self-regulatory capacities, and a sense of self in relation to others. It generated a new conceptualization of the infant as an active, perceiving, social being. It identified new sources of risk in infancy (e.g., maternal depression, attachment disorders, sensory and regulatory disorders). A few infancy researchers also explored the contribution of the infant (or the family's life situation) to the parent-child relationship.

These new findings directed interventionists' attention to the early childhood period and less directly renewed the somewhat wavering faith in the capacity of social science to guide social improvement. They reinforced the global belief that had emerged in the 1960s that experience in the earliest years was the most critical determinant of later outcomes for children. The findings also reinforced the historic American belief in what Grubb and Lazerson (1980) call "parental determinism." This included the general notion that quality of parental care, particularly the early mother-child relationship, was by far the most powerful influence on children's development; and the corollary belief that poor parents lacked the knowledge, skills, and/or internal resources to rear their young children adequately—whether to be successful in school, emotionally healthy, or able to follow the rules of society.

Other theoretical developments provided complementary, and in some ways contrasting bases for early childhood intervention. One was the linkage of ecological theory to child development research (see Bronfenbrenner 1980). Ecologically oriented researchers focused on how factors beyond the mother-child relationship—parents' social support networks, community characteristics, and, at the broadest level, race, social class, and economic arrangements—affected children's well-being and development (and the mother-child relationship itself), and how different kinds and levels of factors mutually influenced each other. Somewhat related to ecological child development research were the new fields of family research and family therapy, which focused on and argued for the whole family as the appropriate unit of research, or concern in intervention.

Nourished by a more complex view of infancy, a greater sensitivity to contextual influences, the field of family research and by the helping principles of the 1960s, early childhood intervention seemed a brand new phenomenon. It offered the potential to address the roots of a range of problems in a range of populations. It seemed a particularly promising approach to addressing the tendency of prevailing services to intervene too late, to be the ambulance service at the bottom of the cliff. It implied the possibility of reducing the need for later expenditure of hundreds of millions of dollars on specialized treatment services. It also captured the interest of the more ambitious service providers in promoting child development in addition to simply preventing problems. Yet early childhood intervention was an approach only in the loosest sense of the word.

In its most general form, early childhood intervention involved the deployment of specially trained community residents and, less commonly, professionals to provide information, guidance, encouragement and emotional support, practical assistance, and sometimes advocacy to families with children from birth to three years of age. Intervention might involve regular home visits over a period of months, or even a few years; sometimes parent support groups at a local community center; and, less commonly, direct services to infants and toddlers in a child development center. The general goals were to strengthen poor parents' ability to protect, nurture, and care for their children. This would in turn improve children's health and development and sometimes enhance parents' own health and psychological well-being. In practice, the interaction of disparate theoretical lenses, different ways of defining target populations, different problems, purposes, and funding streams, resulted in the development of a disparate patchwork of programs. Different theoretical orientations suggested very different purposes and foci for intervention. Some ECI programs were envisioned as serving whole communities or diverse populations of poor families, other focused on a particular problem or population.

It was possible to identify two main streams of ECI practice, one clinical, one community-based. The former was intended to serve young families at heightened risk for, or actually experiencing disturbances in parent-infant relationships. Although families served by clinical infant programs were very likely to be poor, poverty was viewed as a compounding stress rather than as a central factor in working with a family. Clinical infant work had a number of pioneers, foremost of whom was Selma Fraiberg and her colleagues at the University of Michigan's Child Development Project. They developed a tripartite intervention approach that included developmental guidance/supportive intervention, brief crisis intervention, and a new helping modality called parent-infant psychotherapy. Families received one, two, or all three of these, depending on clinical assessment of the family situation, apparent causes of parent-child relationship difficulties, and developmental readiness to enter into a formal therapeautic relationship.

The most innovative of these modalities, parent-infant psychotherapy, drew on theory from both child development and psychoanalysis. As in traditional psychodynamic therapy, the therapist used the positive and negative transference to the helper as a mechanism to illuminate issues and foster change. One difference was that the goal was not a change in personality but in the capacity to nurture. The therapist worked to help the parent recognize the effects of such formative experiences as loss, abandonment, unavailable parenting, and the like on young adults' own capacity to parent. The goal was to help parents recognize, acknowledge, and undo the "painful effects of the past" and to find "new solutions to old problems" (Fraiberg, Shapiro, and Cherniss 1983:60). The presence of the baby during therapeutic sessions provided both an additional source of information about the actual qualities of the relationship and another basis for intervention. In part, it helped the therapist understand to the contribution of the infant to the problems of the parent-infant relationship. She took her cue not only from what she learned of the parent's own nurturance history and the meaning of the baby to the parent (e.g., the feelings that the baby evoked in the parent) but on close observation of parent and infant together.

For most families served in clinical infant programs, the effects of parental psychological vulnerabilities were compounded by extreme youth and poverty and its correlates (e.g., problems with public aid, housing, and so forth). Thus, concrete guidance on caring for infants and action to address poverty-related problems became part of the focus of intervention, requiring the helper to be much more active than would be the case in traditional therapy. Much of the helping for some families was done during home visits, and the team was persistent in reaching out to families that missed scheduled appointments.

Other models of clinical infant work did not employ parent-infant psychotherapy; rather, they infused its principles into supportive work with parents. For example, Sally Provence and colleagues at Yale University developed the Yale Child Welfare Research Program, in which a highly skilled interdisciplinary team consisting of a clinical social worker, nurse, pediatrician, day care worker, and psychologist provided an individually tailored mix of supportive services to young families experiencing parenting difficulties (Provence and Naylor 1983). The program included twice-monthly home visits by the social workers, primary health care, high quality day care, and developmental exams. During the home visits, and in informal activities at a remodeled house in the neighborhood where participating families lived, the social workers focused on attending to mothers' own "psychological neediness and stress" (Provence and Naylor 1983:20). The idea was that before some parents would be able to nurture their children, or tolerate their children being cared for by others, they had to be nurtured themselves.

Clinical early childhood intervention remained modest in size throughout the 1970s and 1980s, concentrated in a few clinical or academic centers where the kind of sophisticated training and supervision needed for such work could occur. Practitioners from the medical and mental health fields interested in infancy received some exposure to clinical infant theory, principles, and methods through the activities of the National Center for Clinical Infant Programs and a handful of academic centers. Some of the ideas and principles underlying this approach—for example, taking one's cues from the observation of parent and infant together—filtered into the broader early childhood intervention community. But the bulk of the community-based social service and child welfare communities, who had the most contact with the growing numbers of young, multiply vulnerable families in low-income communities, had almost no exposure to it.

The other main strain of early childhood intervention, more community-based, was shaped particularly by ecological and family systems theories. These led intervention in a different direction. They suggested the importance of focusing attention on the whole family, of strengthening families' social support networks, and of helping link families to community resources. Systems-oriented theories pointed to multiple, interconnected influences on child development and family functioning. This meant, for better or worse, that interventions needed to be more ambitious and holistic (and led eventually to the current preoccupation with comprehensive interventions). For instance, these theories implicitly argued for addressing simultaneously the interconnected problems of multiply stressed young families—problems as diverse as lack of planning skills, the lack of food, inadequate housing, inadequate health care, the lack of job skills and aspirations, and an emotional unavailability to the infant. At the same time, as Ooms (1996) points out, systems-thinking was "non-blaming," less linear, less cause-and-effect oriented than the traditional linear thinking of developmental researchers. This contributed to a growing focus, at least in the rhetoric, on family strengths.

Much ECI program development during the 1970s and 1980s drew on an eclectic mix of theory and research and thus aimed at a combination of strengthening childrearing (through provision of information, guidance, and feedback on what was observed) and supporting families in their own self-determined childrearing efforts. Over time, intervention theories and designs shifted from a narrow focus on the mother-child dyad to a broader, more diffuse focus on the context of families' lives. One can see this shift in comparing the two best-known federal demonstration programs of that era—the Parent Child Development Centers (PCDCs), a three-site demonstration (Andrews et al 1982); and the later Child and Family Resource Programs (CFRPs), an eleven-site demonstration (Hewett 1982).

In the PCDCs it was possible to see the beginnings of an ecological and systems perspective. Program materials acknowledged the importance of addressing "the complex of problems of poor families." All three PCDC programs provided or linked families to health, social, and other corollary services. Within a framework of common elements the three local programs were given the flexibility to design their approaches based on local needs and circumstances. At the same time their intensive interventions (three to five days a week) were strongly premised and focused on changing maternal knowledge, behavior, and attitudes. (The specific approaches included parenting and child development classes for mothers; maternal observation of and participation in infant nursery activities; and home visits; Andrews, et al. 1982).

The CFRPs reflected the influence of ecological theory and systems ideas much more fully. They were premised on the idea that in order for parenting programs to promote child development, they had to concentrate equally on specific parenting competencies and on the full range of family and neighborhood conditions that impinged on parenting (Hewett 1982). The heart (and for many participating families the extent) of the program was a monthly home visit by specially trained community members, for up to two years. Home visitors tended to focus on helping families gain access to other services and resources, on helping with whatever problems families were preoccupied with at the moment, and generally on supporting families' coping efforts. One key assumption of CFRP was that over time families would be better able to act as their own service brokers and problem managers and that they, as well as the home visitors, would then be able to shift their attention to parenting and child development. For a variety of reasons this assumption did not bear out.

In the late 1970s the idea of early childhood intervention as "family support" coalesced under a new program movement by that name. This movement caught and built on a public feeling (common in American history) that the social fabric was unraveling: family life was breaking down, communal support systems were deteriorating. It also drew on the loss of faith in prevailing helping services and helping professionals and in the tendency of the latter to focus on pathology, to fail to respect families' cultural traditions. Family support programs were envisioned as a means of simultaneously strengthening informal support ties among kith and kin and creating a new model of helping services. They would bring families and neighbors together to provide mutual support around parenting and other tasks. They would build on family strengths and follow families' lead. Staff would be respectful of families' culture and childrearing traditions and serve as a bridge between local childrearing norms and those of the larger society. Programs would be conveniently located, with few barriers to eligibility and participation.

The family support movement had a direct influence on the early childhood intervention field and also began to influence broader service reform efforts. Family support programs sprang up in hundreds of poor and other communities. Even though somewhat global, family support principles reenergized hundreds of small, community-based programs. At the same time the movement created new tensions within the ECI field. For instance, it implicitly questioned the prevailing focus on strengthening childrearing, in some ways muddying the original rationale for ECI programs. In its criticism of formal helpers' historical preoccupation with family problems, the family support movement left its own frontline providers unprepared to deal with the many family vulnerabilities observed or brought to them.

Family support programs were notably ambivalent about whether they were either a form of social service or a new community institution that would supplant the historical role of social service providers. In that light many family support programs viewed staff as community members helping other community members, with little need for a strong knowledge base, training, or supervision. Families could drop in or drop out as they saw fit. During the 1980s, as family support programs in low-income communities began to see and serve greater numbers of multiply vulnerable young families, their diffuse principles and methods would come under tremendous pressure. Without access to the kinds of conceptual tools, detailed "process" descriptions and case vignettes, and intense training and support structures for frontline workers characteristic of clinical infant programs, their staff increasingly felt overwhelmed. Deliberately reconstructing social support systems in support programs was a dubious proposition in communities experiencing dramatic institutional and social breakdown.

In spite of theoretical differences and internal struggles, the early childhood intervention programs that emerged in the 1970s were important for a number of reasons. They infused human development theory and research more directly into the world of social services. The clinical strand offered models and helping principles appropriate to the growing number of multiply vulnerable young families in low-income communities. Collectively, early childhood programs embodied helping principles useful to all kinds of services, whatever the purpose or population: they "met people where they lived," not only physically but psychologically. They provided emotional support, encouragement, and assistance in the framework of families' own efforts to master parenting and other developmental tasks and to cope with the various concrete difficulties associated with poverty. They provided multifaceted support, orchestrated to address a variety of family needs. They were inherently optimistic, focusing on promoting development rather than treating dysfunction, and on work with young families for whom the future was still open. They had the flexibility to respond to the unique patterns of stress and support of different populations in different community contexts. Most considered it their responsibility to reach out to isolated or distrustful families and nurture their capacity to use support. In their diversity, from infant mental health programs at one end to family support programs at the other, they suggested a continuum of services for more and less vulnerable young families. From a systems perspective, they stretched the vision of what had to be included in a continuum of services for poor and vulnerable families.

The principles underlying family-oriented early childhood intervention joined those of the War On Poverty service programs to form the underpinning of what would would emerge in the 1990s as a major effort to rethink social services. The beginnings of this effort could be seen during the late 1980s in proposals in New York, Minneapolis, and a few other cities to reform public social services by creating large numbers of neighborhood-based, preventively oriented family service centers. (Presumably, these local agencies would first form networks and then become little systems, with their own governance mechanisms, authority to negotiate with the large public bureaucracies, and waivers from categorical program constraints.) A number of states developed initiatives along these same lines. A few observers at the time thought they saw the beginning of a shift from the residual model of social services, to a more active developmental one (see Weiss and Halpern 1988:68).

Yet though the principles embodied in early childhood intervention had some influence at the margins of the public service systems, the services themselves made few inroads. Having emerged largely outside the major public helping systems, ECI programs were destined to remain there. Though the concept of early childhood intervention implied a public policy agenda, none developed. It was unclear which of the major public systems—child welfare, education, health, or mental health—would or should take responsibility for funding and managing early childhood intervention services. In some respects they made the most sense as an element of public health services. But the health care system had shown little interest in child development, general family well-being, poverty-related problems, or community-based services. Public health nurses, while continuing to do outreach, had neither the time or inclination to develop ongoing helping relationships with poor families. One could also see ECI services as logically tied to the emerging vision within a segment of the child welfare community of a continuum of supportive family services. Social workers had a long history of supportive helping to vulnerable young families to draw on. Their historic focus on individuals in their social contexts fit the theoretical elements undergirding ECI. Yet, as I will discuss in the following chapter, child welfare services were increasingly preoccupied with demands and pressures that undermined the opportunity to create and sustain a developmental vision.

## Crisis and Reform in Child Welfare Services

Among other things, the 1970s marked the beginning of three decades of constant crisis and repeated reform efforts in urban child welfare services. Some reform efforts would prove more constructive in vision, if not in practice, than others. As I have already noted, the child welfare system was the locus of a renewed vision of a community-based, preventively oriented family service system, with a differentiated, well-integrated continuum of services within each poor community. Yet in practice most reforms were designed or felt compelled to address the symptoms of crisis—increasing pressure on child protection services, growing foster care caseloads, lengthening foster care spells, high rates of return to foster care—rather than patiently trying to build coherent, differentiated local service networks to help the growing number of vulnerable young families. For instance, the not insignificant portion of Title XX funds that went to child welfare services, which might have been used to strengthen supportive services for vulnerable families, was used mostly for foster care. Prevention funds were focused largely on families already in crisis, as were new service models, such as intensive family preservation services.

Also inhibiting reform was the child welfare system's chronic ambivalence about its ideals and mission, particularly the relative balance between (and even the desirability of separating) child and family welfare; the tension between policing and helping functions; and the uncertainty about scope of services. Was child welfare just about child abuse and neglect at the hands of parents (or guardians) or, more broadly, about threats to child and family well-being, especially those threats that accompanied poverty? Was the child welfare system to be a negative force, something people were captured by when they failed their responsibilities, or a positive support, a resource for vulnerable families? Was the child welfare "system" just an investigation, disposition, and monitoring system, or also a service provision system? It was just as conceivable that a state might wish to narrow as that it might wish to broaden who and what was included under the rubric of child welfare, and then hope that some other system would expand to provide supportive services.

Historically, child welfare concerns were not sharply demarcated from general family welfare concerns in services for poor families. It was assumed that the goal of protecting children overlapped—indeed underlaid—those of strengthening family life, facilitating adjustment and coping, and addressing obstacles to self-sufficiency. This lack of differentiation began to break down in the 1960s, under two sources of pressure. First, child abuse and neglect on the one hand and dependency (or nonwork) on the other emerged as distinct social problems, and the fields of child abuse and neglect services (mandated reporting, investigation, placement services, prevention, and treatment) and welfare to work emerged as distinct fields of practice. Second, the federal government created separate categorical funding streams for the two. In the 1970s the historical global objectives of supportive social services for poor families were replaced by two discrete objectives: protecting children from abuse and neglect, and economic self-support. (This split eventually would lead to the explicit removal of child protection as the goal of public assistance, with the passage of the Temporary Assistance to Needy Families Act in late 1996.)

Paralleling the bifurcation in goals was a shift in the locus of service provision. Until the 1960s supportive helping services for poor families had been provided primarily by private voluntary agencies and, more selectively, local public aid departments. (If not always a provider of supportive services, the public aid system historically had at least acted as a kind of switching point, directing families to services.) By the early 1960s the private agencies remaining in poor communities were providing much less noncategorical service than they had in earlier years. The new network of community-based programs created by the War on Poverty and the increased public aid casework stimulated by the 1962 amendments to the Social Security Act compensated partially for this loss. Yet as I have described in earlier chapters, both sources of services were inadequately funded, and both came under attack almost as soon as they emerged. Most notably, the role of supportive services in public aid was barely established before it was undermined by growing caseloads, the splitting off of income maintenance and social service functions, and the changing meaning for remaining services. Supportive services for welfare recipients were coming to be reinterpreted as day care, transportation, and other assistance that enabled people to participate in work preparation activities, to seek and hold jobs. (Moreover, the policy goal of helping people leave welfare—to the extent that it was implemented at all—was rapidly becoming the purview of labor economists, vocational trainers, adult educators, and other manpower specialists.)

The patchwork of problem- and population-specific programs—for instance programs for pregnant and parenting teens, and various early childhood intervention initiatives—was adding to the mix of supportive service available in poor communities. Yet this heterogeneous collection still had only a modest presence and was largely unconnected to significant funding streams. Public health nurses continued to do some early outreach and home visiting, but their contacts with poor families were sporadic in nature.

Complicating the effects of a shift in the locus of service provision was the problem of a society producing growing numbers of multiply vulnerable young families, with no components of the service system having clear responsibility for identifying, reaching out to, and supporting those families. Though the majority of new ECI programs were well located for early identification of and outreach to vulnerable families, few saw that as their mission, and fewer still had the capacity to serve such families. The worsening situation of many poor families was certainly not the responsibility and problem of the child welfare system alone—nor even the responsibility of the helping system as a whole. With such a diffuse, multifaceted problem, no single intervention or reform focus would have been adequate. Yet by default, and to a lesser extent design, the child welfare system was becoming the major public system with at least an implicit charge to provide helping services to poor families. It made a certain amount of sense: the majority of children at risk for compromised parenting were so partly, and sometimes largely, for poverty-related reasons.

The problem was that existing public child welfare systems were themselves ill-equipped by virtue of mission and staffing to provide supportive helping services to poor families; furthermore, they were increasingly overwhelmed by their child protection mandates and growing foster care caseloads. Already in the early 1960s Kahn (1964:18) had noted that "while we don't separate children from families for economic reasons as a matter of public policy, we tolerate a very predictable chain of events which leads us to this as an inevitable consequence." Later observers asked how a system whose main activity centered around breaking up families could take the lead in creating family-centered services (Weissman 1978) or in providing differentiated responses to varied family situations. In summarizing a series of major studies of foster care in the 1960s and 1970s, Lindsey (1994:35) writes that they illuminated "an almost Kafkaesque system, in which the removal of children from their parents merely aggravated individual pain and suffering, which the agencies seemed neither to understand nor appreciate."

Much of the focus of developments in child welfare services during the 1970s in fact centered around struggling with such systemic dysfunctions, responding to new mandates to investigate reports of child abuse or neglect, and managing growing foster care caseloads. There nonetheless were at least a few developments that supported the goal of service provision to poor and vulnerable families, and a few proposals that implied or suggested a basic rethinking of child welfare. For instance, in 1974 the federal Child Abuse Prevention and Treatment Act was passed, creating a regular, if modest stream of funds for preventively oriented services. This legislation in turn led some states to create their own prevention and service provision funding streams.

## A Dream and an Experiment

One distinctive proposal for child welfare reform emerged in 1971, when the Citizens' Committee for Children of New York issued "A Dream Deferred," a report harshly critical of New York City's child welfare system. The report argued that the concept of child welfare had been inappropriately narrowed to mean child placement and that efforts to prevent the need for placement had been half-hearted, small-scale, and ineffective (Citizen's Committee 1971). It noted that there was little supportive services being provided to poor families, including the most vulnerable ones. It argued that a system built around the process of child placement "cannot create programs and policies that emphasize promoting the welfare of children" in their homes.

"A Dream Deferred" recommended a "new" kind of family service system, with primary responsibility delegated to "locally based general family service social workers," who would work from "neighborhood offices of a reorganized public department" (Citizens' Committee 1971:21). The family service workers would be "outposted" in schools, settlement houses, health stations, housing projects, and the like and were to work closely with community institutions. The collective goal was to identify vulnerable families (and potentially vulnerable ones, such as those on welfare), mobilize and coordinate resources and supports for them, and monitor their well-being and progress. The report also urged the voluntary service sector to "update its service approaches, to enrich and expand what it offers, to share its expertise and strengthen the whole" (Citizens' Committee 1971:453).

The report, like similar reports that would appear every five to ten years thereafter through the 1980s and 1990s, had little influence on New York City's child welfare system. But it did stimulate some innovation at the margins. For instance, it played a role in the creation of the Lower East Side Family Union (LESFU), a collaborative initiative of five settlement houses on Manhattan's Lower East Side. The motivating force behind the union was Harold Rue of the Henry Street Settlement, who also chaired the Citizen's Committee, as well as the committee of Lower East Side settlement directors.

The LESFU model combined ideas from "A Dream Deferred" with those from the 1960s, adding a few of its own (Weissman 1978; Fanshel, Finch, and Grundy 1992). At the broadest level it was intended to mobilize the Lower East Side community in Manhattan to support vulnerable families. In part that meant forging a coherent network out of disparate local services and focusing that network on the most vulnerable families, particularly those whose children were at heightened or immediate risk of removal from the home, and those families not yet involved with specialized agencies. The primary goal was prevention of placement. Although it would serve troubled and overwhelmed families, LESFU was to be a "union" of providers and clients: the families served would have substantive roles in shaping both their own services and the design of the program itself. The "family union was to be an organization of clients that would serve as an ongoing interest group or watchdog for children's services and as a source of mutual support and help for its members" (Weissman 1978:45).

At the heart of the model were three teams of paraprofessionals, each composed of a social work associate (the lead team member), a homemaker, and a housekeeper, supervised by a social worker with a graduate degree. It was presumed that paraprofessionals from the community would be more likely than professionals to know or be able to learn which neighborhood families were in trouble and to "expect families to succeed" (Fanshel, Finch, and Grundy 1992:6). Each team was staffed with members of a particular ethnic group—Chinese, African American, Hispanic (primarily Puerto Rican)—reflecting the ethnic mix of the area. The teams were charged with case finding; case management—linking families to needed services, bringing together the specialists serving a family to assure shared goals and coordinated actions; and, not least, providing direct helping services, primarily through home visits. There was to be a contract developed between each family and all the providers working with that family, including the LESFU team. That contract was supposed to reflect a shared, negotiated understanding of family problems, resources, and support needs, as well as the responsibilities of all parties.

The Lower East Side Family Union started work with families in May 1974. The first years were difficult, raising questions about almost every element of the program's strategy. Some of the problems revolved around staff roles and responsibilities—for instance, the lack of clear differentiation and boundaries in the roles of team members; others around staffing choices. The use of paraprofessionals in the critical generalist case manager role did not work well. The case managers were reluctant to call specialists together for meetings, feeling themselves to be of lower status and less competent. They did not feel qualified to evaluate the specialized services families were receiving. They also tended to work around, rather than address directly the parenting problems present in many of the families served (Fanshel, Finch, and Grundy 1992:192). This may have been partly due to the negotiated nature of the service contract, which encouraged clients to decide on the issues they themselves considered pressing. But the tendency of paraprofessionals to avoid or "not see" problems in emotionally laden domains such as parenting had already been observed in the 1960s, and it is not clear why the LESFU program developers ignored this information.

Within the group of paraprofessionals, those who had more experience to start with proved more effective than their less experienced peers in key aspects of practice, including risk assessment and "[the] ability to see families as a whole, to manuever local and public agency workers to help clients, and to write records in a concise manner" (Weissman 1978:61). Although other providers—specialists—appreciated the availability and efforts of the case managers and their team, that appreciation did not translate into willingness to give up prerogatives.

Over time at least some of the staffing and staff role-related issues were worked out. The teams settled into the kind of helping common to paraprofessionals working with inner-city families: practical assistance with daily tasks, help with specific problems, emotional support and encouragement, mediation with public service systems, efforts to to teach parents to plan and anticipate more and react less. Although such help was exhausting and frustrating with families who often were self-destructive and prone either to constant conflict or crisis or extreme passivity, it was, at the least, concrete. Program design problems of other sorts nonetheless persisted. There were problems with the idea of a service contract. For one thing, some, if not much of what other agencies provided was on an emergency basis. At a minimum, services were fluid, shifting, and difficult to predefine. Some providers were reluctant to sign a contract because they felt their word should be trusted and/or simply did not want to be dictated to by the Union.

It was difficult to locate vulnerable families not already involved with the specialized service system. Very few referrals, less than 10 percent came from within the settlement network, undermining the idea of neighborhood-based agencies as early warning sources that would spot families heading for crisis. It was difficult also to determine whom to try to serve. It proved impossible to identify specific families in which children were likely to be removed if no intervention occurred. While families referred to LESFU had plenty of problems, starting with inadequate income, no employment, and inadequate housing, and proceeding to difficulties with parenting, adult relationships, and behavioral problems in older children, these problems did not necessarily put children at immediate risk of removal.

Over time it became less clear exactly what the goal of intervention was, beyond helping address the variety of specific problems identified in and by families. Perhaps that modest goal was the best one. As Fanshel, Finch, and Grundy (1992:228) note, relieving "the psychological stress that beleaguered parents experience, which makes them . . . vulnerable to engaging in destructive interactions with their children . . . should not be dismissed as bandaids." Nonetheless, the problems of most of the participating families were not resolvable at some predictable point in time.

Indirectly, the LESFU experience suggested that the vision outlined in "A Dream Deferred" embodied, or perhaps hid issues that were more complex than expected. The idea of infusing poor neighborhoods with networks of parent aides and homemakers was not a bad one, especially if those workers were clear about what they were doing and were supported by other service elements in addressing crises and emergencies—for example, bringing a caregiver into children's homes for a day or two (Lindsey 1994:50). Yet it proved hard to create integrated services by either case management or contracts. It proved hard to know when to intervene or when it would be inappropriate to use prevention of placement as a goal, organizer, and engine for intervention efforts. This objective was simply not suited to the chronic, sometimes diffuse and fluctuating difficulties of many poor families. Not least, the concept of shared responsibility for child protection—among individual community members, the community at large, and specific helping agencies—was too ambiguous.

The LESFU initiative had not required or called for, although its approach implied, changes in public child welfare services in New York City. The Family Services division of the city's child welfare agency was supposed to provide the kinds of ongoing supports provided by LESFU, and it did in fact increase funding for parent aides and homemakers during the later 1970s and early 1980s. But any intentions it had to provide community-based prevention services were increasingly swamped by open child welfare cases, many referred by the juvenile court.

# CHAPTER EIGHT

# Retrenchment Without Renewal

*The old family and children's service program, an open-ended casework service for low-income families and children with needs and problems, has no place in this department. We need to make it clear that we don't have the resources here to do everything and must take on the priority task of helping people who fall below the minimum line.*

—an administrator of Maryland's child welfare system

*Some jobs just cannot be done properly.*

—Michael Lipsky

By the early 1980s efforts to sustain the vision of a neighborhood-based family service system, with a well-differentiated continuum of services, were increasingly constrained by a host of external pressures. These included a series of fiscal crises in many cities and states; a growing number of very vulnerable families living in distressed and depleted communities; mounting pressure from the public to identify and investigate abuse and protect children; a growing rejection of the goals and assumptions that had framed social welfare activity since the late 1930s; and continuing erosion in public faith in services and public support for service providers. The large public agencies responded to these pressures by becoming even more bureaucratic, focusing on procedures and tightening control over how resources were used (McGowan 1990).

As always, pressures on and within services converged mostly on front-line providers, and thus on their clients. A new profile of human service work emerged that included increased paperwork and bureaucracy, growing caseloads of very vulnerable families, less supervision, and pressure to close cases quickly (in part due to growing waiting lists, in part to changing reimbursement patterns). By late in the decade some observers were describing front-line practice, particularly in the major public systems, as impossible.

Within urban child welfare systems, almost 90 percent of funding—the principal potential public funding source for supportive services—went to substitute care (53 percent), protective services (25 percent), adoption services (6 percent), and disposition of juveniles (5 percent) (Kamerman and Kahn 1989). Placement prevention and reunification preoccupations consumed what few discretionary resources were not being consumed by voracious foster care systems and distracted the child welfare community from the task of conceptualizing and implementing a continuum of supportive services for vulnerable families. Broad, as opposed to targeted prevention and early intervention efforts, which would have eased some of the pressure on mainline services, remained at the very margins of the service system.

## Growing Pressures

The 1980s were characterized by a widespread urban fiscal crisis that was compounded by federal policy. Many older cities had a declining tax base. Instead of helping with this loss, the federal government dramatically cut its aid to cities. During the 1980s the percentage of city expenditures covered by federal aid fell from 22 to 6 percent (Weir 1993:8). Beginning in the late 1970s federal expenditures on Title XX had decreased, in inflation-adjusted dollars. In 1981 Title XX became part of a social service block grant, further diluting its dollars and identity. There was also a shift in the use of available public dollars for services, away from counseling, child and family services, and, to a lesser extent, day care and into health care, mental health, and residential services of various kinds (Fabricant and Burghart 1992:124–125).

When the effect of local and regional recessions, tied to a changing national economy as well as to the business cycle, was added to these losses, the effects on social service budgets could be dramatic. Lipsky (1984) argues that the strategy of letting inflation and budget reductions put "natural" pressure on human service agencies was deliberately intended to force service reductions. He called the results—which included narrowed eligibility, larger caseloads, longer waiting lists for services, less outreach, and the closing down of neighborhood offices—bureaucratic disentitlement. (Other effects included less time and resources for the support and development of frontline staff.) It shifted responsibility for the consequences from elected officials to the human service community.

Meanwhile, during this period the nature and correlates of family poverty were also changing. Poverty was becoming ever more closely linked to out-of-wedlock childbearing, single parenthood, and residence in urban neighborhoods of concentrated poverty. Life in such neighborhoods had never been easy. Beginning in the late 1960s and accelerating into the 1970s and 1980s, it became significantly worse, as the toll of decades of public and private sector disinvestment became apparent, and the outmigration of middle-class families intensified. Housing stock, schools, and other physical infrastructure was becoming so deteriorated that nothing short of massive investment would rehabilitate it. Many inner-city neighborhoods experienced the breakdown of the social, religious, and economic institutions that had historically provided a framework of norms and goals, as well as supports, for nurturing and providing for children. Informal social networks were forced increasingly to focus on members' basic surivival needs, leaving less energy for emotional and instrumental support and social regulation.

The majority of inner-city families continued to cope as best they could with the diminishing resources available to them. Yet with less support and margin for error they were more susceptible to unexpected events, disruptions, and crises. Moreover, a growing proportion of young adults living in inner-city neighborhoods were embarking on parenthood and family life with a host of vulnerabilities. These young adults had personal histories marked by adversity in many spheres, including disruptions in caregiving, inadequate nurturance or rejection by parents, parental substance abuse, family violence, sexual abuse, and difficulties in school (Halpern 1997). Such histories led not only to parenting vulnerabilities but often to difficulties in many domains of family life—adult relationships, work, education, health, housing, substance abuse, and managing financial and other resources. For some young adults the effects of multiple vulnerabilities were compounded by the availability of crackcocaine, and the dramatic increase in family and community violence that accompanied its appearance in the inner city.

Societal anxiety about the worsening situation of vulnerable families was projected once again onto the social service community (Valentine 1994:73). Indeed, such projection seemed to accelerate geometrically during the 1980s and early 1990s. Periodic, but highly publicized case tragedies seemed to impugn the competence and even the intentions of child welfare workers and the service system as a whole. Each death of a child at the hands of parents or guardians fueled another round of anger, which was then displaced on overwhelmed, minimally trained, and inadequately supported frontline protective service workers.

At the same time the idea was emerging that the social welfare state had reached a kind of limit. The longstanding, but recently latent battle about the limits of state intrusion into family and community life was reengaged. The Reagan Administration gave voice, and therefore legitimacy to an emerging conservative critique holding that government itself was the source of many societal problems. This would cripple social reform initiatives for the remainder of the century, and would lead in the late 1980s and early 1990s to a shift in the locus of reform efforts to the states. It would lead also to efforts to "re-privatize [sic] social and personal problems," asking families and communities to once again assume the burden of mutual support (Fabricant and Burghart 1992:227).

The public climate created by the Reagan Administration eroded what political will remained to support adequate funding for services and provided fertile soil for new avenues of criticism. One suggested that since services were ineffective, it was a waste of public resources to fund them adequately (see Orfield 1991:525). Others argued that helping professionals and the bureaucracies in which they worked were at best inflexible and at worst self-serving. Still others argued that helping professionals deliberately kept poor and vulnerable people dependent because they benefited from the latter's "clienthood." One asked why the situation and well-being of many poor families worsened during the 1970s and early 1980s, a period of expanded social services (Mead 1986:47)? Even program or family success stories were turned against prevailing services, used to argue either that the exception proved the rule or (since they often involved private agencies) to further discredit the competence of the public service sector.

Mingled with the undue criticism were genuine, longstanding issues that were being raised again by more sympathetic critics. Why was it that those most in need of supportive services were precisely those least likely to have access to them? Why were the least experienced workers put in situations requiring them to make the most difficult decisions in society? Why was it so difficult to sustain a supportive, not to mention a developmental perspective in work with children and families? Why were there still so few pathways between categorical programs, not to mention service systems?

## Service Agencies Respond

Public and private agencies were in different positions in relation to these various population, political, financial, and conceptual pressures, and reacted differently. Public child welfare agencies were most sensitive to political pressures to prevent further case tragedies, interpreting such tragedies as signs of a need to tighten up: to take in and process greater numbers of families, and to document their actions fully, in order to protect themselves in the event a case went wrong and came to public attention. They were sensitive also to pressure from their budget offices to prevent "disallowances" by federal and state auditors that resulted from either procedural and paperwork slip-ups (by supervisory or frontline workers), or serving unreimbursable clients, or providing unreimbursable services (Berlin undated).

The Federal Adoption Assistance and Child Welfare Act of 1980 was providing some new monies for preventive services. But these monies were by and large intended for the prevention of foster care placement and the reuniting of children already in placement with their families. Thus, while continuing to proclaim the importance of community-based prevention, outreach, and early childhood intervention, public agencies for the most part narrowed their prevention focus to families showing signs of, or with histories of, serious difficulties.

One reflection of this narrow focus was the embrace of an innovative service model (with roots in the multiproblem family demonstrations of the 1950s), known as intensive family preservation services. These were short-term, crisis-oriented services, designed to prevent child placement (or, less commonly, re-placement) in families considered to be at imminent (but needless) risk of having children removed. The model was premised on the notion that it was possible to identify or pinpoint such imminent risk and within a short period—a matter of weeks—substantially address the problems contributing to it. Proponents argued that by "reducing the number and incidence of removals a strong family preservation capacity" could free up resources to be used to build a full continuum of services (Nelson 1991:216–217).

The strengths of intensive family preservation services included a preference for highly professional staff; small caseloads; a clear theoretical framework translated into clear intervention techniques; a focus on the whole family and the way it was functioning, as well as on individual family members; a focus on the full range of family problems; and a balance between therapeutic and concrete services. Because they fit the preoccupations of child welfare authorities, such programs expanded rapidly during the 1980s. By one estimate they grew in number from 20 programs in 1982 to 269 in 1988 (Biegel and Wells 1991:xiii). At their peril, they ignored the Lower East Side Family Union experience (described in chapter 7), which had suggested strongly that placement prevention was a dubious and overly narrow objective, relying on the impossible task of accurate targeting and timing. (Proponents of focusing services on those at imminent risk might have done better to focus on homelessness rather than child placement, since the events leading up to the former are somewhat more predictable and the meaning of the outcome less ambiguous.) In addition, family preservation models were ill-suited to the largest group of vulnerable families—young inner-city families, with a variety of vulnerabilities and chronic, stubborn problems that came to the fore at unpredictable moments and that certainly were not susceptible to interventions of short duration.

By far the most significant response of the public agencies to various external pressures—a response driven both by political demand and by the desire to create a buffer between themselves and the public—was to shift more of the tasks of serving poor and vulnerable families) to private agencies. This meant survival for some agencies, more resources for others—but at a price. One stream of new public resources was categorical federal funds (Mostly Medicaid and Title IV-E funds) intended for children already in foster care. Thus agencies were increasingly forced to organize themselves to become managers of foster care caseloads. Other resources came from state and municipal funding streams for assessment, case management, casework, and homemaker or other services for particular categories of families. Both sources of funding usually involved purchase of service agreements, and required an emphasis on improved productivity and efficiency, as well as greater accountability. These requirements in turn created pressure to standardize and proceduralize management and frontline practice and to drop or shrink services that could not be reimbursed. Private agencies, like public ones, protected themselves from audits by creating paper trails demonstrating that they had followed procedures and had documentation for every action their staff had taken. Frontline workers were reigned in.

Private family service agencies also had to seek constructive responses to the growing numbers of very vulnerable families in the communities they served who did not fit or fall into particular categorical programs. This was an old mission—historically, agencies had always tried to set aside funds for broadly targeted prevention services intended to serve the general, "undifferentiated" mix of families in poor communities, with the overall idea of "keep[ing] something from happening" (Hess, McGowan, and Meyer 1995:133)—complicated by the new pressures on services. Thus providers worked to get neighborhood families that came in for help into a categorical program. Providers also had to find ways to deal with the nonreimbursable support needs of families in one or another categorical program. For instance, they used more broadly targeted programs provided by the agency—a Head Start program or parent support group—as a resource for families in one or another specialized category. These responses, while adaptive, sometimes had their own costs, such as increasing the burden on frontline workers in already fragile programs. Moreover, they tended not to address systematically the complicated, long-term support needs of critical populations—vulnerable families with infants and very young children who had not yet come to the attention of child welfare authorities, or families who had struggled ineffectively for a number of years, and were failing in their efforts to keep their eight-, nine-, or ten-year-old children on track.

## Effects on Frontline Practice

Already by 1980 it was observed that helpers were coming to view themselves as "victims of the same [forces] that victimize their clients" (Lipsky 1980:183). This sense of victimization only worsened during the next decade and a half. At one level it was derived from the strain of working with greater numbers of very vulnerable families, under difficult community conditions. Berlin (undated:5) described the new and intensified poverty-related problems as "like a tidal wave surging over the decks" of child and family service agencies. Whereas in earlier times a frontline practitioner might have had a few very vulnerable families in her caseload, now she might have a sizable number. This meant less diversity in a typical caseload and more clients calling or walking in in crisis, week in and week out. One frontline worker with sixteen years of experience told Fabricant and Burghart (1992:138): "There are just so many more chaotic families. The parents are so needy and clearly not in control . . . often I don't know where to start with the issues of housing, food, violence, or drugs. . . . All of this just adds to the pressure I'm feeling."

Work with vulnerable families sometimes led frontline providers to doubt themselves. Helping under such circumstances was emotionally depleting and sometimes distressing. Confronted with a host of complex family problems, it was sometimes hard to know where to begin. It could be hard even to make and maintain contact with families. Parents might be indifferent, wary, or hostile to offers of help. Providers increasingly encountered situations in which they were not sure they "[had] what it takes to assist the client" (Rein 1983:143). Over time the stresses and strain of work with vulnerable families could threaten frontline workers' commitment to their work, allegiance to their agency, and identity as growing helping professionals. At the same time providers found it increasingly difficult to put faith in some of their clients, without worrying that such faith was misplaced—especially parents whose own pressing needs and neediness conflicted with their parental identity and responsibilities (Hess, McGowan, and Meyer 1995). The best interests of individual family members and the family as a whole were not easy to discern in growing numbers of families.

The stressful effects of work with vulnerable families were exacerbated by the increasingly unsupportive social and organizational context in which that work took place. As one practitioner told Hess, McGowan, and Meyer (1995:13), "It is appalling how little people know about this kind of work and how little they recognize the importance of it. I find that very hard." The accumulating number of seemingly senseless rules and procedures, and the need to document every action also communicated distrust to the frontline worker, either from his or her own agency or the public agency funding his or her activities.

Those with case management responsibilities of one kind or another (including eligibility determination) were particularly affected by the changing conditions of work. It was not uncommon for such workers to spend a third to a half of their time on paperwork, and their supervisors even more. Larger caseloads, increased paperwork, and the loss of role discretion undermined the ability of frontline workers to customize their work with clients, be flexible in their response to crises, and maintain the mental energy to think about their caseloads as a whole and make adjustments to their work. Their availability to clients was increasingly circumscribed and their ability to stay in touch diminished. It became increasingly difficult for service workers to figure out how and whether "to carry out or not carry out all or part of their many-sided duties" (Orfield 1991:521).

Lack of time became an increasingly common theme in the literature on frontline practice with poor families: time to make critical decisions, to analyze and think about cases; time to follow up on referrals made and to help clients locate resources; time to really listen to what a client was saying in what may have seemed a rambling description of a problem or a monosyllabic response (Lipsky 1980; Fabricant and Burghart 1992). Weissbourd (1996:153) offers the following anecdote, involving a respected physician in Boston's South Community Health Center: "I was with Hass when, after seeing his usual long succession of patients one morning, he asked a mother how she was doing. She mumbled, while dropping her head and staring at the floor, that she was O.K. Next to her name on his chart, he simply jotted down 'O.K.' "

Supervisors experienced the same time pressures as their frontline workers, with parallel consequences, including less time for individual supervision, case review, and discussion. Lack of adequate supervision was particularly serious in protective services where many workers were "inexperienced and young—in their mid-twenties," and needed guidance from supervisors to confirm their judgments (Weissbourd 1996:191).

The combination of time and resource pressures, larger caseloads with greater percentages of vulnerable families, less discretion, more seemingly meaningless paperwork and procedures, less supervision. and fewer opportunities to process and be supported in work with families contributed to a cluster of frontline behaviors that Sieber called "fatal remedies" (cited in Dressel 1984:8). These behaviors included focusing on procedure; claiming less discretion than one actually had; not suggesting alternatives that would demand increased work; stereotyping clients in order to reduce the need to individualize; redefining (i.e., narrowing) the range of supports a client was seen to need; choosing—and rationalizing the choice of—some clients for greater attention than others; and ignoring problems, including suspected client fraud, that would require a lot of paperwork (Lipsky 1980:140–149).

In interviews with fifty-three frontline workers in a diverse sample of child and family service agencies in New York, Fabricant and Burghart (1992:132–166) found frontline workers affected in a range of ways by the social and bureaucratic forces impinging on them. Workers noted constant pressure to move clients along "from step A to step B," and to overschedule and overbook (on the theory that they would have cancellations). One case-worker who was supposed to have twenty-three "case contact" hours per week was required to book thirty-three or more hours. When, as happened, all or most clients showed up, it was overwhelming. Workloads and time pressures led to exhaustion, to work that was not as deep, regular, or sustained as it needed to be, and sometimes to disengagement:

> "At the end of the workday I'm just not as alert. I'm exhausted. I'm just not there for the client."

> "When clients come late I'm glad.... My schedule is such that I'm really fatigued....Ultimately I just tend to space out in many more of these sessions or I don't take it where it should go therapeautically."

> "I just don't have the time to learn about or apply the critical pieces of class, culture, or race to my clients . . . these clients have different experiences and orientations that need to be tapped and understood. But who has the time for this . . . work?"

Providers who worked with poor families had always had to cope with the frustration of being unable to address the basic conditions of clients' lives. Now they could not even strive for modest achievements, those characteristic of interpersonal helping, and be nourished enough by such achievements to keep on with the work. Without time and mandate to develop sustained helping relationships, they could not begin to get at therapeutic issues, nor could they follow through on efforts to link clients to badly needed resources.

The continuing reliance on (shifting) categorical funding streams, some originating at the federal level, others at the state or local level, undermined whatever coherence and continuity private providers tried to bring to their work with families. McGowan (1990:71) described the difficulty the Brooklyn Bureau of Community Service had in referring families in its prevention program to its homemaker aide program, because the latter was funded by a different branch of the city's child welfare agency. Categorical programming obliterated both the history and breadth of service to a family, and the capacity to stay with families over time. When a case was opened, there was little capacity for a new provider to learn a family's history of involvement with various services. Combined with resource scarcity, categorical programming sometimes turned agencies against each other, leading each to feel that the others made its work more difficult, that it had to fight them for information or resources for its clients. Frontline workers in one New York City community agency told observers that it was both exhausting and demoralizing to constantly have to fight and beg for the most basic resources for poor and vulnerable families (Hess, McGowan, and Meyer 1995:19). Not least, categorical programming left untouched the question of who was responsible for vulnerable children and families in a general sense rather than when they presented with particular circumstances.

When a frontline provider or supervisor was constantly forced into positions that made it impossible for her to use her knowledge and experience, this inevitably weakened her commitment to the work. Rein (1983:152) argued that for many, the pressures and contradictions of practice were leading to a "separation of meaning and action." The routine activities and procedures of the agency continue, but the "complex structure of actions is partly unshielded and unjustified in an ideological and emotional sense. . . . People keep on doing their jobs but they are no longer sure they know what they are doing." The largely implicit feelings in frontline workers, which resulted from the knowledge that they were not doing what they should and could be doing and from the discomfort of being forced to behave toward clients in ways that they knew were not constructive, were called by Rein "practice worries." At some point, for some workers, the strains of such worries were converted to burnout and turnover. The latter in particular was hugely costly to services, not just in the loss of continuity of relationships with families but also because of the loss of the reservoir of experience available to the service community.

## Conclusion

The 1970s and 1980s were characterized by a complicated interaction between shifting federal and state priorities; public social service systems' efforts to cope with growing pressures; and the emergence of new service ideas and approaches, largely but not entirely outside those systems. The federal government's preoccupation with administrative reform—service integration, better use of data—lacked substance. These tools of the new "public administrators" bore no message about the purpose of services. (The social workers and child development specialists who had staffed and usually led federal human service agencies until the mid-1960s had had their biases, but their preoccupations were usually substantive.) The commitment to devolution and local priority-setting, while a healthy one, lacked mechanisms for assuring that an appropriate share of resources would go to poor families and communities.

The federal government did play a major role in one substantive development that profoundly affected the supportive services landscape. That was the permanent split in theory, policy, and practice between family dependency concerns and child welfare concerns. The loss of this historical connection meant that public aid was no longer a doorway to supportive services nor had much connection to the private agency network that provided such services. This not only left an already overwhelmed child welfare system with the task of orchestrating and funding supportive services, it also contributed to the overall fragmentation of the social service system.

Continued policy fragmentation and problem-specific specialization during the 1970s and 1980s contributed to the difficulty in forging a coherent sense of services. These trends left the service system more complex than ever and also left frontline providers with narrower mandates and roles than ever. At the same time those mandates, notably in public aid and child welfare, were ambiguous. Fragmentation complicated the task of generating a coherent narrative of what services were about and a clear articulation of appropriate expectations.

One dominant substantive reform concept of the era, family-oriented early childhood intervention, offered much conceptual promise. The principles and practices of the clinical infant programs, combined with those of family support programs, provided a strong base for work with the growing group of multiply vulnerable young families. Yet most of those within this program movement did not see work with such families as their mission. Moreover early childhood intervention was both a diffuse and notably decentralized program movement. By the late 1980s it was still unconnected to any of the major public systems, and its funding remained a tiny percentage of total funding for social services for poor families. Other substantive reforms of the era were notable for being problem- and population-specific, and in that sense arbitrary "points of engagement in the matrix of [poverty-related] social problems" (Galper 1975:77). It was hard even to evaluate their overall impact, as problems ebbed and flowed, populations changed, and preoccupations shifted. The other notable program movement of the era, intensive family preservation services, offered some interesting concepts and principles but was in many respects ill-suited to the emerging profile of young, multiply vulnerable families in poverty.

Taken together, developments in supportive services during this period probably pushed things further from the ideal of a coherent continuum of services that was preventively oriented, family-centered, community-rooted, and largely noncategorical. Although this ideal animated many reform proposals and some reform efforts, by the end of the 1980s it still had no policy or system base. Moreover, the rhetorical commitment to a broad vision of services within the child and family service community was no match for the growing secular pressures on service providers.

One final development in supportive services during this period bears noting again. Throughout the century there had been a tendency to become more critical of services during times of heightened value conflict or societal shift or crisis. This critical perspective had now become chronic. A vicious cycle had been set in place: inadequate support and belittlement of services debilitated them so greatly that they were deemed all but irrelevant, which further limited support for them. Lifeless concepts such as accountability, standards, and proceduralization were used to provide structure, to keep things moving, to keep providers from falling apart under the pressures they were experiencing. Any new money tended to go to new categorical purposes and programs, pulling agency support and some of the best people from existing services.

By the late 1980s it was becoming clear to even the most entrenched bureaucrats that their narrow responses to the unprecedented pressures on services were counterproductive. But it was also clear that no responses of the service system, whether more or less constructive, could alter the larger ideological processes at work in society, which would continue to grind down whatever residual faith existed in formal helping efforts or in and social welfare activity generally. More thoughtful observers pointed out that after all, services largely had done what society asked them to. The responsibilities of more advantaged, secure members of society toward the poor had been "mediated through a vast division of labor," carried out mostly by helping professionals (Ignatieff 1985:10). By its nature, this process could never yield the sense of social cohesion of more "natural" approaches to meeting social needs. The 1990s nonetheless would bring an intensified effort to reconstruct such natural approaches and shift the locus of service provision once again to communities.

# CHAPTER NINE

# New Paradigms, Old Problems

*Until you fix individual problems and do old-fashioned casework, forget
about the community stuff.*
—"Voices from the Field," Chapin Hall Center for Children

*The more people turn to services the weaker their community becomes.*
—from a concept paper by a traditional family service agency
in Pittsburgh

*Local politicians became interested in these new approaches "to offset cuts
in expenditures by improved methods of working and to defend local
services by making them more relevant and answerable to the citizen."*
—Roger Hadley

In the 1990s the century-long struggle to find and sustain a constructive
role for helping services for poor families has again taken a new turn. In the
face of organizational crises, cost containment pressures and outright funding reductions, shifting policy frameworks, and public skepticism about efforts to address social problems, the decade has witnessed a renewed wave
of service reform. As in the past, some reform has been been initiated by the
service provision community itself, as it attempts to be responsive to changing family and community conditions, ideas and concerns in the air, and
funding priorities. Philanthropic foundations and the federal government
have played a role. For instance, in 1993 Congress authorized $930 million
to states over five years for family support and preservation services. State
governments have been surprisingly active; municipal governments less so.

The problems driving service reform in the 1990s are not new. On one
side is the continuing need to find a useful response to the most vulnerable
families; on the other the accumulated dysfunctions of the service system
itself, ranging from the timing and philosophy of services to their organization and funding. After thirty years of occasionally intense, frequently
sporadic reform, poor families still encounter "an inaccessible, highly unco-
ordinated array of narrowly focused services and benefits, targeted on dif-

ferent and often conflicting goals . . . [with] inconsistent eligibility criteria and conflicting rules" (Gerry and Paulson 1995:3). They "must carry their life stories around to several places and give each agency a different part of the story" (Institute for Educational Leadership 1994:5). Families experience a lack of program and staff continuity in their lives; providers experience the same lack of coherence in their funding and mandates.

In a Campaign for Children "Issues Brief," the National Governors Association noted that by the time federal and state dollars reach local communities, service providers "confront a large number of small pools of funds for which families must be determined eligible on a case-by-case basis." Determining, documenting, and monitoring eligibility waste large amounts of time. The brief notes that case management does not help much as a strategy for improving services to vulnerable families when case managers must spend most of their time reacting to the problems created by categorical programs.

One would think that, given developments described in the previous chapter, any remaining visions of a neighborhood-based family service system, with a well-differentiated continuum of services, would have been crushed. But that is only partly the case. That modest portion of the vision acknowledging that it might be necessary to provide skilled, patient, interpersonal help to some families on a long-term basis did largely dissipate. The even more modest portion suggesting that an adequately rich continuum of services requires adequate funding is also dead. What survived, and has become magnified, is a collection of principles, characterized by some as a "new paradigm" for services. In policy paper after policy paper, proposal after proposal, one sees the call for services to be preventive, holistic, flexible, individually tailored, family-centered, empowering, and culturally sensitive. To these are added the call for services that are mission-focused, yet also continuous, comprehensive, noncategorical, integrated, and collaborative. What has also survived is the remarkably robust impulse to tie services more closely to the life of poor neighborhoods.

The "new paradigm" in services is not exactly new. The principles reflect ideals that have appeared and reappeared throughout the century. In different eras they have been promoted individually or attached to different service movements: the settlements of the Progressive era, the "multiproblem" family demonstrations of the 1950s, the new services associated with community action in the 1960s, and the early childhood intervention and family support movement of the 1970s and 1980s. In no previous era, however, have these principles been so repeatedly lumped together in all kinds of reform proposals or descriptions of specific initiatives This has had a dramatic (some might say hypnotic) effect; it is almost as if no one had wanted these things for services before.

Some proponents of the new paradigm recognize that best practice will not just happen by stating a set of principles over and over again, or by packaging them in a request for proposals, or by presenting them in in-service training workshops. They recognize that the behavior of frontline providers, their supervisors and agencies is strongly shaped by organizational and systemic factors, particularly approaches to funding services. For instance, the evaluator of a family support initiative in Minneapolis noted that, in spite of participating programs' best efforts to create and sustain a strong mission, "the politics of funding create mission chaos.... It's hard to stay mission-focused when every funder wants your mission to be whatever they are willing to provide money for this week" (Patton 1993:16).

Nonetheless, after thirty years of almost constant reform efforts, those responsible for the management of human services remain surprisingly unsure about how to stimulate, organize, and bring about systemic reform. (To a lesser extent they also remain unsure about what a reformed service system would look like and how exactly it would operate, beyond reflecting some particular set of ideals.) There is a growing belief that reform cannot be imposed from the top down and must to some extent be demand-driven. The staff director of a major human service reform initiative in Illinois noted that "only a huge and potent groundswell of grassroots effort will move public officials to make meaningful reform" (cited in Preister 1996:12).

There has been a continued tendency, found in past reform eras, to locate reform initially in specific local institutions or agencies and use those as a base for influencing the larger service system. The idea is that participants will identify the local obstacles to systemic coherence and develop strategies to make the local system work better as a whole. These strategies can then be expanded to other settings or be taken up in a statewide reform initiative. (This is similar to the idea of testing and then replicating a particular type of service model). Schools have been a surprisingly popular base for incubating system reform, a step beyond the newly popular notion of schools as community centers or as the hubs of local service systems. Other types of local institutions or clusters of institutions have been used as well, including Head Start programs, settlements, family support programs, and traditional casework agencies.

A related variation of bottom-up system reform has been to base what is intended eventually to be statewide cross-system reform in one or more local community "collaboratives." Drawing on different constituencies in the community, the collaborative is supposed to figure out the new relationships, arrangements, and agreements between agencies and systems that will be needed to create a more coherent service system, with the results theoretically serving as a model for the rest of a state. This approach is being used, for instance, in the statewide human service reform effort in Illinois.

Many visions of a reformed service system that have emerged in the 1990s draw on the historical ideal of community-rooted services. As at previous points over the past thirty years, there has been a modest movement to involve community residents in the planning, governance, and provision of services. Some current proponents of this movement urge a fundamental shift in authority away from large bureaucracies to community structures. There also are two newer dimensions to the effort to make services more community-oriented. One is an interest in "interweaving [sic] formal and informal care and control" (Adams and Nelson 1995:1). In part that implies shifting responsibilities historically assumed by formal human services providers—for example child protection—to community residents and community-based institutions. In New York City the commissioner of the Administration for Children's Services has proposed using "neighborhood networks of churches, medical centers and social service organizations [to] handle the care and monitoring of troubled families" (Sexton 1996:1).

The other new dimension that has some roots in the past seeks to tie service provision and reform to broad community development concerns such as housing, safety, economic enterprise, and community organization. Service agencies and service reform initiatives are adopting community-building as a new mission and/or philosophy, reshaping the activities of their staff and the nature of their relationship to low-income communities. (On the other side of the equation, those, such as community development corporations, who have traditionally been involved in community development activity, are increasingly looking to provide services and/or to focus on such traditional service goals as supporting and strengthening families.) In some cases service agencies (and community development organizations) are addressing their new goals by adding staff and activities to their own organizations; in others by developing new collaborative relationships. This new trend in social problem-solving reflects in part a recognition of the powerful relationship between the well-being of inner-city families and that of their local communities, and in part a sense of limitations by those working within each tradition—whether trying to support and strengthen families one by one, without attending to the social ecology shaping those families' beliefs, behavior, and aspirations or trying to strengthen a geographic place as a whole, without attending to the individuals that shape that place.

It is not clear what percentage of child and family service agencies have embraced a community-building mission at some level. Most agencies that provide child welfare services are so tied to the categorical purchase of service framework that they have little energy for diffuse new missions. Many serve children and families spread out across large numbers of communities. Many are struggling with cuts in funds for preventive and community services, the presumed source of fuel for a community-building mission. The number that have embraced (or reembraced) this mission, at least in part, is nonetheless growing. In addition, the larger organizations and networks from which child and family service agencies take their cues about innovation have jumped on the community-building bandwagon. For example, Family Service America has begun a major initiative to promote what it calls community-centered family service among the 280 traditional casework agencies that constitute its membership. And New York City's network of thirty-five settlements has embraced community-building as a priority (Hirota, Brown, and Mollard 1997).

A different approach to systemic reform has focused on creating a proper framework for accountability in services. Proponents of this approach are nonetheless using the concept differently. Some, connected to the larger movement to tie services to their communities, focus primarily on making services more accountable to the communities in which they reside. Others focus on benchmarks (of progress) or on outcomes. Gardner (1995) argues that a critical flaw in the service reform efforts of the 1960s and 1970s was a failure to specify the community-level child and family outcomes to which they wished to be held accountable. It has been argued that so-called outcome-based accountability would simply put more pressure on already overwhelmed frontline providers; and that the effects of services are often both very individualized and difficult to quantify. Proponents counter that the key to outcome-based accountability is appropriate benchmarks or outcomes; that it can be used as a quid pro quo to give frontline providers more discretion; that it can provide a focus for communities' efforts on behalf of children; and that it can illuminate whether investments in children and families are adequate (Schorr 1997). It remains to be seen whether outcome-based accountability can be used in a constructive and helpful way.

It has also been argued that successful system reform will not occur until reform is built on an understanding of two things: how and why service systems allocate resources as they do (Wulczyn 1996); and how funding patterns constrain reform efforts themselves. For instance, public service systems and private providers have been reluctant to mount or embrace initiatives whose approach to services prevented federal or state reimbursement (Berlin undated). There is in fact a growing movement to use change in service financing approaches and priorities as a spur to or a key component of system reform. Some system reforms, such as decategorization and decentralization, imply or require financing reforms almost by definition. Others, such as making services more community-oriented, would be more effective if accompanied by such reform. (Where, for example, are funds that would allow service agency staff to engage in community development activities to come from?) According to Cutler (undated:18) examples of financing reforms designed to support current system reform proposals include: putting significant amounts of service delivery resources under the control of "consumers," whether families or communities; shifting funding across system boundaries through flexibility at the state, city, or neighborhood level; and pooling significant amounts of funding (i.e., putting funds under the shared control of multiple agencies). Some would predicate financing reforms on some form of accountability, although it is not clear who would or could be accountable in each case.

### Changing Perspectives on Poverty: A Shifting Social Welfare Framework

As in the past, debates about the purpose and organization of services have been influenced by prevailing thinking about poverty and poor people. In particular, there has been a newly intensified debate about the nature and causes of persistent poverty. One line of argument in this debate has refocused attention on the geographic dimensions of poverty, something that was minimized in the 1970s and 1980s. With some exceptions (e.g., Lemann 1991; Massey and Denton 1993), the renewed focus on the social geography of poverty has not addressed the historical policies and practices that have contributed to the concentration of poor people of color in particular neighborhoods. Rather, most writers have focused on its destructive effects, in the creation of what Stark (1987) called "deviant places." In another example of the American tendency to mix apples and oranges in social thinking, the recognition that urban poverty is concentrated in particular neighborhoods has contributed to the push for community-based and bounded service reform.

A quite different set of arguments holds that a growing proportion of poverty is due to the behavioral choices (if not the values) of poor people, which are exacerbated by social policies that are too permissive, fail to enforce social norms and expectations, and/or are perverse in their incentive structure, as well as by social service providers who are too nonjudgmental and too noncommittal about right and wrong (Himmelfarb 1991; Mead 1986 1994; Payne 1996). Poor people are at best demoralized due to permissive programs that keep them from acting on their [moral] beliefs; at worst they are betrayed by the lack of social pressure to behave morally in the face of "contrary temptations" (Mead 1986:23; 1994:333).

Two implications have been drawn from this line of argument. One, not surprisingly, argues for social policy and practice that communicates clear, unambiguous behavioral expectations of poor people. It suggests a much greater role for social service personnel in monitoring poor peoples' behavior and enforcing social norms. States such as Michigan and Wisconsin have already begun using public aid caseworkers for these purposes. A few observers have recommended what they call a preventive monitoring role with respect to child welfare—for instance, recommending that families with certain high risk profiles be identified, visited, and assessed on a regular basis by protective service workers, regardless of whether there is any evidence of abuse or neglect.

The other implication drawn from the moral-behavioral perspective on poverty harks back to the nineteenth-century notion that alleviating hardship and deprivation can undermine individual will: "Extreme forms of suffering are indeed incapacitating and therefore harmful. But intermediate levels of deprivation—or the anticipating of such—motivate constructive choices; therefore aiming to reduce such moderate deprivation is unhelpful" (Payne 1996:51).

The idea that help can have perverse effects and, conversely, that withholding help can be the most helpful course of action has been applied primarily to welfare reform, leading to the ideas of time limits and "capping" grants (not increasing them when subsequent children are born). Yet it has sometimes been directed to other policy domains. For instance McDonald (1994:59) argued that services that strove to support and strengthen parenting in vulnerable families contributed to illegitimacy, because they implicitly assumed "a nonjudgmental approach to family formation."

The new lines of argument about poverty and poverty-related social policy have become part of something larger. The 1990s are bringing shifts, perhaps fundamental shifts, in the American social welfare system. If the United States began the twentieth century thinking that laissez-faire had "outlived its usefulness" (Rochefort 1981:573), it is ending the century believing that government has outlived its usefulness. William Bennet and Dan Coates, two prominent conservatives, recommend "diverting a share of welfare spending directly to private and religious antipoverty charities" (Sviridoff and Ryan 1996:2). In his second inaugural address, President

Clinton reflected public sentiment when he noted that government was neither the problem nor the solution.

One sign of changing public beliefs about social welfare has been the lack of protest over the demise of the AFDC program and its historical mission of protecting vulnerable children. Its replacement, Temporary Assistance to Needy Families (TANF), does not have protecting children as its mission, which if anything can be defined as requiring states to focus their welfare systems (and services) on moving welfare recipients into the workforce as quickly as possible. With the passage of TANF, a quarter century of debate about the extent, nature, and locus of public responsibility for the well-being of poor and vulnerable families would seem to have ended. President Nixon's argument that basic family supports are a national responsibility and service delivery a state or local responsibility has been repudiated.

Yet the complexities and ambiguities of TANF are almost incalculable. The shape, purposes, and human consequences of the reformed American social welfare system may remain hazy for years. That is in part because within the strong welfare to work mandate states have considerable flexibility to shape their own programs. It is not yet clear whether states can or will develop philosophies at odds with TANF. It is not clear whether they will assume responsibility for protecting children from destitution, and if so whether they will they do so by supporting families or removing children from their families. Put more directly, it is not yet clear how many poor families will be forced off the welfare rolls (by virtue of status or behavior) before the head of household has found full-time work; neither is it clear what states will do with or for families forced off the rolls but unable to support themselves. It is also not clear what types of health insurance entitlement and child care subsidies, if any, will be afforded poor working families, and what kinds of supports states will provide people to help them stay attached to the workforce.

There is an expectation, one that carries echoes of nineteenth-century practices, that families unable to support themselves but ineligible for public assistance will be taken care of by their own relatives or by private charities. This is a new component of privatization (and one quite different from "purchase of services"). But as one Massachusetts teen mother, ineligible for welfare because she refused to live with her parents (who refused to help her and themselves were on the verge of eviction) and bounced from shelters to other family to foster care to friends, told a reporter, "Some teens don't have nobody to turn to" (Vobejda and Haveman 1997:6; in addition, Massachusetts had to contract with two social service agencies to track down young families who had lost benefits to see how they were faring).

As the earliest evidence from TANF, and more definitive findings from state and local experiments that have TANF-like elements, come in, a few patterns are becoming evident. One is that frontline workers in public aid offices are bearing the brunt of the pressure to make welfare reform work. Their performance is now being evaluated on the number of families leaving their caseloads and their willingness to sanction those who do not follow new rules. These pressures, combined with inadequate retraining and lack of guidelines for making determinations, have led in some jurisdictions to high levels of incorrect sanctioning (i.e., reducing or halting aid payments and Food Stamps to a family). One report found that "44 percent of the penalties imposed in the first five months of Milwaukee's [new welfare] program were later overturned when officials discovered they had made errors" (DeParle 1997a:A10). A second early finding, from a number of states, is that only half of those leaving welfare find jobs in the period immediately after they leave, and for those who do find jobs, wages are typically well below the poverty line. A third finding—which was in fact already clear from child care research—is that there is a critical shortage of even minimally adequate, let alone good quality child care for poor infants and toddlers whose young mothers are being pushed into the workforce.

Still another finding from TANF and TANF-like experiments is that while the pressures of sanctions and time limits are motivating many welfare recipients to seek jobs, the majority of those who find jobs on their own lose them within months, if not weeks. Many people need job retention and reemployment assistance (see Herr, Halpern, and Wagner 1995). The threat of sanctions and time limits are also having little or no effect on a sizable group of welfare recipients, who take no action to seek work until, and even after, they are sanctioned. For this group, leaving welfare will be a gradual, often difficult process, likely to take years. People in it will need customized, carefully constructed pathways, starting with low-risk opportunities to acquire the basic skills and dispositions needed to hold on to a job (e.g., the ability to adhere to a schedule) and moving gradually to more demanding, worklike activities. They also will need regular monitoring and support, if they are to keep moving from step to step (Herr, Wagner, and Halpern 1996). To be helpful to both those likely to need assistance keeping jobs and those not yet ready to work full-time, public aid offices will have to reinvent themselves as welfare to work offices.

In addition to profoundly altering the American social welfare framework, the 104th Congress and President Clinton decided that eliminating budget deficits "take precedence [sic] over all social protection goals" (Kamerman 1996:453). Two approaches are being used to meet deficit reduction targets. One is funding ceilings on programs for the poor and vulnerable, called "capitated" funding; the other is straight funding cuts. (Capitated funding was the federal government's quid pro quo for allowing states greater flexibility in use of federal funds through block grants.) The effects of the funding ceilings theoretically will not be felt until states experience the next recession. (Historically, increased federal funding has helped to level things out during recessions. Fixed ceilings on federal funding mean that such compensatory support will no longer be forthcoming.) Gary Stangler, the director of Missouri's social service department, sees preventive services as most at risk when the next economic downturn comes (Stangler 1995): "The gravity in block grants will pull the funding to the maintenance and subsistence payments in cash welfare, foster care and adoption assistance. The gains that states have been able to make in preventive services will be most at risk."

In a similar vein, most of the cuts that accompanied the new federal legislation will not be felt for a few years, because they are back-loaded. Yet some effects are appearing already. Thousands, or perhaps hundreds of thousands of legal immigrants have been cut off from Food Stamps. Immediate 15 percent cuts in state social service block grant appropriations have in turn been passed on by state and city agencies to community agencies already overwhelmed by a combination of prior cuts and increased demand for a range of basic family supports (a demand created in part by welfare reform). No one knows what effects these changes in public assistance will have on state and municipal child welfare systems. Many of these systems are under court supervision due to their inability to fulfill current mandates to protect children, implement permanency goals, provide helping services to troubled families, and fulfill various other missions. If, as is possible, children in newly destitute families become de facto or de jure wards of the state, by simple virtue of their family's ineligibility for public supports, this would exacerbate systemic crises. There has been a growing dialogue within the child welfare community about whether the jurisdiction of child welfare authorities should be narrowed to focus on the identification and prosecution of the small or moderate percentage of vulnerable families in which parents clearly do not have children's interests at heart. (The great bulk of vulnerable families presumably would then be identified and served by nonstatutory agencies.) Certainly this possibility would become an impossibility if child welfare systems were to become responsible for destitute children and families.

It is less clear than ever where the responsibility for monitoring and supporting child and family well-being lies. Some argue that such responsibility should reside at the community level (Gerry and Paulson 1995:5). Others argue for the principle of "shared responsibility" (first articulated by Robert Moroney 1986). The philosophy of devolution and privatization is already affecting child welfare policy and practice. As I have already noted, it is being translated into an emergent movement to shift responsibility for identifying, monitoring, and helping vulnerable families to community-based institutions and neighbors. The underlying thesis—that community residents will be willing to involve themselves in the lives of their troubled neighbors—is currently supported only by anecdote. It is worth pursuing, but with great care.

The potential, then, for wholesale reform of child and family services appears to be great in some respects, constrained in others. Many pieces of the child and family welfare puzzle have been thrown in the air. The various reform impulses of the 1990s—making communities the locus of service governance, organization and provision,and financing reform; using social policy explicitly to mold poor peoples' behavior; shifting responsibility for welfare to states, private charity, even neighbors—do not all sit well together (and are only just beginning to be related to each other in a few jurisdictions). Financing reform in particular is still mostly rhetoric, and its potential is likely to be constrained by escalating funding pressures. None of the current reform strategies are designed or intended to address directly the problems—described in chapter 8—that are undermining conditions of frontline practice. None draws on the obvious fact that if frontline workers were treated as full, complex human beings, with strengths and vulnerabilities, they would be more likely to treat the families they serve with the same respect. The related possibility that this is the key to restoring poor families' faith in services is also ignored.

## In Search of Coherence: Some Current Strategies

Within the larger framework of uncertainty about the future of social welfare, social service providers struggle on, as do the families they serve. The new paradigm principles enumerated earlier—flexible, individualized, holistic, strengths-oriented, family-centered, culturally sensitive services—continue to fertilize innovation in practice. Beyond efforts to incorporate the discrete principles, it is possible to observe a striving for coherence, at many levels, from individual family to program or agency to local community to larger service system. In general case management is much less emphasized than before as a vehicle for forging more coherent services. Some agencies have focused, reasonably, on assuring a measure of coherence among their own offerings. More ambitiously, there has been a renewed wave of reform efforts, combining a push for such longstanding goals as service decategorization and service integration with the 1960s goal of decentralization.

## A Thickening Web of Best Practice Principles

The new paradigm concepts form the main strands of a thickening web of related concepts and principles. Additional strands have been articulated for specific systems (including child welfare, maternal and child health, and mental health; see e.g., Lourie 1994); in specific service movements, notably family support and family preservation; and in model programs. Collectively, these new principles gather under the umbrella of "best practice."

The current interest in best practice has a number of sources. It arises partly out of the findings of program evaluation and partly out of a sense of the limits of program evaluation. It constitutes an implicit argument that although services as a whole seem ineffective, cumulative experience has yielded principles upon which to build more effective services. It comes from Americans' need to be reassured that there are technical solutions to complex, longstanding, unresolved problems. The interest in best practice stems also from the fact that not every local agency has the capacity to or interest in replicating promising program models wholesale. Rather, it seems more feasible to identify the things that make those models successful and use those to shape everyday services.

To cite just a few examples of the kinds of principles emerging to constitute best practice: good services are seen to reach out to families unable or unwilling to seek help themselves; to communicate through their actions both reliability and an unwavering commitment to families served; to work within a framework of small, incremental goals and achievements; to identify a clear mission and organize program resources and activities around it; and (at the same time) to recognize that, whatever the focus of a helping effort, it is important to consider people in the full contexts of their lives (see e.g., Halpern 1997). Good services (and service providers) view families as active partners in addressing family difficulties; they also draw community members and institutions into the task of supporting, nurturing, and caring for families. Program or agency leadership pays close attention to staff development, as well as to the working conditions of frontline staff.

The various new paradigm principles and their corollaries are seen to have implications for professional roles in general and for specialists in particular. Some have argued that these principles imply fewer formal services and less of a role for professionals and specialists (on the grounds that they are inherently unable to provide the rapid, individualized response and the practical help with everyday life tasks that characterize more informal supports). Others argue that they imply primarily new models for the helping professional, who would use his or her expertise differently. For instance, professionals would have to learn how to elicit client strengths, such as "cultural and personal stories, narratives and lore" (Saleebey 1996:305) and to work in partnership with nonservice institutions. One proposal calls for "flexible specialists," who learn to perform functions and assume responsibilities outside their specialty. Flexible specialists would be better able to address vulnerable families' interconnected problems, especially making fewer and more appropriate referrals (i.e., neither too many nor too few; O'Looney 1996:142).

Another staffing concept, intended to contribute to a coherent local service system, is that of multidisciplinary teams under some form of unified supervision. Teams can strive to foster system coherence indirectly, by enhancing coherence for individual clients (much the way case management does). The model here might be that used in mental health, which has a modest tradition of using multidisciplinary teams to develop treatment plans for new clients and review the progress of existing clients. A more innovative vision for teams has system coherence as part of their mandate. The model here can be found in the British experience with the "patch approach" to delivering statutory services (Adams and Krauth 1995). Under this community-centered model, teams of specialists (from social services, health, and housing) and generalists, working out of the local office of a statutory (public social service) agency were responsible for all families within some geographically defined area. Their philosophical charge was to "find creative ways of meeting statutory responsibilities in individual cases while working proactively in the neighborhood." The idea was to "pick [sic] up signs of trouble early," forestalling family crises, and to involve other community institutions in supporting the statutory agency's child and family welfare mission (Adams and Krauth 1995:87).

Surrounding the specific qualities of service and staffing strategies are concepts that paint a picture of ideal local service systems. One is the notion of a local continuum of services. This notion has two dimensions. The first focuses on a continuum in types of services available to families in a community at any moment in time. Some models envision a core of nonspecialized supportive services for parents, and perhaps direct care for children, surrounded by specialized services such as mental health or substance abuse treatment. For instance, a Missouri group called Visions for Child at Risk mounted an initiative to have family therapists and outreach workers added to the staff of family support centers. Such a continuum might be anchored by family support services and/or intensive family preservation services, each element embodying the common principles in its own fashion. The second dimension of continuity is focused on assuring that particular families have continuous services over time, according to the age of their children and to the parents' own related support needs, from the prenatal period through adolescence.

Closely related to the concept of a continuum is that of comprehensiveness. Some use this term in reference to what individual families need, or to the approach that should be taken in serving individual families. Others use it to describe an ideal for a local service system, to argue the need for an adequately differentiated array of types of services, or a critical mass of services. Still others use the term in reference to specific programs or agencies—for example, arguing that good programs for vulnerable families provide comprehensive services. (That usually turns out to mean providing a few things oneself and referring families served to other services, with whom one might or might not have some kind of cooperative agreement.)

*Creating Coherence at the Agency Level*

Although the different dimensions of coherence in supportive services are usually viewed as attributes of local service systems, they can be seen as relevant to individual agencies as well. Historically, for instance, settlements have argued that their array of services increases the likelihood of continuity in services to a family over a period of years. Children may pass from a settlement's early childhood programs to its after school and then youth programs. During the course of this progression, staff come to know and participate in the full life story of both children and parents. Children and parents gradually come to see the settlement as an integral part of their support network, calling on settlement staff for advice and help with problems, even when they are not formally enrolled in a particular service.

McGowan (1990) discusses the efforts of a number of traditional child and family service agencies in New York City—including Leake and Watts, the Brooklyn Bureau of Community Services, Good Shepherd, and St. Christopher-Otille, a large, multisite agency that sponsors the Center for Family Life—to do what they could internally to develop a coherent approach to serving families. Their efforts address some or all the elements touched on above—how staff perceive their roles, the ways in which staff work together, the deliberate envisioning of a continuum of services, and how various individual services relate to each other to create continuity and comprehensiveness.

McGowan's description suggests that these agencies tended to start out as traditional child welfare agencies who broadened their sense of mission and service array in an effort to be more responsive to both vulnerable families and the communities in which they were located. The agencies strive to balance attention to concrete needs and clinical services and to develop a service mix that includes positive developmental supports—for example, a mother-toddler play group, an after school program, a theatre group, or a summer camp program—as well as specialized child welfare services. They cross over system boundaries when they see the need; for instance, developing a dropout prevention program or a specialized housing program for homeless teen parents. Management pays close attention to which types of decisions need to be made centrally and which belong at the level of individual programs. They use various strategies to counter the isolating effects of categorical funding and try to view categorical funding streams as pieces of a puzzle that it is their responsibility to assemble in a coherent way.

As they have turned to the problem of coherence, these agencies have adopted multiple strategies. The Center for Family Life (CFL) uses a single intake for all families, regardless of which service they are seeking. Both Good Shepherd and CFL encourage and have good mechanisms for "intra-agency" referral (McGowan 1990; Hess, McGowan, and Meyer 1995). The Center for Family Life also tries to minimize "diagnostic or categorical" barriers to participation in its programs by tapping multiple funding streams (McGowan 1990). In all these agencies, staff from different programs or divisions meet regularly and work in informal or formal teams around families receiving multiple services. They also try to balance "sharing responsibility" with "professional autonomy" (McGowan 1990:95). One way these agencies interpret comprehensiveness is to grow and develop in a coherent way by paying attention to how their various services relate to each other and by thinking carefully about the role of satellite centers. Efforts to grow focus as much on filling gaps in the continuum of programs within the agency, and responding to emergent problems or populations, as on responding to Requests for Proposals from various funding sources.

*Varieties of System Reform*

Although service reform efforts beginning in the late 1980s and continuing into the 1990s have shared many philosophical premises, they have varied in ambition, emphasis, and strategy. Some efforts have striven primarily to increase access to services, others to promote service integration, others to democratize governance, and still others to recreate whole new service systems within the boundaries of particular local communities, counties, or whole states. There are no mutually exclusive categories into which it is possible to sort reform efforts. I have chosen to discuss three categories that

reflect differences in the way particular reform efforts begin: at a particular
site, with a particular model, or within a particular local community. As will
be seen, even these overlap.

SITE-BASED REFORM.    Site-based system reform bases a broad reform
agenda in a particular local service institution—for example, a school. (This
is not the same as asking a particular type of service institution to take on a
broader mission.) The chosen institution might be used as a convenient
base for launching a reform effort, or it might take the lead in trying to
bring a variety of service agencies together. Initiatives employing this strategy rarely include reform of governance or financing from the outset.
Rather, they set in motion and then try to build on more discrete reforms,
such as redeployment of some modest set of funds or an agreement between
two agencies to coordinate services.

One notable site-based initiative with system reform aspirations is New
Beginnings in San Diego County (Philliber Research Associates 1994; Institute for Educational Leadership 1994). The long-term goal of this initiative is to create an integrated service system in San Diego County and to
restructure and refocus public services so that they are more preventive,
family-centered, and holistic in orientation. The initiative is built on a
school-based family service center in one school (other centers are being
developed). The center is staffed by a family service advocate, a mental
health specialist, a nurse practitioner, and a community development specialist (or community organizer). Center staff provide information and referral, parenting supports, adult education, some counseling, some basic
health services, and case management for selected families. As in the Lower
East Family Union model described in chapter 8, the family service advocate is supposed to bring together all the specialized providers working with
particularly vulnerable families for "multi-agency case consultation." The
school-based service center is supposed to serve families of children enrolled in that particular school first, then other families in the school's attendance area. Families also are assessed and designated to receive varied
levels of service.

Surrounding the direct services of the initial and subsequent centers is
a countywide strategic plan for shifting services toward prevention, for creating cross-agency accountability for child and family outcomes, and for
addressing obstacles to interagency collaboration. A range of mechanisms
has been created to weave services together more closely: an "institute"
whose mission is to promote collaboration and train providers to do it;
memoranda of understanding between agencies; joint training sessions for

providers from different agencies; joint use of facilities; release time for staff to consult with peers from other agencies; collaborative grant writing; and concrete recognition and rewards for staff to work collaboratively. Agreements and mechanisms were supposed to be developed to make it easier for staff from different agencies to share information. One such mechanism was a "consolidated index" of families served by different agencies (reminiscent of that developed by the Charity Organization Societies a century earlier). There also was a long-term goal of developing an integrated data system for the whole county. Finally, two broad principles undergird the whole initiative: reliance on existing resources rather than special or temporary funds and changing the existing system when problems arise, not by-passing it.

The early progress of the New Beginnings initiative revealed many of the dilemmas of employing a new paradigm philosophy in work with vulnerable families. More fundamentally, it revealed the dilemmas inherent in using specific sites or local human service institutions as a base for systemic reforms. Most families sought the center out for a discrete purpose—a child's health problem, academic problems (a desire to have a child tutored), or a referral for after school care. As a result, it was hard to build the long-term relationships with relatively less vulnerable families that would allow staff to catch developing problems early. Relatedly, staff were forced to spend disproportionate time with a small group of families in crisis, which also undermined their mission of prevention. With these families, it was difficult to maintain a strengths perspective. It was sometimes hard to hold on to the belief that parents were doing the best they could, or even enough, to help themselves and their children, when the evidence seemed to contradict this assumption.

The New Beginnings center was intended both to provide direct services and to be a hub of research and development—"to learn what was required [sic]" to provide good services to vulnerable families (Philliber Research Associates 1994:2), and to invent or discover the principles needed for broader system change (Institute for Educational Leadership 1994). The staff was better suited for, and was forced by the urgency and number of family support needs to focus on the first of these tasks. Like the community action agencies of the 1960s, the center itself had little leverage to alter the policies and practices of other providers or to get funding freed up for the New Beginning initiative itself. For instance, the family center staff were not able to get child protective services to share information about children or families served by the center who might have been involved in the child welfare system. In other words, there was little connection between staff energies that were focused on providing good services to a defined population of families and the larger system change focus of the initiative.

During the course of the initiative other reform efforts in San Diego have started up, diverting the energy of some stakeholders and raising the question of which initiatives would fit into which others. (This problem—what someone called the "multiplication of collaboratives"—has become ubiquitous.) Collaborating agencies kept one foot in and one foot out of the New Beginnings initiative. They were especially reluctant to share funds. A 1994 evaluation report noted great progress in creating a collaborative spirit among the participating agencies but little or no progress in achieving concrete service integration goals, such as shared intake, data, or funds (Philliber 1994).

MODEL-BASED REFORM.    This strand of reform efforts builds a more ambitious agenda on the back of a particular type of or approach to service provision. The particular service model chosen is usually perceived as a central building block and philosophical guide for the reformed service system.

In the late 1980s and early 1990s Milwaukee undertook a child welfare reform effort that built on three models—family support, family preservation, and the Patch approach described earlier in this chapter (Hagedorn 1995; Hagedorn directed this initiative.) The idea was to create structures and conditions that would in turn change the core tasks and behavior of public social service workers. In two target neighborhoods public child welfare workers were organized into units of twelve to fifteen "generalists." A geographically tied caseload belonged to the whole unit, and particular caseworkers were responsible for staying with families through the whole case disposition process. The units were "outstationed in buildings located in the neighborhoods they served and housed alongside financial assistance workers" (Hagedorn 1995:130). Staff from other public agencies, such as job training and public health, were also at the site.

Although the whole unit would work together to share decisions and make service plans, there would also be pairing off of frontline providers to provide intensive family preservation services to some families. In the abstract, the units were supposed to have authority to respond in individualized and differentiated ways to different families. An additional element of reform was the hiring of neighborhood coordinators, whose job it was to help create neighborhood councils to which these units would be accountable in some form (Hagedorn 1995:148).

This particular reform, created and spurred by a reform commissioner, foundered on the rocks of resistance from three groups of key stakeholders—long-term administrators, the union representing child welfare workers, and individual frontline workers themselves. Hagedorn (1995:149) writes that "it was hoped that outstationed social workers, freed from the isolated and cynical bureaucratic chatter in a large office building, might be more open to hear pained neighborhood voices." Yet even this modest goal was hardly achieved. Hagedorn (1995:122) offers the example of a family that walked in to a neighborhood outstation housing one of the pilot units, asking for help. Since there had been no child abuse referral, the supervisor refused to help the family, arguing that the unit was already over-burdened with mandatory cases. In discussing frontline workers' responses to the initiative, Hagedorn (1995:136) writes that "while reform had its supporters, most workers believed they were pawns in another useless reorganization that in the end would change nothing. They were basically right." He notes also that the demands of workers' day-to-day routines were stronger than the ill-defined promise of the new approach to child welfare services.

COMMUNITY-BASED SYSTEM REFORM.    A number of service system reform efforts in the 1990s have been community-based or community-oriented. The common premise, as stated by the director of one initiative, is that "local change builds system change" (Brettschneider 1995; although few initiatives spell out exactly how this process is intended to occur). Initiatives almost always begin with creation of some kind of community-level planning process and may also create a local governance mechanism. At the same time they vary in the degree to which the ultimate aim is to completely "deconstruct" the prevailing centralized, categorical service system and reconstruct it as a genuinely bottom-up system, with authority and legitimacy residing within local communities (see Nelson, cited in Bruner and Parachini 1997:5). In concrete terms, current initiatives vary in the extent to which there is an intent to "start from scratch" and fundamentally rethink services in or beyond the geographic area; the extent to which public service dollars flowing to a community (or its residents) are redeployed or freed up for the use of the initiative; the extent to which community residents control either or both the terms of the initiative itself—its goals, strategy, use of funds, hiring, firing, etc.—and the shape and content of whatever reformed service system emerges. Initiative also vary in the extent to which prevailing government obligations, rules, and laws are put in abeyance in the geographic area defined for the initiative.

Most initiatives in this heterogeneous category do not strive to create a fully community-governed and managed service system. Rather, they use local communities primarily as a frame for geographically bounding the focus of a reform effort. An example can be found in Illinois, which as of this writing is in the early stages of a major state reorganization of its social service system, using community-level reform in selected local communities to test both how the pieces of a new system might work together and the feasibility of handing some control over to local communities. The community collaboratives it has created for the initiative, called federations, have mostly a planning mandate; there has been little freeing up or decategorization of public dollars for use in locally directed ways.

Other initiatives in this category do use the concept of community as the foundation and organizer for decentralizing the governance of services (sometimes including the management of categorical funding). Local governance is seen as a response to the increasingly common complaint that "no one is in charge of local community services for children and families. No one governs the totality" (Center for the Study of Social Policy 1991:4). An example of initiatives designed to foster local governance would be Kansas City's Local Investment Commission (LINC), whose aim is to "devolve responsibility for the design and operation of services to neighborhood leaders" and residents and to shift service funding from categorical to noncategorical programs (Orland, Danegger, and Foley 1997:10). This initiative is led by a commission composed of business leaders, community leaders, and residents of poor neighborhoods; one element of its evolving plan has been the "professional development" of these laypersons on topics related to human service management and delivery. (Another example of an initiative intended to promote local governance, Agenda for Children Tomorrow in New York City, is described later, as I turn to a discussion of ties between services and community-building).

As in past decades some community-based initiatives have focused on one particular system, usually child welfare, and others on the child and family services system broadly defined to include child welfare, early childhood services, mental health services, and in some cases schools. Child welfare-related initiatives continue to be motivated by the cost of growing foster care caseloads and a general sense of crisis in child welfare systems. Most have experimented with ways to combine family support services and/or intensive family preservation services with a community focus to shape a redesigned service system.

In the late 1980s Iowa undertook an initiative in two counties (since extended to several more), which combined the use of family support and family preservation services with the decategorization of various child welfare funding streams; the aim of this initiative was to prevent placement and reduce foster care caseloads (Busey 1995). The general idea of the Iowa

Decategorization Initiative was that more flexible funding would free up resources that could be redirected to preventive services and strengthen the ability of IFPS workers to respond to emergencies. Decategorization would increase the flexibility and discretion of frontline providers and spur creativity across all the components of the local service systems, providing incentives for providers to rethink their approaches and work together more closely. The initiative was sold to skeptical state administrators and legislators by combining decategorization with funding caps. The argument was that while decategorization would encourage providers to think, act, and approach their work differently, funding constraints would force them to do so.

As in the Milwuakee initiative, one of the two counties also incorporated the Patch approach into its strategy, focusing on a low-income neighborhood of about 10,000 residents in Cedar Rapids (Zalenski 1996). The Patch team in that county consisted of social workers from child protective services (CPS) and staff from a local settlement, housing, juvenile probation, the homemaker program, and the health department. The CPS workers were outposted to family support centers, where they presumably would be able to monitor vulnerable children and families more closely and informally, identify problems requiring CPS intervention earlier, and work more closely with community-based services providers.

Anecdotal evidence suggested that participation on the Patch team appeared to free up team members to think and act differently, to alter the way they understood and went about their work (Adams and Krauth 1995). They were more willing to tackle tasks falling outside their formal roles; more willing to listen to and give vulnerable families (i.e., those suspected of abuse or neglect) the benefit of the doubt; more inclined to work in the community; and more inclined to reflect on what they were observing in their work. Response time to particular family problems decreased in many cases. At the same time the "Patch" work remained more of an add-on than a defining organizer for services. Team members continued with preexisting responsibilities, procedures, and so forth and reported to management in their own separate agencies. The service system surrounding the Patch teams was much less affected than the Patch team members themselves. The effort also barely moved the county toward the philosophical ideal of shared responsibility for families, among formal and informal institutions within a whole community.

The overall effects of decategorization in the two counties also were reportedly modest (Busey 1995). Some service gaps were filled. Some vulnerable families were reached earlier. Providers paid a little closer attention to what was available to be mobilized for families. But foster care caseloads did not go down. For one thing, the short-term IFPS model once again proved ill-suited for poor, vulnerable young families not in crisis but with long-term, shifting support needs. For another, many "mandatory reporters" of suspected child abuse and neglect were not involved in the initiative and thus continued generating reports to be investigated at the same rate as before. For still another, CPS investigation and decision-making guidelines did not change to reflect the new more holistic approach to assessing and working with families. (That has since changed, and Iowa is experimenting with new approaches to protective services that would lead to a more differentiated set of responses to vulnerable families.) In a different vein, preventing out of home placement seemed too narrow and limited an engine for service reform. Not all or even most of what providers did related to that goal.

At a practical level, it took an enormous amount of ongoing effort—effort that had little to do with the nature and quality of service provision—to make the decategorization of child and family services work. In one county the planning committee met two and a half to four hours every week for the first four years of the project (Busey 1995:8). Subsequent decategorization initiatives in other states have confirmed the labor intensiveness of the task, as well as the importance of allocating resources to "capacity-building"—preparing staff at all levels to work in new ways.

## Linking Services and Service Reform to Community Development

During the 1990s there has been a renewal of the historical urge to make services more community-oriented: to embed them more in community life; to make them more responsive to community priorities; and, most ambitiously, to directly take on one or more aspects of community development, such as housing development and rehabilitation, public safety, economic redevelopment, and/or community organization. This urge has found expression alongside, and sometimes been interwoven with, efforts to implement the new paradigm principles I have already discussed. It overlaps with (and can be difficult to distinguish from) neighborhood-based service system reform, differing primarily in its explicit emphasis on community-building as an objective.

The expression of a renewed community orientation can be viewed on a continuum from modest gestures to the wholehearted assumption of a community-building mission. For instance, at the level of individual agencies it includes relocating service sites, and even agency administrative offices, to poor neighborhoods (as a gesture of commitment and a way of strengthening neighborhood infrastructure); reorienting agency priorities to reflect those of particular communities served; involving community residents as service providers (for philosophical and/or job creation reasons); and connecting with local institutions outside the service system (e.g., with a library to do a book club or an after school program). It involves support for recreating traditional, informal associations, such as block clubs (Sviridoff and Ryan 1997). It includes hiring community organizers; providing technical assistance and space to resident groups or organizations doing community organizing; assuming leadership for strengthening ties among community groups and institutions; and taking direct responsibility for housing rehabilitation or public safety campaigns, or for seeding microenterprises, or for transporting community residents to jobs. Community-building activities are sometimes undertaken alone, more often in partnership with other organizations.

Within broader service reform initiatives, the expression of a community-building philosophy or mission has tended to start with the development of community councils. These councils decide what service priorities ought to be and how to use public service dollars; negotiate with service providers about their future role in the community; and tie service reform to broader community development objectives. (The existence and activity of the councils, and the fact of turning responsibility for services over to the community are viewed as expressions of community-building in and of themselves.) As with discrete services agencies, the community-building approach has included direct involvement in one, a few, or many domains of community life—housing, public safety, civic association, and economic development. (In a few initiatives, service reform is itself viewed as a form of community-building.)

Some have argued that community-building is as much a philosophy or lens that infuses all the work of an agency or initiative as it is a particular set of activities. For instance, a provider who employs a community-building lens in his or her work with individual parents might be more apt to view those parents as potential partners and resources in achieving a particular service goal. He or she might be more apt to ask what the parents can be encouraged to contribute to the agency in return for services provided to a child, thus not only creating a framework of reciprocity but also building civic involvement through volunteering.

*Rationales for Attention to Community-Building*

The disparate expressions of the drive to link services (or service reform) and community-building have been motivated by an equally disparate, and sometimes contradictory set of assumptions and concerns. It is argued that the local communities in which most poor families live are weak, in effect an additional risk factor for families, and therefore in need of attention from service providers. It is also argued, however, that those local communities are an untapped resource for supporting families, too long ignored by service providers. Some hold the growth of services as partly responsible for the deterioration of local communities. Some view the decline in services as an important element of local community deterioration.

Perhaps the overarching rationale for service providers to pay attention to community-building is that one cannot look at, try to understand, or try to help families in isolation from the contexts in which they are embedded. Particularly for poor families, individual and family well-being are tightly, if not inextricably, linked to the well-being of the communities in which they reside. No matter how good a discrete helping service, its influence will be limited if there is no attention to the larger social ecology of peoples' lives—whether as risk factor or resource. (Indeed at some point in their careers, many individual service providers who work with poor families also have experienced a crisis of meaning and meaningfulness about their work, with some concluding that the only way to make an impact is by attending to the broad forces shaping clients' lives. The new community orientation of agencies is in part a collective expression of this individual crisis.)

Attention to the contexts of poor families' lives has been compelled in part by the extraordinary deterioration of those contexts, as I discussed in chapter 8. The 1990s have brought a renewed awareness of the geographic dimensions of poverty, in particular of the increasing concentration of risk factors within poor urban communities and, equally important, the loss of protective factors (Halpern 1995:200). If more and more families in a particular neighborhood are vulnerable, that leaves fewer and fewer families with the resources to support their more vulnerable members. More vulnerability has also meant more crime, as well as more public (and private) violence. These in turn have contributed to a decline in sense of community (i.e., of emotional safety, sense of belonging, and identification), in reliance on community norms to guide childrearing, and in social trust. The loss of investment and trust extends in some cases to community services.

Closely tied to renewed attention to the geographic dimensions of poverty, family vulnerability, and its correlates is attention to the geographic dimensions of service needs, the organization of services, and service expenditures. To cite just two statistics illustrating the former: In New York City the "rate of placement" of children into foster care is 1.45/100 children in the poorest neighborhoods versus .29/100 children in the wealthiest

(Wulczyn 1996:204). In a number of New York City's poorest neighborhoods almost 10 percent of families are reported for child abuse and neglect each year (Agenda for Children Tomorrow 1996:17–23; although many of these are not substantiated, these reporting rates still suggest high levels of family vulnerability). A recognition of concentration effects for both poverty itself and for service needs has led to the idea that since we now know what works in social services, "if we could manage to concentrate and integrate resources and program knowledge in particular communities over a sustained period of time," we could get significant impacts (Kubisch, Weiss, Schorr, and Connell 1995:2).

Looking at the organization of services through a geographic or local community lens raises all kinds of issues. First it focuses attention on what the service system looks like in a particular community, what service infrastructure exists, and how that system works as a whole to respond to vulnerable families in the community. A community lens illuminates what pieces of the service system need to work together and where gaps are. It focuses attention on issues of location and ownership of services. It has been argued, for instance, that locating and "owning" services outside the communities in which their clients reside has made them less responsive to both those clients and their communities. Service managers are less likely to hear from community residents—who after all know their own lives best—about their support needs and priorities. An agency located far from, or rooted outside a client's community might have little sense of community programs and resources potentially helpful to that client. The child welfare system might place a child in foster care so far from where parents live that it is almost impossible for them to visit him or her (Brettschneider 1995). For their part, poor people are thought to have less sense of identification with services whose roots and loyalty lie outside the community. (Conversely, services rooted inside their communities and well-respected by community members appear to some to be ideal vehicles for community-building initiatives. They have credibility among residents. They are often viewed as neutral organizations, not aligned with one or another power base. They have systems for financial management and control in place. Their executives may have experience in managing innovative initiatives.)

It has been argued that services have to be made "more vulnerable to pressure from clients and community organizations" (Hagedorn 1995:149). Service design and reform have been too driven by service providers whose primary interests have been in their continued survival and control over resources. Even when motivated by a genuine desire to improve services, providers have had too narrow a vision of problems. They have placed too much emphasis on knitting together, rebundling, and regrouping a relatively small range of programs and too little on the things of primary concern to neighborhood residents: jobs, transportation, good schools, safety, convenient stores, and so forth (Anderson 1994).

Another, paradoxical argument for a community-building philosophy within services holds that it would help society rethink (i.e., reduce) the role of services in problem-solving. Services are seen as having crowded out, or even repressed informal communal mechanisms for supporting, socializing, and controlling families. One critic asks whether services "might not actually be the cause of the current social disarray rather than its principal solution" (McKnight 1997:123). Another argues that "problems like delinquency, long-term dependency, and family violence cannot be left to the helping professions" (Polsky 1991:221), but should be addressed primarily by "ordinary citizens," the residents of poor communities themselves, with some financial and technical back-stopping. Services—especially those rooted outside the communities they serve—have weakened local communities by causing residents to look outside the community for solutions to their problems.

It has been argued that a community-building lens would lead service providers to look at the effects of their helping approaches differently; for example, it might help them to recognize that they may be weakening rather than enhancing their clients' capacity to solve their own problems. This argument is part of a general attack on "clienthood," which is seen either to exacerbate poor peoples' feelings of dependence, powerlessness, and lack of self-worth or, at best, to teach them to cope better with toxic environments and unjust circumstances. Moreover, clients in most human services have historically been isolated from one another, reducing the likelihood that they would see their situation as "a reflection of social structure" (Lipsky 1980:118)or see each other as sources of support. (In the 1980s family support programs had recognized and acted on this in a modest way, bringing parents together to identify with each other as well as share common concerns.) As a Chicago civil rights organizer put it, "all those people who are passing through social service agencies are potential actors in the community, as opposed to just clients or victims" (Obama 1995).

A community-building lens presumably would also lead service providers to focus much more on identifying and using the social resources, or assets embedded in communities (peoples' talents, energies, and time; social networks and civic associations; and churches and strengths-oriented services, such as family support centers or Head Start programs). Unlike physical or financial resources, which are depleted by use, the more a social resource is used, the stronger it becomes and the stronger the social fabric of the community becomes. (This so-called "asset-based" approach to community-building is very different from traditional community organizing, which tries to mobilize the latent political "resources" of a poor community to demand more assets—services, investment, infrastructure—from those in power.)

There are also two finance-related arguments for making services more community-oriented and rooted. The first holds that the public and private dollars spent on services in poor communities really belongs to the residents of those communities and should be used in their interest, according to their priorities (even if those priorities do not include funding traditional specialized services). They should be used also to create jobs for local residents, who should be hired to provide services. Service dollars should also should go to community-based agencies. For instance, in planning for the Milwaukee child welfare reform described earlier in this chapter, it was found that less than 1 percent of the purchase of service dollars in Milwaukee's public child and family service system "went to agencies located within . . . target areas, where 25 percent of [its] clients lived" (Hagedorn 1995:65). The second, ironically, holds that "there isn't enough money anymore to be providing services on an individual basis to all of the people that need them in the way we have traditionally done. Therefore you have to think about other ways you can improve the circumstances in people's lives" (Kubisch, cited in Herszehorn 1996:39). In other words, creating stronger communities, or participation in community-building activities, is a kind of substitute for adequate services.

*Examples of Community-Building Activity in Different Types of*
*Service Agencies*

Examples of agencies that have adopted a community-building mission or philosophy, or simply engaged in one or more community-building activities can be found in almost every category of supportive services—settlements, family service agencies, family support programs and other early childhood providers, and even youth-serving organizations. Some activities are occurring within agencies, but an increasing number are occurring through partnerships with organizations that have historically focused on community development.

SETTLEMENTS. There are currently over 800 settlements operating in cities throughout the United States. (Many of these are actually neighborhood centers, initiated over the past thirty-five years that have joined the settlement movement; United Neighborhood Houses 1991:4). Settlements in many cities are making efforts to decrease their reliance on categorical funding and reclaim their heritage as important community institutions. They have increased community representation on their boards. They have provided an institutional home—served as fiscal agent, provided space, sometimes staff assistance—for community organizations. A few settlements have embraced community-building as their overall mission or philosophy, with the idea that it could serve as a guiding framework for all their disparate activities. Some settlements are developing partnerships with nonservice institutions, such as community development corporations, to promote community-building ends. For instance, the Kathryn Tyler Neighborhood Center in Cleveland runs the family support and child care services of a local community development corporation.

The resource exchange, in which community residents perform a service for other community residents and get paid in "time-dollars," is an innovation that may have originated with the Grace Hill settlement in St. Louis but has now expanded to other settlements (as well as other community-based agencies). The service provided can be almost anything—"fix a car, watch a baby, move furniture, or stay with an infirm parent" (Husock 1992:53.) The time-dollars generated can in turn be used to purchase services or, more selectively, basic goods such as diapers, food stuffs, soap, etc. A few settlement houses also have started microenterprise programs, as part of their adult or youth programming. (Microenterprises are small businesses that can be operated by one or two people with modest start-up capital, usually providing a service or manufacturing a good that is locally valued—for example, making school uniforms or braiding hair.)

New York City's thirty-five settlements, under the umbrella of United Neighborhood Houses of New York, have undertaken an initiative to improve their responsiveness to children and families and incorporated community-building as an important component of this effort. One member, Forest Hills Community House, reportedly hires all staff with the notion that they will need to be—or to think like—community organizers. Another, Kingsbridge Heights, set out to alter its organizational structure and culture "to support a new set of staff roles and relationships with community participants" (United Neighborhood Houses 1995:15). Still another, the Citizen's Advice Bureau (CAB), demonstrates the importance of taking community-building where you find it (Hirota, Brown, and Mollard 1997). CAB has worked with a building that was about to be removed from the city's cooperative management and ownership housing program, for failure to comply with program rules. That would have meant an increase in rents, as well as loss of control over management. The building was not working as a co-

operative—there was a lot of distrust among tenants and attendance at tenants' association meetings was well below the 65 percent needed to remain in
the program. CAB first had to gain the trust and support of tenants, which
it did by using them to staff its new office in the building; starting some services (a mother-child support program; HIPPY, a home-based preschool
program); and helping address chronic building problems such as unlimited
access to the roof, which attracted drug dealers. The CAB staff also worked
with tenants to help them understand their new responsibilities as owners,
including supervising maintenance workers and collecting rent. When the
city formalized its threat to remove the building from the program, CAB
staff helped tenants develop a strategy for responding to that threat.

FAMILY SERVICE AGENCIES    Some unknown percentage of traditional
casework agencies are also striving to become more community-oriented, if
not to formally embrace community-building. As with settlements, this
takes many forms, depending on opportunity and agency proclivity. Sviridoff
and Ryan (1996:5–8) cite a range of examples, taken from a study undertaken
for Family Service America, a membership organization for some 280 family service agencies. These include a major family service agency in Bridgeport, Connecticut, which has moved its headquarters to one of Bridgeport's
poorest neighborhoods and reconceptualized its home health aid program as
partly a job program for low-income residents of that neighborhood; an
agency in Kansas City that has hooked up with a local housing project to
develop a youth services; and a major casework agency in Minneapolis that
has undertaken an initiative designed to "build peer relationships with
clients, to transform clients into community contributors, to increase accountability to the community."

Another example is provided by the Children's Aid Society of New
York, which has focused a modest portion of its energies and resources on
improving the quality of life and trying to create a strong community in one
particular square block in Harlem with some 500 apartments. The block
was chosen for its proximity to one of the Society's community centers,
some of whose staff have focused their efforts (and experience) on reaching
out to residents of this block and linking them to various resources. Children's Aid also joined with a small, neighborhood nonprofit, which is doing
tenant organizing. This organizing is focused on pressuring landlords to re-
pair and maintain apartments and on helping a sizable group of squatters in
a few buildings gain legal rights to their spaces. In addition, the agency has
developed closer ties (and provided resources) to a homeless shelter across
the street from its community center (Herszehorn 1996:39).

FAMILY SUPPORT PROGRAMS AND AGENCIES. As with settlements and family service agencies, the evidence of the involvement of family support programs and agencies in community-building is largely anecdotal. Family support programs have always hired community residents and brought young parents together for mutual support, both of which are considered expressions of community-building. Some programs provide child care for working families (a critical element of community that is not usually considered a community-building activity). Stokely (1996) cites a number of examples of community-building among family support programs in California: a group of family support agencies in Del Paso Heights worked to foster a range of mutual assistance activities within that community, including community gardens and a volunteer exchange network. In Marin City, a family support initiative, Families First, has developed a working relationship with the local community development corporation. The latter is responsible for hiring the program's paraprofessional home visiting staff from among community residents and also links participating families to job training and jobs, housing, and other resources. At the same time the knowledge about "community conditions that keep families in poverty and distress," gleaned by Families First's home visitors, is being shared with other community agencies and institutions involved in community development, through formal mechanisms developed for that purpose (Stokely 1996:37). In San Francisco, "the Good Samaritan Family Resource Center is partnering with Mission Housing Development Corporation, a nonprofit housing developer operating in the same community, to develop twenty-two units of affordable housing" (Stokely 1996:35). A number of California's family support centers have incorporated welfare to work activities, including hiring employment counselors and job developers and running job clubs and job fairs; and a number are supporting microenterprise and self-employment initiatives, particularly for immigrant populations.

*Linking Neighborhood-Based Service Reform with Community-Building*

The two neighborhood-based system reform initiatives described earlier—Milwaukee's Child Welfare Reform and the Iowa decategorization initiative—did not make community-building an explicit objective. Their goal was the provision of better services and the neighborhood was the canvas for their activities. In an increasing number of neighborhood-based service reform initiatives, community-building is taking a much more prominent place, either as a goal or distinct element or interwoven with service reform in a way that makes it hard to tell the two apart.

AGENDA FOR CHILDREN TOMORROW (ACT). This initiative emerged from a blue-ribbon panel report not all that dissimilar to "A Dream Deferred," the 1971 report that had led to the Lower East Side Family Union (see chapter 6). This new report, "Untangling Family Services," published in 1988, criticized the fragmentation of prevailing services in poor neighborhoods and recommended the "creation of a locally-based planning process to coordinate the efforts of human service and economic development programs in designated neighborhoods" (Agenda for Children Tomorrow 1995).

The ACT Implementation Project derived from this recommendation. The immediate goal of ACT is more accessible, easy to use services: "a family needing child care, income support, counselling and educational assistance should be able to find help at a single location in its own community . . . regardless of which 'door' it entered" (Agenda for Children Tomorrow 1995). The ultimate goal, as stated by Eric Brettschneider, ACT's staff director, is "to foster neighborhood-based integrated services, which are community driven, asset based and prevention oriented" (Brettschneider 1995). Reform is aimed at all service systems, except for education. Reformed services should be part of a larger network of less formal supports and eventually embedded in broader community development strategies. One important by-product of ACT's reform activities would also be new structures for "planning and resource allocation" in each ACT neighborhood (ACT 1997a). The project is housed in the mayor's office and directed by an oversight committee composed of high-level representatives from city agencies, private agencies, community groups, and funders.

The project began in 1990–1991 by developing profiles of New York City's ten most vulnerable neighborhoods, based on low birth weight and infant mortality rates (and possibly child abuse and neglect statistics). Drawing on these profiles, the oversight committee and staff identified and began working with community representatives to form "collaboratives." Five local communities were selected for an initial round of activities, kicked off by the strategic planning retreats of the collaboratives. Led by an ACT-supplied planner, each neighborhood coalition was encouraged (or perhaps directed) to "find 10 policies to change or programs to develop about which the government and non-government collaborators could agree" (Brettschneider 1995). These projects would work toward some tangible successes, which were seen as the building blocks of system change. The priorities developed by the collaboratives varied; the most prominent were quality child care and early childhood services, employment opportunities, entrepreneurial opportunities for youth, and increased access to maternal and child health care (Agenda for Children Tomorrow 1995:6). Two communities, Bushwick and Washington Heights, have since focused on early childhood services, in particular the development of a model to help children make the transition from day care and early childhood programs to school and to train providers on both sides of that transition to help it work smoothly. Washington Heights and Mott Haven have focused on employment creation, through job-training and job placement for community residents and assistance to small, fledgling businesses. Mott Haven and Jamaica have developed plans to mobilize community institutions to address environmental concerns

ACT central staff and collaboratives have been helpful service brokers in a number of instances. For example, a home visiting program for new parents in Washington Heights, Best Beginnings, owes its existence partly to the efforts of the local ACT collaborative to overcome community suspicion of "outsiders" coming in to impose services (in this case the Society for the Prevention of Cruelty to Children and Columbia Presbyterian Hospital; Agenda for Children Tomorrow 1996:26). ACT also has been a successful magnet for other funding sources and initiatives. (This has meant that some activities in the participating neighborhoods are based less on local priorities than on those of ACT's external funders.) In addition to foundation support, ACT has secured funding from the city's Community Development Agency and the Human Resources Administration. The ACT neighborhoods were chosen as target neighborhoods by a state initiative called the Neighborhood-Based Alliance (NBA), an initiative similar in purpose and design to ACT. Under NBA, categorical funds from a number of state agencies are channeled to the state's Department of Social Services, which in turn channels "decategorized" money to a lead agency in each neighborhood selected to participate. Under the guidance of a neighborhood advisory council, that agency then subcontracts with a variety of community agencies to provide specific services (Chaskin and Garg 1994:17). Individual ACT neighborhoods received grants from Americorps, the State Department of Mental Health (for prevention activities), and the federal government (for substance abuse prevention, and delinquency prevention).

ACT appears to be making very slow progress toward its goal of reinvented service systems in (not to mention beyond) the target neighborhoods. Like its sister initiatives, ACT was intended by its leadership to be a spur for system reform: "Driven by the success of the [target] communities, bureaucracies would begin to reform themselves to support local need" (Brettschneider 1995). It is not clear, though, that the modest reforms potentially achieved in these neighborhoods will be able to influence basic policies, practices, and conditions throughout the city's child and family service system. In some respects ACT has been more successful in helping its local communities understand and respond to external policy and funding changes—for instance those following the reorganization of New York City's child welfare system—than in shaping those changes. Nonetheless, during 1997 one event occurred that promises to enlarge ACT's influence on the larger service system. The newly appointed commissioner of New York City's new child welfare agency, the Administration for Children's Services (ACS), asked ACT to assist the agency in "designing a neighborhood-based child welfare system" (ACT 1997b). ACT moved its offices to ACS and has proposed a number of specific reforms, including regular case conferences involving ACS staff and local voluntary providers who have contact with vulnerable families (Agenda for Children Tomorrow 1997b:4–8). Thus far most of the influence has come from ACT's leadership and less from the local communities and their collaboratives, but there are efforts to use data from the collaboratives to guide citywide changes.

ACT also has demonstrated only modest progress in its goal of expanding the work of the collaboratives to include economic development, housing, and related issues. ACT is perceived by observers to be primarily about social service reform, and its move to the Administration for Children's Services will only heighten that perception. Director Eric Brettschneider has noted that "ACT has been timid" about economic development and housing, adopting a strategy of of "using human services as the back door" to get at these issues (Agenda for Children Tomorrow 1997a:16). Still, beyond the inherent value of the collaboratives themselves, each has participated in some way in community development activity. The Washington Heights collaborative has worked jointly with the Neighborhood Based Alliance staff to create a Community Development Credit Union. The Bedford Stuyvesant collaborative is working with other local organizations on land use planning. There has been some work in crime prevention in a couple of the neighborhoods. One can argue that the youth employment efforts of a couple of the collaboratives support community-building. One can argue as well that the neighborhood-level data generated by ACT is an important foundation for community-building.

PARTNERSHIP FOR NEIGHBORHOOD INITIATIVE.    An initiative that has thoroughly mixed community-building and service reform together is the Partnership for Neighborhood Initiative (PNI), in Palm Beach County, Florida. The partnership involves just about all the public human service agencies that operate in Palm Beach County (notably the State Department of Health and Rehabilitative Services and the county health department); the MaCarthur Foundation; the local United Way and the local community foundation; and the Children's Services Council, which oversees monies generated by a special county tax targeted for child and family services. The principal goal of PNI is "to develop healthier, more competent communities in Palm Beach County by reshaping the delivery of health, human, and training services at the neighborhood level and by developing neighborhood-based leadership and involvement (Hamilton:1, undated). The initiative has been guided by the belief that service providers were too powerful and unaccountable; services were too splintered; and that there was too much emphasis on "specialized" (treatment) services and not enough on "primary" (preventive, developmental) services.

The strategy for bringing about system reform through PNI is both bottom-up and top-down, with the two processes theoretically combining to create a coherent vision and plan. Low-income neighborhoods (or groups representing such neighborhoods), of no less than 500 residents and no more than 5,000 residents, were invited to apply to the partnership. Those neighborhoods selected—three so far—were provided a community organizer hired by the initiative, who hooked up with or if necessary developed a core leadership group, which in turn pulled neighborhood residents into a strategic planning process—identifying key local issues, setting priorities, developing a plan for addressing priorities. Although the boundaries of the planning process were unclear, the resulting plan ideally was to reflect a reorientation of child and family services, placing greater emphasis on primary services (and therefore less on specialized ones) and describing how primary and specialized services would function together as a coherent whole. The bottom-up service reform planning process was seen also as serving two additional purposes. It would be a vehicle for community empowerment that included leadership-building, greater resident participation in community affairs, and a better organized community. And the perspectives of the local neighborhoods on services problems and needs would provide data that the large systems could use to rethink services countywide.

The quid pro quo for the participating neighborhoods was a commitment from the various public agencies and service funding sources to reorient their services/resources to reflect neighborhood priorities and goals. In addition to incorporating the perspective of the local communities, the partnership agencies were responsible for tackling the administrative, organizational, and funding issues inherent in a reformed service system. Although still in process, the funders and participants in PNI have already faced and begun to grapple with a number of issues springing from the initiative's assumptions. While a local community (leaders and residents) may indeed serve as a kind of conscience for service providers, reminding them of the importance of preventively oriented services, it is not equipped to envision and design, let alone nurture a reformed service system. The locally focused problem analyses and plans of five small sites do not add up to a vision, let alone a plan for a reformed service system. Locally defined problems and plans in the three PNI sites have had only a tangential relationship to child and family services. For instance, one neighborhood identified drug activity and prostitution as its key problems and identified the improvement of land use and physical infrastructure (i.e., water, sewage, and roads) as local priorities. Another defined public transportation for seniors and school busing as key problems. The third was concerned about job creation (Chapin Hall 1997:14, 21, 25). Within the child and family service domain, community priorities in the three sites reflected a not surprising interest in the basics—more and better child care, after school programs and youth services, decent health care, job training and placement opportunities, some family support services.

While the leadership of different public service systems or institutions have bought in to the aims of the initiative, through participation on the steering committee, they appear to have held back on a both a significant commitment to reform of their own services within the county and a commitment of funds to PNI. This may be due in part to larger developments in state services, including welfare reform, funding cutbacks, the move to managed care in child welfare and health care (which tends to reduce flexible funds for prevention services), and the impending break-up of the Department of Health and Rehabilitative Services. Moreover, one steering committee member told this author that no mechanism was created to nurture the commitment of lower-level service staff to the initiative.

Perhaps for all these reasons, during the first few years of the initiative the views of the major partners about its purpose have shifted. Already in mid-1995 the evaluator noted that "the steering committee [consisting of the major partners] now view PNI as an initiative designed to promote community development with some role for health, human and training services. . . . Most of the committee also recognize that this view represents an evolution from the early central role of health, human and training services" (Richman and Ogletree 1995:12). To the extent that system reform emerges in the county in coming years, it will probably be shaped more by external pressures and the vision of those at the top of the partnership than by the community-building activities of PNI. The initiative is still evolving.

But its early history raises questions about the mixing of service reform and community-building agendas.

## Current Reform Trends: Promise and Limitations

Kahn (1964) long ago pointed out with respect to the child and family services that "lacking true working systems, ideological slogans dominate." The concepts shaping service reform in the 1990s—the new paradigm principles, tying services to community life and organizing them at the community level—may be more than ideological slogans. They provide a diffuse vision of good services and an ideal service system. They have contributed to a slight shift in funding, toward early childhood programs and preventive services generally, as well as toward agencies with a base in poor communities. They have introduced new ways of thinking about the role of services—for instance, the notion that services "represent no more than a single strand in the complex web of relationships" and institutions that provide social support and social control in communities (Hadley, Cooper, Dale, and Stacy 1987:96). They have helped breach the walls in public policy that artificially separate different aspects of peoples' lives—for instance, housing quality, neighborhood safety, and parents' ability to care for their children.

These new concepts are beginning to influence state social service policy, although they have not yet provided the leverage to alter prevailing practices in child and family services. Moreover, they do not address adequately the problem of building appropriate service strategies and agency structures to support frontline practice for the most vulnerable families. And they do not provide a clear sense of what we want to accomplish with services for poor and vulnerable families. As I have noted earlier, they hardly acknowledge that it might be necessary to provide skilled, patient, interpersonal help to some families on a long-term basis. In this regard, a sharper analytic lens must be applied to both family support and family preservation if they are to stand as core models for refashioned services. While each model provides a few elements of the skilled, stable, and long-term, relatively intensive yet flexible help needed by vulnerable families, neither provides all those elements—family support not being skilled enough, family preservation not long-term enough. Neither model is well-suited theoretically or practically to address deeply rooted parental vulnerabilities.

The individual new paradigm principles could benefit from a more analytic lens also. For instance, a strengths orientation is indeed a helpful counterweight to one that focuses just on vulnerabilities. Among other things, it forces the provider to examine resources in clients' lives not usually considered in formal assessments; for instance, coping patterns rooted in particular cultural traditions. But misused, as it seems at times to be, it can be as damaging as the contrasting orientation it is supposed to replace. Telling people that "you know you can do it," "you're smart—you can do whatever you want"; providing "a steady stream of praise" (Weissbourd 1996:152) can be condescending or worse. Being family-centered has helped providers understand and then learn to work with families as systems. But the concept can easily be— and often is—misinterpreted as implying that children's and parents' needs are identical, whereas it should mean something more subtle. It should mean recognizing that it is almost impossible to address and meet children's needs without attending to those of their parents, and that while children and parents have distinct needs, they are to some degree intertwined in the family system.

Viewing families as partners can also be a confusing and potentially misleading concept. Certainly one goal of good helping is to forge an alliance with clients in the service of a set of mutually determined objectives. Partnership implies openness and mutuality, and at times—but not always—honesty about one's own uncertainty as a helper. Yet beyond these attributes, helping relationships are defined by different roles and different kinds of power. Democracy is more useful as a political principle than a therapeutic one. Moreover, individual helpers have their own styles, patterns of strengths, and limitations. The explicit or implicit imperatives of some of the new paradigm principles do not always fit those—a reality that should be respected. For example, not all—or even most—caseworkers are suited to such tasks as "helping [sic] families engage in collective action" (Sviridoff and Ryan 1996:v). Those promoting the new paradigm principles must attend to the possibility that they may be increasing pressures on already overwhelmed frontline providers.

As has ever been the case with service reform, frontline workers, most knowledgeable about (if not always able to articulate) the conditions of practice and the support needs of families, remain little consulted about reforms that will profoundly affect their work. (This is illustrated clearly in the Milwaukee child welfare reform initiative.) Moreover, little attention has been paid in reform initiatives to the fears of frontline workers: the loss of a role for their expertise and experience, and sometimes the loss of their positions; the need to establish a whole new set of relationships; the fear that someone or some group is sitting in an office or community center somewhere and deciding their fate without consulting them. One study of a small group of New York City settlements that shifted their mission toward community-building noted such frontline staff fears as an increased amount of work, the loss of their role and identity, involvement in unresolvable community problems, and the loss of definition and structure in their work with clients (Hirota, Brown and Martin 1996:21). In one of the settlements, Kingsbridge Heights, frontline staff pointed out the irony in the nondemocratic, top-down imposition of the new mandate to shift to a community-building approach that emphasized participatory democracy.

At a broader level, the major ideas and impulses driving service reform in the 1990s are sometimes not consistent. The more or less centralized planning and control required for service coordination and integration clash with the decentralization implied by community-rooted services. Concepts (and values) such as collaboration, service integration, and decategorization are not unmixed blessings. Collaboration has proven exhausting and time-consuming, and as often as not has added little to the quality of frontline services to families (Patton 1993). Not all complexity is needless. It helps professionals and families find a niche; in addition, when one program or agency is deteriorating, another might be growing. Nor is all fragmentation needless. Take the seemingly inefficient and frustrating practice of each program having its own intake. Common intake presumably would devolve to first-line, community-based agencies, as well as to emergency programs such as shelters. If such agencies had to collect all the information needed to determine eligibility for public assistance and other government programs, it would drain already overwhelmed staff resources (O'Looney 1996:189).

No one would defend the all-or-nothing approach to eligibility in categorical programs; it does, however, meet certain needs—helping define purposes and services and helping predict and control caseloads—that would still be relevant under conditions of greater flexibility in eligibility. Noncategorical services would still need to define, and therefore predict and control caseload size, which in turn shapes funding and staffing demands. In his evaluation of an innovative network of family support programs in Minneapolis, Patton (1993:47) notes that they were "constantly pushing up against and having to figure out where to set boundaries: Who's eligible? What services are allowable for a particular family? When is a participant 'out' of the program?"

There is a tendency within current reforms to simply tear down or replace traditional ideas or services. That may be a natural instinct, but it is surely the wrong one. Rather, as Bane (undated:17) notes, "we should think of comprehensiveness and flexibility in terms of pushing out the boundaries of traditional [well defined] services, rather than of replacing them with new, all purpose programs."

## Tying Services to Community-Building

Some skeptics argue that the recent efforts to tie services and service reform to community-building reflect just one more instance of service providers outwitting their critics by adapting to the fad of the moment (see e.g., Polsky 1991). One report notes that service providers, facing "shrinking budgets and diminishing public esteem," are "anxious to make more relevant a chaotic patchwork of programs" (Anderson 1994). My view, however, is that whatever disengenuousness there is in current reform efforts lies elsewhere. The motives and behavior of service providers, like anyone else's, have always been a mixture of idealism, altruism, and self-interest. Many agency heads and staff have persisted in participating in specific community initiatives in spite of extraordinary demands on their professional and personal time, little in the way of financial returns, and the lack of respectful treatment. As one conference discussant noted, family service agency administrators "don't know where to go to work with the community; every time they turn to one community representative, they get slapped by another" (Family Impact Seminar 1996:3).

If there is disengenuousness in the current situation it lies elsewhere: first in propounding the idea that we are going to do more community-building initiatives because we do not have the resources to provide individual services to all who need them; and then in not funding those community-building initiatives adequately. (A related piece of disengenuousness is in asking local communities that have been neglected, excluded, and disinvested in for generations to take responsibility for their own revitalization, with some relatively modest outside resources thrown in; see Halpern 1995.) Instead of funding, one finds an emphasis on process. One evaluator noted that reform initiatives that emphasize community-building are "not about solving any particular problems like child care or drugs or whatever, but about generalized problem-solving capability" (Stone 1995:15). The logic involved begins to resemble a kind of shell game. As the executive director of New York City's Federation of Protestant Welfare Agencies noted, "There is no way these communities can be serviced without money. Everybody knows, if we want to be honest and the truth be told, if you want to address these problems you have to have money" (McLaughlin, cited in Herszehorn 1996:39).

It should be noted as well that where there are some resources for innovation and reform, they can often be fruitfully used for purposes more
closely tied to the main work of services. Most settlements and family service agencies these days lack the resources to interrelate their existing programs, follow-up with children and families who have complicated problems, start a desperately needed new service, or develop linkages to other
agencies. They should not in addition be forced to worry about what available new money tells them to worry about.

Putting aside the financial issues in current efforts to tie services to community-building, the strategy is proving to have inherent strengths and limitations. Well-established and respected service agencies are often a strong
base from which to initiate a community-building effort, especially if they
also have strong management. (At the same time even strong agencies are
often stretched to the limit these days, and one more major task can knock
them off balance.) Some assumptions and purposes within the community-building movement make sense. There is much inherent value in compelling service designers and providers to pay attention to what families
have to say about their lives; in sensitizing service providers to the informal
resources and local institutions to which vulnerable families might be
linked; in finding ways to strengthen ties among community members; and
in turning the attention of important community institutions (that might
be otherwise preoccupied) to child and family well-being.

Other purposes are more questionable. For instance, an emerging les-
son—seen most clearly in the case of the Partnership for Neighborhood Initiative—is that while reforming child and family services and doing community development are complementary, even overlapping tasks, they are
not to be confused with each other. Community residents can help providers
be more sensitive to when, where, and how they provide services. There is a
tension between the sense that we know what best practice is and what good
services ought to look like, and the belief that we will learn what a reformed
service system should be and do through listening to the voices of community residents in poor neighborhoods. Even when the goal is promotion of
self-help and mutual assistance, these do not magically take form based on
good intentions. As the leaders of one initiative noted, "self help and mutual assistance programs are not likely to develop spontaneously, especially if
there are high levels of despair and alienation in the neighborhood. These
activities must be initiated, organized and nurtured by skillful people, working together with neighborhood residents (Del Paso heights Model 1992).

One senses that current initiatives have done little more than glance
backward at historical experience before charging ahead. For instance, the

community action experience of the 1960s taught (among other things) that promoting participatory democracy and reforming services were in many respects apples and oranges. The same seems to be the case for communi-ty-building and reforming services. Like participation, community-build-ing offers the potential to make reform more sensitive and responsive to the concerns of service "consumers." The residents of poor communities know their own realities the best. They often have a good idea of what can and cannot be done, what will and will not work in a particular neighborhood context. But they are often ill-equipped to offer ideas and strategies for ad-dressing problems in the organization and financing of services. (Relatedly, there is accumulating evidence that it is not so much the participation of a small number of community members on a governance entity that strengthens a community and nurtures individual development as wide-spread, "lower level" participation in various local institutions; an argument made by Sviridoff and Ryan 1996.)

The argument that services and broader problem-solving efforts have to grow out of the uniqueness of local communities is belied to some extent by the extraordinary similarity among current community initiatives. Why do they look so alike and develop so similarly? Why, after going through a strategic planning process, do the governing collaboratives of initiatives continually rediscover that what community residents want are more and better quality services: these typically include day care and early childhood education, youth services (including after school programs, tutoring, and mentoring programs), assistance finding jobs, family support programs as well as counselling, substance abuse treatment, and other specialized ser-vices. It is hard to see what would make the list different. Strategic planning probably has other rationales and benefits; if this is so, residents of poor communities should be informed of those before they devote endless hours to meetings.

There also are limitations to the strategy of focusing efforts on recon-ceptualizing and reorganizing at the community level. Many of the most important influences on both services and local communities reside at a higher level—administratively and politically. While it is true that one can "see" the match or mismatch between systemic features and families' sup-port needs and priorities at the community level, it does not follow that that is the best level to at which to reorganize. For one thing, while many of the problems with prevailing services are visible at the neighborhood level, they are not for the most part rooted there. Relatedly, local government, which has a great deal of influence over reform, is typically weak or absent at that level, as is leadership in discrete public service systems. Reform efforts limited to the boundaries of a neighborhood, or series of neighborhoods, or even a county, inevitably run up against the lack of change in the larger systems in which local services are embedded. For instance, almost no community-based reform efforts have been able to get commitments from major categorical programs for funding reforms that would free up significant resources, let alone gain authority for control of such funds.

A problem that is loosely related to the problem of the level of focus is that in current community-based service reform initiatives there has been a lack of clarity about who is responsible for service outcomes under the reformed local system. For many of the reasons already discussed, the idea of making local communities responsible for child and family well-being is as problematic as it is superficially attractive. It only makes sense if a host of conditions are met: e.g, community is defined much more clearly; poor communities are afforded far more resources and control of resources than they currently have access to; political decision-making becomes more decentralized; and the like. (The same communities cannot be both fonts of untapped assets and places in which the accumulation of risk factors and vulnerability has overwhelmed those community institutions that have historically provided social support and social control to families.)

Finally, a fundamental tension in the current generation of efforts to tie services to community is their ambivalence about the value of services as an element of community and as a positive support for families. There seems to be a prevalent sentiment that services are an important cause of community deterioration and that communities are weak because "service-producing institutions" are so strong (McKnight 1995:ix). Yet, if anything, one contributing factor to the deterioration of many inner-city communities has been a decline in the quantity and/or quality of supportive services. (Put differently, services are as susceptible as the families they serve to community conditions.) The critics of services who have stressed their dependency-inducing quality have mistaken the temporary and bounded psychological dependency that is part and parcel of helping relationships for a more deeply rooted feeling of inefficacy, which has little or nothing to do with a discrete helping experience. (A more extreme version of this latter criticism holds that helping professionals needlessly create dependency solely to make sure that they will continue to have jobs; see McKnight 1995:98. This argument is so insulting to the thousands of underpaid, overworked front-line helping professionals, struggling to do what they can for vulnerable families that it hardly merits a response.)

There are many good reasons for services to attend to the ecology of life in their communities. But to be healthy resources for families in highly stressed communities, services also need ties outside those communities. They need a certain amount of separateness. A de facto local service monopoly that "could in some instances be of poor quality" is not necessarily the best helping situation for vulnerable families; such families may need "escape channels"—options outside the local community (McGowan 1990:218). In a parallel vein, frontline providers and their supervisors get some of the psychological nourishment they need to continue difficult work in part through their sense of identification with other "communities" than those in which they work every day; notably that of professional colleagues. The issue in all of this is balance, the need to develop a middle ground. Yet that has proven the most difficult task of all in American service—and broader social welfare—reform efforts. Historical and current arrangements have many problems, but they are not all bad. We do not have to repudiate them in order to be able to move ahead.

# CHAPTER TEN

## *Where to from Here?*

*If the nation had deliberately designed a system that would frustrate the professionals who staff it, anger the public who finance it, and abandon the children who depend on it, it could not have done a better job than the present child welfare system.*

—National Commission on Children

*I was looking for someone to talk to so I wouldn't hurt myself or my child.*

—a young mother in New York City

*I don't remember a moment that's been worse.*

—a settlement house director

We have now had more than a century of experience with supportive social services for poor families. This experience has been marked by much good and some harm, but most of all by a chronic sense that arrangements for providing help were inadequate and needed reform. There have been many reasons for the persistent desire to reform services—changing social conditions, new knowledge and ideas, the identification of new social problems, and the redefinition of old ones. Underlying these have been longstanding concerns over efficiency and effectiveness, the need for more preventive services, and better coordination among providers. Reform efforts have yielded many helpful new approaches and programs. Nonetheless, such efforts have not brought us closer to a service system that is coherent in purpose and design, and responsive to families, especially poor families.

This is not an indictment of services. For one thing, I believe that the responsibility of analysts, like that of politicians, administrators, and the public, is to support the work of those at the front line, not make it even more difficult. For another, I disagree with those, such as McKnight (1996) and Polsky (1991), who view services as fundamentally destructive. There is no question that services and service providers have at times misread poor families' lives and behavior. Service providers have at times been too intrusive, at times unavailable when most needed. They have needlessly withheld access to public or private supports and needlessly broken families up in the name of child protection. They have contributed to a kind of inequality for poor families not often noted: that of being unilaterally subject to the judgment of others, of not having the power to judge in return (Ignatieff 1985:45).

Yet services and service providers have also provided substantial, largely unmeasured volumes of emotional support, guidance, and practical assistance to poor families over the past century. They have helped their clients come to know and understand themselves better, to cope with problems more effectively. They have modestly softened the effects of financial hardship and insecurity. They have helped poor families gain access to the kinds of family support and problem-solving resources that more economically advantaged families simply purchase when needed (Epstein 1993). No one can say whether these benefits outweigh what harm services have done. I suspect they have.

Services first emerged and continue to be relevant in part because they meet real support needs and address real problems not being met or addressed by other social institutions. Unquestionably, there is much more formal care and helping, and much less informal care and helping than there was a century or a half century ago. Yet, as I have argued earlier, services have been much more a correlate than a cause of the decline in informal supports. It has been argued that formal helping is more contingent than the informal kind and therefore presumably more subject to abuse or withdrawal at the whim of those doing the helping (Hardin 1990). But no one knows whether families or churches or ethnic associations stuck by their vulnerable members any more than have service providers.

We have now, as at other moments in the past, a number of promising ideas and elements to work with. We have plenty of best practice principles and interesting program and agency models. We know that the heart of services is caring relationships, not rules and procedures. We know that we must seek ways to provide help that do not undermine peoples' sense of dignity. We are beginning to appreciate the need to help in ways that are empathic but do not insist on or assume a common interest between service providers and recipients. We are learning to design services that give at least a modest measure of voice and actual control to poor families served.

Systems-thinking (especially with respect to families) and community-mindedness are beginning to have an impact on the way services are organized, managed, and provided. Policy makers and funders are worrying more deliberately and systematically about how their discrete efforts relate to others (although they are not yet acting on that worry). Service providers are becoming more sensitive to the larger set of relationships and institutions in the lives of their clients and becoming more likely to consider and work with families in the context of the demands and resources in their communities. As a staff member at the Center for Family Life told Hess, McGowan, and Meyer (1995:9), "when I see a family beginning to deteriorate, falling apart, I can almost visualize pulling in nets or supports to keep them going." There seems also to be a recognition that, as Ignatieff (1985) notes, the formal social welfare mechanisms used in modern societies to meet the needs of vulnerable families cannot satisfy more subtle human needs—for choice; a sense of belonging, of social membership; a sense of dignity. Yet the question remains: Why, after nearly a century of effort, has the United States made only modest progress toward a good enough, let alone a good service system for poor and vulnerable families? Why has the experience of providing and receiving help so often been a difficult one? Why, as Lipsky (1980:40, quoting Margaret Landau) observed almost two decades ago are "most goals in social services . . . more like receding horizons than fixed targets"?

I have argued in this book that there are many explanations for the modest progress and the continuing struggles within services for poor families. One is rooted in the attitudes and preoccupations of helpers themselves. Like other Americans, service providers have too often used their own fears and wishes, rather than the complicated realities of poor families' lives as the template for policy and practice. A second explanation, tempering the first, is found in the inherent uncertainties and dilemmas of formal helping under conditions of poverty. Providers may have been self-concerned, but they have also genuinely struggled—in every era—with the question of how to interpret and address the chasm between their own lives and experiences and those of families they serve. They have struggled with how to view families, what questions to ask, what to focus on, how to construct a serviceable narrative of poor families' lives. They have struggled with issues of control over problem definition, with issues of power and authority. They have tried to walk a fine line between attending to the aims of society and responding to the priorities of families served, while maintaining some control over the definition and form of their work. Providers have struggled to solve insoluble problems and struggled with the discrepancy between what they had to offer and what they believed families really needed.

Another explanation for modest progress can be found in the resistance of the large service bureaucracies that took shape in the 1950s to the pressures for reform that began in the 1960s and continued intermittently in the ensuing decades. The service bureaucracies have tended to respond to external pressure by closing up rather than opening up. They have absorbed periodic federal efforts to reorganize services; been unmindful toward scores of foundation initiatives designed to demonstrate alternative approaches to supporting and helping families; and been unresponsive toward public and media criticism, except to exert greater control on their frontline providers. Resistance has been made more possible by the sometimes decontextualized, often ambivalent, invariably ahistorical approaches taken to reform. Reforms have often been launched with little attention to the likely political, organizational, and social forces with which they would have to contend. Reform proponents have made little effort to study and learn from similar efforts in previous eras.

One purpose of the book in fact has been to illustrate the enduring, and constraining, influence of early frameworks and choices about goals, methods, and ways of organizing services. My purpose has not been to raise "what if" questions—what if community-based approaches had prevailed over the quest to become scientific; what if more effort had been made to understand the lives and perspectives of immigrants, or to develop helping approaches that could work constructively with uncertainty. Rather, it has been in part to emphasize that early frames and choices, no matter how naturally rooted in and flowing from their time in history, have had consequences. Perhaps more important, this book will serve as a reminder that the dysfunctional arrangements and dilemmas with which service reformers have wrestled in recent decades have deep roots.

Indeed, some of those roots—and, it can be argued some of the most fundamental reasons for the continuing struggle within services for poor families—originate outside the service system. The evolution of social services has been bound up with Americans' struggle to find a way of thinking about and addressing poverty-related social problems. Are they best understood as problems of adjustment or of exclusion; of cultural mores or blocked opportunity? More broadly, services have been buffeted by Americans' contending visions of society. We will not let go of competing values that stand in each others' way: liberty and fraternity, individual and collective responsibility. Grubb and Lazerson (1980:44, 271) argue that "because the expansion of public responsibility has always been accompanied by an ideological commitment to private responsibility for familial and economic decisions," expressions of the former have often had a peculiar, ambivalent cast. Or as Schorr (1986:11) describes it, "our search for community is overlaid on the pursuit of happiness; under stress it is subject to being shed." At different times, services have been asked to act on starkly contrasting analyses of social problems, and visions of society. At times they have been asked to take a kind of in-between position, reconciling irreconcilable mandates, splitting the difference, filling the vacuum created by ideological extremes. In both cases, services have been an inviting target for criticism from those holding opposing ideological views.

Doubts about services for poor families have accompanied every notable development in their history. Since the late 1960s these doubts have escalated, and those who serve the poor have had to struggle with the question of why they should do work that was not valued or respected by society. At the century's end American society has still not articulated why services are needed, what kind are needed, and what should be expected of them. Should services be more narrowly and residually conceived, or more should they be conceived more broadly as important developmental supports to families? Should they be woven more into the social fabric of community life? Who should define the purposes and emphases of services, and what process should be created to do so?

At the same time that some argue for the ineffectiveness, even the harm of services, others argue that we need a critical mass and continuum of services in distressed neighborhoods. Arguments are made that poor people receive second-class services and simultaneously that perhaps community members could provide services better than those with preparation and experience. One observer argues that we have been unduly pessimistic about the potential of services (Schorr 1988). Another argues that we have been unduly optimistic and accuses service providers of sustaining the "the myth of social efficiency . . . that scientific social cures are possible, are cheap, and are consistent with prevailing social arrangements" (Epstein 1993:189). He suggests that service providers know—at some level—that services cannot solve poverty-related social problems, but are keeping quiet about it, "in return for continuation of their modest funding" (Epstein 1993:8).

More advantaged Americans simultaneously expect too much and too little of services for poor families. Providers know from long experience that individual or family change is extraordinarily difficult to bring about; that when it does occur it is gradual, fragile, reversible. They know that in the flux of families' histories, circumstances, and experiences, services play a modest role yet they have failed to communicate this experience. As a result, policy makers, funders, and the public at large still expect services to have significant effects—because no other expectation has been defined.

### An Extremely Modest Vision

I find that I am not one for prescriptions. As Katz (1995:7) notes, "no set of recommendations flows directly from any historical analysis. Understanding the origins and dimensions of a social issue can lead in very different policy directions." That said, I believe a first step toward a viable future is to articulate a set of touchstones for thinking about services, to guide both general debate and specific reform efforts. Policy makers and reformers must respect and attend to the interests of different stakeholders in the service process. They must balance attention to innovation with attention to doing existing things well. They must acknowledge and work constructively with complexity, as well as with differences in ideology and interests. In our societal debates about services we must refrain from splitting—good people from bad, right ideas from wrong. In order to get reform strategies right we have to examine honestly and understand adequately both what services have accomplished and why they have struggled. Not least, we have to work from the premise that there are no shortcuts to strengthening supportive services for poor families.

Those who manage and provide services have to acknowledge that there are moral dilemmas in formal helping, especially under conditions of poverty and social exclusion. To what extent, for instance, should those who help do so within the framework of a particular set of moral preferences? If so, whose preferences should those be? Peoples' morality is bound up in and flows from their personal histories as much or more than from societal mores. Helping relationships are defined in part by societal demands on both helpers and helped, in part by the preoccupations and daily realities of families served, and in part by helpers' own decisions about what is most relevant. Helpers do best when they have the opportunity to balance demands: to help poor families in their self-determined efforts to manage and balance the many functions of family life and to support them in their efforts to grow and develop in both self-directed and socially valued ways.

When larger frameworks and systems are incoherent, as they have been and remain, efforts to hold things together, let alone improve them, seem to fall disproportionately on the backs of smaller components of those systems; in the case of supportive services, on individual agencies and frontline providers. These days, both seem to feel too much on their own: responsible but without the unambiguous support and resources to carry out their responsibilities. As a presenter at a recent child welfare conference put it: "Our work is demanding and draining; persons we serve are in difficult and sensitive situations. Each year we are asked to do more with less. Every day seems to present a new set of obstacles: more paperwork, re-organizations, cutbacks and multiple priorities."

Therefore a central preoccupation of service systems surely should be frontline providers who feel secure in the purpose and amount of their work and in the boundaries of their responsibilities. Providing responsive, consistent, individualized care is physically and emotionally exhausting under the best of circumstances. Providers at least have to feel that their jobs will not change or disappear suddenly at the whim of a political appointee who has latched on to the idea of the moment. They have to feel secure in order to acknowledge uncertainties and "practice worries." That means, in part, that we have to stop blaming and tearing down frontline providers, attacking their beliefs and assumptions as well as their actions. The basic internal task of each succeeding level of the service system should be to support the one below it, to make it possible to strive to do good work.

Policy makers should not—as they seem to be doing with managed care—repudiate programs and agencies as building blocks of good local service systems. Agencies that serve families need to be invested in and nurtured, so they in turn can invest in and nurture staff, who in turn can effectively look after the families they serve. (Musick and Stott 1990:664, describe this as a "chain of enablement.") Moreover, if policy makers are going to be periodically, or constantly putting new demands on organizations, they have to be strong organizations to start with.

Substantively, it is critical to develop more subtle, differentiated policy in the child welfare and welfare to work domains. It is critical to refrain from viewing vulnerable families as all good or all bad. There is a difference between a parent who has little confidence he or she is doing a good job and one so overwhelmed, angry, and preoccupied that his or her children are in real danger. I question whether the latter can and ought to be a "partner" to the helping professional, let alone "help" with the work a service agency is doing in a particular neighborhood. We have to refrain from assuming that all young parents should be required to work (just as we should refrain from excusing all young parents from work). Some young parents are best suited to be urged and supported to work; others to care for their young children now and work later. For some families, requiring parents to work is the best pathway to improving children's well-being; for others not so.

Frontline providers in child and family services need the preparation and flexibility to approach work with different families in distinct ways, using a range of clinical tools. New policy developments have to be sensitive to the fact that a growing proportion of young adults in poor communities are embarking on parenthood and family life with personal histories marked by adversity in many spheres (including disruptions in caregiving, inadequate nurturance, parental substance abuse, family violence). Such histories create profound obstacles to most developmental tasks, including parenting, forming healthy and stable family relationships, and, more selectively, doing well at work (see Halpern 1997).

Families certainly should not be defined by their vulnerabilities and problems—it is difficult to know what a particular vulnerability means to an individual or to predict who will function adaptively in the face of it. Yet the social service community should not abandon long-term helping efforts and therapeutic work for especially vulnerable families, as seems to be occurring in redefining services as little more than case management. (The other critical components of care for such families include respite care (therapeutic, as well as regular developmental), day care for young children, and crisis/emergency services.)

There has been a crucial theoretical element missing from intervention approaches for multiply vulnerable families in recent years. As valuable as they are, family systems and crisis intervention theories are like two legs of a three-legged stool. There is a small but coherent body of work that remains largely unknown to the community-based social service and child welfare communities, but that offers substantial promise as the third theoretical leg for future helping efforts for multiply vulnerable young families. I described this work, called variously a clinical infant or infant mental health approach, in chapter 7. It combines child development theory, psychodynamic theory, and elements of family systems and crisis intervention approaches (see e.g., Fraiberg, Shapiro, and Cherniss 1983; Provence and Naylor 1983). It is built on a sensitivity to the way in which parents' pasts— "ghosts in the nursery"—intrude on the present, while viewing the present (including the depradations and hardships associated with poverty) as real and important. When embodied in programs, its elements include direct developmental services for both parents and young children, as well as long-term (often three years or more), therapeutic relationships, built on a foundation of responsiveness to concrete support needs, crisis intervention when necessary, and attention to the parents' own developmental needs. The therapeutic work balances attention to present, real difficulties in the parent-child relationship and family relationships; the roots of those difficulties in parents' earlier histories; and parents' and young children's distinct needs, without putting these elements in opposition to each other.

Given the imperative of a much fuller response to very vulnerable families, I would still argue against the residual vision of services, since they, like any other institution, cannot possibly function well as a last resort. I would argue for somewhat greater investment in services that support and nurture families that are coping, recognizing that such investment is inherently inefficient and that its benefits are likely to be diffuse. In addition to their modest, but crucial benefits to individual families, such normal or normalizing services provide important infrastructure in distressed local communities.

The ideological and financial pressures on and within services make it that much more critical to articulate appropriately modest expectations. Their effects should be conceptualized and measured in the most modest of units. Decisions to invest in services should be made on a realistic basis, since overpromising bears costs that undermine their foundations. Hardin (1990:538) argues, in my view sensibly, for a limited view of services: "What one can do as a professional is to provide care within reasonable limits. Some of these are limits of personal energy, ability, and time. But some of the limits are social constraints." Or as Adams and Nelson (1995:8) note, "the beginning of wisdom in reinventing human services may be a recognition of their marginality."

Finally, it is urgent that government, civic, and religious leaders, service providers, and citizens come together to debate the basic questions about services—their purposes, emphases, tasks, societal role—and to debate the appropriate expectations of services. This debate should have occurred a long time ago; it should have occurred again as American society was recently preparing to fundamentally alter our social welfare system. Services may work at the margins of family and community life. The support they provide may be modest. Yet that modest support, in its way, is critical.

Vaclav Havel noted recently, with reference to the relationship between Eastern and Western Europe, that one half of a room cannot remain forever warm while the other half is cold (Havel 1996:40). This is an apt metaphor for the consequences of failing to recognize and address poverty as a characteristic feature of American society. It can be argued that the task of strengthening supportive services pales before the more basic one of reconstructing the relationship between poor families and the larger society of which they are a part. Much of the difficulty experienced by poor families, as well as those who would try to support them, stems from the basic climate of distrust, punitiveness, and resource scarcity in which both must struggle to function. The notion that the poor are at some level responsible for their situation has translated into the view that spending money on supportive services for poor families should not be necessary; that it is, in effect, a needless expense. The climate surrounding poor people is, if anything, worsening. The public, and therefore the politicians who follow its lead, seem to be in an ungenerous mood. As one observer noted, the current thinking is that "less is more"; this bodes ill both for poor families and those who would provide supports for them.

Still, it can be argued that the current difficult context makes the task of finding a useful way of framing, organizing, and undertaking helping services that much more important. For even as they are criticized, even amidst continuing philosophical confusion, supportive services will continue to bear a disproportionate share of communal efforts to support poor families' in their own efforts to cope, to meet needs, and to grow.

Abott, Edith and Sophinisba Breckinridge. 1921. "The Administration of the Aid to Mothers Law in Illinois." Washington, D.C.: Children's Bureau Public Document # 82.

Adams, Paul and Kristine Nelson, eds. 1995. *Reinventing Human Services: Community- and Family-Centered Practice*. New York: Aldine de Gruyter.

Adams, Paul and Karin Krauth. 1995. "Working With Families and Communities: The Patch Approach." In ibid.

Agenda for Children Tomorrow. 1995 (April). Progress report: July 1992–June 1994. New York City, Mayor's Office of Education and Human Services.

——. 1997a. Evaluation Design Document. New York.

——. 1997b. Progress Report: February 1996–June 1997. New York.

Albee, George. 1980. "The Fourth Mental Health Revolution." *Journal of Primary Prevention* 1 (2): 67–70.

Alexander, Leslie. 1972. "Social Work's Freudian Deluge: Myth or Reality?." *Social Service Review* 46 (4): 517–538.

Allen, Jack. 1994. "The Discourse of Homeless Families." *Journal of Social Distress and the Homeless* 3 (2): 175–184.

Anderson, Gary (with Harold Weissman). 1990. "Child Abuse and Neglect: Wicked Problems and Professional Paradigms." In H. Weissman, ed., *Serious Play*. Silver Spring, Md: National Association of Social Work.

Anderson, Kenneth. 1995. [retrospective on Christopher Lasch's work]. *Times Literary Supplement*, September 22, p. 4825.

Anderson, Maxwell. 1994. "Service Integration Needs Neighborhood Governance." In *Strategies for Distressed Neighborhoods*. California: Center for Integrated Services.

Andrews, Susan and Colleagues. 1982. "The Skills of Mothering: A Study of Parent Child Development Centers." *Monographs of the Society for the Study of Child Development* 47 (6).

Austin, David. 1988. *The Political Economy of Human Service Programs*. Greenwich, Conn.: JAI Press.

Balogh, Brian. 1996. "Introduction" in *Journal of Policy History* 8 (1): 1–33.

Bane, Mary Jo. Undated. *The Federal Role in Improving Services for Children*. Cambridge: Kennedy School of Government, Harvard University (mimeo).

Bane, Mary Jo and David Ellwood. 1994. *Welfare Realities*. Cambridge: Harvard University Press.

Beck, Bertram. 1972. "Community Control: A Distraction Not an Answer." In F. Lowenberg and R. Dolgoff, eds., *The Practice of Social Intervention: Goals, Roles, and Strategies*. Itasca, Ill.: Peacock.

Beck, Bernard. 1967. "Welfare As a Moral Category" *Social Problems* 14 (3): 258–277.

Beller, Kuno. 1979. "Early Intervention Programs." In J. Ofosky, ed., *Handbook of Infant Development*. New York: Wiley.

Berger, Peter and Richard Neuhaus. 1977. *To Empower People: The Role of Mediating Structures in Public Policy*. Washington, D.C.: American Enterprise Foundation.

Berkowitz, Edward and Kim McQuaid. 1989. "Bureaucrats as Social Engineers: Federal Welfare Programs in Herbert Hoover's America." In D. Critchlow and E. Hawley, eds., *Poverty and Public Policy in Modern America*. Chicago: Dorsey.

Biegel, David and Kathleen Wells. "Introduction." In K. Wells and D. Biegel, eds., *Family Preservation Services*. Newbury Park, Cal.: Sage.

Berlin, Gordon. undated. "The New Poverty Among Families: A Service Decategorization Response." New York: MDRC.

Blau, Peter. 1965. "Orientation Toward Clients in a Public Welfare Agency." In Meyer Zald, ed., *Social Welfare Institutions*. New York: Wiley.

Bocage, Myrna, Homonoff, Emeline, and Priscilla Riley. 1995. "Measuring the Impact of the Fiscal Crisis on Human Service Agencies and Social Work Training." *Social Work* 40 (5): 701–705.

Boggs, Marjorie. 1930. "A Staff Discussion of Relief." *The Family* (July): 149–152.

Borris, Eileen. 1992. "The Settlement Movement Revisited: Social Control with a Conscience." *Reviews in American History* 20: 216–221.

Boulding, Kenneth. 1961. "Reflections on Poverty." *Social Welfare Forum*. New York: Columbia University Press.

Bowles, Dorcas. 1972. "Making Casework Relevant to Black People: Approaches, Techniques and Theoretical Implications." In Lowenberg and Dolgoff, eds., *The Practice of Social Intervention*

Boyer, Paul. 1978. *Urban Masses and Moral Order in America*. Cambridge: Harvard University Press.

Brace, Charles Loring. 1872. *The Dangerous Classes of New York.* New York: Wynkoop and Hallenbeck.

Brandt, Lillian. 1905. "On the Verge of Dependence." *Charities and Commons* 15: 462–468.

Bremmer, Robert. 1972. *From The Depths: The Discovery of Poverty in the United States.* New York: New York University Press.

Brettschneider, Eric. 1995 (July). "Defining ACT (Agenda For Children Tomorrow)." New York City: Mayor's Office of Education and Human Services.

Brisley, Mary. 1924. "An Attempt to Articulate Processes." *The Family* 5 (October): 157–161.

Bronfenbrenner, Urie. 1980. *The Ecology of Human Development.* Cambridge: Harvard University Press.

Brown, Gordon. 1968. *The Multi-Problem Dilemma.* Metuchen, N.J.: Scarecrow.

Brown, Prudence. 1995. *Settlement Houses Today: Their Community Building Role.* Chicago: Chapin Hall Center for Children at the University of Chicago.

Bruner, Charles and Larry Parachini. 1997. *Building Community.* Washington, D.C.: Together We Can Initiative.

Bruno, Frank. 1933. "Social Work Objectives in the New Era." *Proceedings of the National Council of Social Work.* Chicago: University of Chicago Press.

Buell, Bradley. 1952. *Community Planning for Human Services.* New York: Columbia University Press.

Burtless, Gary. 1995. "Employment Prospects of Welfare Recipients." In D. Nightingale and R. Haveman, eds., *The Work Alternative.* Washington, D.C.: Urban Institute.

Busey, Elizabeth. 1995. *Improving Children and Family Services in Iowa.* Seattle, Wash.: Cascade Center for Public Service.

Bush, Malcolm. 1988. *Families in Distress.* Berkely: University of California Press.

Butler, Stuart and Anna Kondratas, 1987. *Out of the Poverty Trap: A Conservative Strategy for Welfare Reform.* New York. Free Press.

Cahan, Emily. 1989. *Past Caring.* New York: National center for Children in Poverty.

Carson, Mina. 1990. *Settlement Folk.* Chicago: University of Chicago Press.

Center for the Study of Social Policy. 1991 (September). *Building a Community Agenda: Developing Local Governing Elites.* Washington, D.C.

Chambers, Clark, 1963. *Seedtime of Reform.* Ann Arbor: University of Michigan Press.

———. 1985. "The Historical Role of the Voluntary Sector in Human Service Delvery in Urban America." In Gary Tobin, ed. *Social Planning and Human Service Delivery in the Voluntary Sector.* Westport, Conn.: Greenwood.

———. 1992. "Uphill All the Way: Reflections in the Course and Study of Social Welfare History." Social Service Review (December): 492–504.

Chapin Hall Center for Children. 1997 (January). The Partnership for Neighborhood Initiative. Chicago.

Chase-Lansdale, Lindsay and Maris Vinovkis. undated. *Whose Responsibility: An*

*Historical Analysis of the Changing Roles of Mothers, Fathers and Society in Assuming Responsibility for Poor Children*. Chicago: Chapin Hall Center for Children at the University of Chicago.

Chaskin, Robert and Sunil Garg. 1994. *The Issue of Governance in Neighborhood-Based Initiatives*. Chicago: Chapin Hall Center for Children at the University of Chicago.

Cherniss, Cary. 1986. "Different Ways of Thinking About Burnout." In E. Seidman and J. Rapaport, eds., Redefining Social Problems. New York: Plenum.

Cicirelli, Victor. 1969. *The Impact of Head Start*. Athens, Ohio: Westinghouse Learning Corporation with Ohio University.

Citizens' Committee for the Children of New York. 1971. "Toward a New Social Service System." *Child Welfare* 50 (8): 448–459.

Clark, Kenneth and Jeanette Hopkins. 1968. *A Relevant war on Poverty*. New York: Harper.

Cloward, Richard and Lloyd Ohlin. 1960. *Delinquency and Opportunity*. Glencoe, Illinois: Free Press.

Cloward, Richard and Irwin Epstein. 1965. "Private Welfare's Disengagement From the Poor: The Case of Family Adjustment Agencies." In Meyer Zald, ed., *Social Welfare Institutions*. New York: Wiley.

Cmiel, Kenneth. 1995. *A Home of Another Kind: One Chicago Orphanage and the Tangle of Child Welfare*. Chicago: University of Chicago Press.

COFI (Community Organizing and Family Issues). 1995 (Summer). *COFI Notes*. Chicago.

Cohen, Robert. 1976. *"New Careers" Grows Older*. Baltimore: Johns Hopkins University Press.

Coles, Robert. 1964. "Journey Into the Minds of the Lower Depths." *New Republic* (February 15): 11–12.

Connell, James, Anne Kubisch, Lisbeth Schorr, and Carol Weiss, eds. 1995. *New Approaches to Evaluating Community Initiatives: Concepts, Methods, and Contexts*. New York: Aspen Institute.

Coontz, Stephanie. 1992. *The Way We Never Were*. New York: Basic Books.

Coyle, Grace. 1935. "The Limitations of Social Work in Relation to Social Re-Organizing." *Social Forces* 14 (October): 94–102.

Crocker, Ruth. 1992. *Social Work and Social Order: The Settlement Movement in Two Industrial Cities, 1889–1930*. Urbana, Ill.: University of Illinois Press.

Cutler, Ira. undated. *The Role of Finance Reform in Comprehensive Service Initiatives*. Washington, D.C.: The Finance Project.

Davis, Martha. 1996. "Welfare Rights and Women's Rights." *Journal of Policy History* 8 (1): 144–165.

Degler, Carl. 1980. *At Odds: Women and the Family in America from the Revolution to the Present*. New York: Oxford University Press.

Del Paso Heights Model. 1992 (June). "Proposal." Sacramento, Cal.: Office of the County Executive.

DeParle, Jason. 1997a. "U.S. Welfare System Dies as State Programs Emerge." *New York Times,* June 30, pp. A1, A10.

——. 1997b. "Success and Frustration as Welfare Rules Change." *New York Times,* December 30, pp. A1, A16–A17.

Devine, Edward. 1904. *The Principles of Relief.* New York: MacMillan.

——. 1907. "The New View." *Charities* (August 3): 461–464.

Diggins, John Patrick. 1994. *The Promise of Pragmatism.* Chicago: University of Chicago Press.

Dressel, Paula. 1984. *The Service Trap.* Springfield, Ill.: Charles Thomas.

Dubey, Sumati. 1972. "Community Action Programs and Citizen Participation: Issues and Confusions." In Lowenberg and Dolgoff, eds., *The Practice of Social Intervention.*

Dugger, Celia. 1995. "Budget Cuts Imperil Efforts to Save Families." *New York Times,* May 12, pp. A1, A15.

Dunham, Arthur. 1938. "Public Assistance in the U.S." In Russell Kurtz, ed., *The Public Assistance Worker.* New York: Russell Sage Foundation.

Edin, Kathryn. 1993. *There's a Lot of Month Left at the End of the Money: How Welfare Recipients Make Ends Meet in Chicago.* New York: Garland.

——. 1991. "Surviving the Welfare System: How AFDC Recipients Make Ends Met in Chicago." *Social Problems* 38: 462–474.

Ehrenreich, John. 1985. *The Altruistic Imagination: A History of Social Work and Social Policy in the United States.* Ithaca, N.Y.: Cornell University Press.

Epstein, William. 1993. *The Dilemma of American Social Welfare.* New Brunswick, N.J.: Transaction.

Fabricant, Michael and Steve Burghart. 1992. *The Welfare State Crisis and the Transformation of Social Service Work.* Armonk, N.Y.: M. E. Sharpe.

Family Resource Coalition, 1995

Family Resource Coalition. 1996. "Guidelines for Family Support Practice." Chicago.

Family Impact Seminar. 1996. "Strong Families, Strong Communities: Making the Connection." New York: Meeting at the Ford Foundation, March.

Fanshel, David, Stephen Finch, and John Grundy. 1992. *Serving the Urban Poor.* Westport, Conn.: Praeger.

Fischer, Joel. 1976. *The Effectiveness of Social Casework.* Springfield, Ill.: Charles Thomas.

Foster, Helen. 1958. "Family-Centered Services Through Aid to Dependent Children." In *Social Welfare Forum.* New York: Columbia University Press.

Fraiberg, Selma, Vivian Shapiro, and Deborah Cherniss. 1983. "Treatment Modalities." In Justin Call, Eleanor Galenson, and Robert Tyson, eds., *Frontiers of Infant Psychiatry.* New York: Basic Books.

Freeman, Joshua and Colleagues. 1992. *Who Built America?* Volume 2. New York: Pantheon.

Galper, Jefffrey. 1975. *The Politics of Social Services.* Paramus, N.J.: Prentice Hall.

Gardner, Sydney. 1995 (December). "Babes, Bathwater, and Muddy Waters." Hand-snet: Children, Youth and Families Forum.

Garfinkel, Irwin and Sara McLanahan. 1986. *Single Mothers and Their Children: A New American Dilemma.* Washington, D.C.: Urban Institute.

Garten, Nina and Herbert Otto. 1964. *The Development of Theory and Practice in So-cial Casework.* Springfield, Ill.: Charles Thomas.

Garvin, Charles, Smith, Audrey and William Reid. 1978. *The Work Incentive Expe-rience.* Montclair, N.J.: Allenheld, Osman.

Gaylin, Willard, Ira Glasser, Steven Marcus, and David Rothman. 1978. *Doing Good: The Limits of Benevolence.* New York: Pantheon.

Geismar, Ludwig. 1957. *The Family-Centered Project in St. Paul.* St. Paul, Minn.: Minnesota Historical Society.

Geismar, Ludwig and June Krisberg. 1967. *The Forgotten Neighborhood.* Metuchen, N.J.: Scarecrow.

Germain, Carel. 1970. "Casework and Science: A Historical Encounter." In R. Roberts and R. Nee, eds., *Theories of Social Casework.* Chicago: University of Chicago Press.

Gerry, Martin and Ronelle Paulson. 1995. *Realizing a New Community Vision: Community-Based Networks of Children's Services and Family Supports.* New York: Aspen Institute.

Gettleman, Marvin. 1963. "Charity and Social Classes in the United States." *Amer-ican Journal of Economics and Sociology* 22 (April/June): 313–336.

Gil, David. 1976. *The Challenge of Social Equality.* Cambridge, Mass.: Schenkman.

Gittens, Joan. 1986. *The Children of the State: Dependent Children in Illinois, 1818–1980s.* Chicago: Chapin Hall Center for Children at the University of Chicago.

Gladwin, Thomas. 1961. "The Anthropolist's View of Poverty." *Social Welfare Forum.* New York: Columbia University Press.

Glasser, Ira. 1978. "Prisoners of Benevolence" In W. Gaylin, I. Glasser, S. Marcus, and D. Rothman, eds., *Doing Good.* New York: Pantheon.

Glazer, Nathan. 1971. "The Limits of Social Policy." *Commentary* 52: 51–58.

Goldberg, Gertrude. 1969. "Non-professionals in Human Services." In C. Grosser, W. Henry, and J. Kelly, eds., *Non-professionals in the Human Services.* San Fran-cisco: Jossey Bass.

———. 1980. "Community Service Society of New York: Part II: Implementation of Radical Change." *Social Service Review* June: 202–219.

Gompers, Samuel. 1919. *Labor and the Common Worker.* New York: Dutton (cited in Ann Withorn, *Serving the People: Social Services and Social Change.* New York: Columbia University Press, 1994).

Goodin, Robert. 1985. *Protecting the Vulnerable.* Chicago: University of Chicago Press.

Gordon, Jesse. 1978. "WIN Research: A Review of the Findings." In Garvin, Smith, and Reid, eds., *The Work Incentive Experience.*

Gordon, Linda. 1988. *Heroes of Their own Lives.* New York: Penguin.

———. 1990. *Women, the State, and Welfare.* Madison: University of Wisconsin Press.

———. 1994. *Pitied But Not Yet Entitled: Single Women and Welfare in History*. New York: Free Press.

Gottlieb, Naomi. 1974. *The Welfare Bind*. New York: Columbia University Press.

Graebner, William. 1980. "The Unstable World of Benjamin Spock: Social Engineering in a Democratic Culture." *Journal of American History* 67 (3): 612–629.

Greenberg, Polly. 1990. *The Devil Has Slippery Shoes*. Washington, D.C.: Youth Policy Institute.

Grob, Gerald. 1973. "Welfare and Poverty in American History." *Reviews in American History* 1 (March): 42–52.

Grosser, Charles, Henry, William, and James Kelly (eds.). 1969. *Non-professionals in the Human Services*. San Francisco: Jossey Bass.

Grubb, Norton, and Marvin Lazerson. 1980. *Broken Promises*. New York: Basic Books.

Hadley, Roger, M. Cooper, P. Dale, and G. Stacy. 1987. *A Community Social Worker's Handbook*. London: Tavistock.

Hagedorn, John. 1995. *Forsaking Our Children: Bureaucracy and Reform in the Child Welfare System*. Chicago: Lake View.

Hall, Helen. 1971. *Unfinished Business*. New York: MacMillan.

Halmos, Paul. 1970. *The Faith of Counselors*. New York: Schocken.

Halpern, Robert. 1988. "Parent Support and Education for Low-Income Families: Historical and Current Perspectives." *Children and Youth Services Review* 10: 283–303.

———. 1990. "Parent Support and Education Programs." *Children and Youth Services Review* 12: 285–308.

———. 1991. "Supportive Services for Families in Poverty: Dilemmas of Reform." *Social Service Review* 65 (3): 343–364.

———. 1993. "The Societal Context of Home Visiting and Related Services to Address Poverty." *The Future of Children* 3 (3): 158–171.

———. 1995. *Rebuilding the Inner City: A History of Neighborhood Initiatives to Address Poverty in the United States*. New York: Columbia University Press.

———. 1996. "Parent Support and Education Programs: What Role in the Continuum of Child and Family Services?" In Ira Schwartz, ed., *Family and Home-Based Services*. Lincoln: University of Nebraska Press.

———. 1997. "Good Practice With Multiply Vulnerable Young Families: Challenges and Principles." *Children and Youth Services Review* 19 (4): 253–275.

Hamilton, Gordon. 1934. "Casework Responsibility in the Unemployment Relief Agency." *Proceedings of the National Council of Social Workers*, pp. 389–398. Chicago: University of Chicago Press.

———. 1948. "Helping People: The Growth of a Profession." *Journal of Social Casework* 29 (8): 291–299.

Hamilton, Ralph. Undated. "Partnership for Neighborhood Initiative." Palm Beach, Fla: The MacArthur Foundation. (Posted on "Handsnet" on the Internet.)

Handler, Joel and Ellen Hollingsworth. 1971. *The Deserving Poor: A Study of Welfare Administration*. Chicago: Markham.

Handler, Joel and Yeheskel Hasenfeld. 1991. *The Moral Construction of Poverty: Welfare Reform in America*. California: Sage.

Hardin, Russell. 1990. "The Artificial Duties of Contemporary Professionals." *Social Service Review* (December): 528–42.

Havel, Vaclav. 1996. "The Hope for Escape." *New York Review of Books* 43 (June 20): 38–40.

Heclo, Hugh. 1996. "The Sixties' False Dawn: Awakenings, Movements and Post-Modern Policy Making." *Journal of Policy History* 8 (1): 34–63.

Heineman (Field), Martha. 1980. "Social Casework Practice During the Psychiatric Deluge." *Social Service Review* 54 (4): 482–507.

Herr, Toby and Robert Halpern. 1993 (November). "Bridging the Worlds of Head Start and Welfare to Work." Chicago: Project Match, Erikson Institute.

Herr, Toby, Suzanne Wagner, and Robert Halpern. 1996 (December). "Making the Shoe Fit: Creating a Work Preparation System for a Large and Diverse Welfare Population." Chicago, Illinois: Project Match, Erikson Institute.

Herszehorn, David. 1996. "Healing Neighborhoods with Comprehensive Community-Building." *New York Times*, December 8, p. 39.

Herzog, Elizabeth. 1972. "Facts and Fictions About the Poor." In Lowenberg and Dolgoff, eds., *The Practice of Social Intervention*.

Hess, Peg, Brenda McGowan, and Carol Meyer. 1995. "Practitioners' Perspectives on Services to Families and Children in Big Cities." In Kahn and Kamerman, eds. *Children and Their Families in Big Cities*.

Hewett, Kathryn. 1982. "Comprehensive Family Service Programs: Special features and Associated Measurement Problems." In J. Travers and R. Light, eds., *Learning From Experience*. Washington, D.C.: National Academy Press.

Himmelfarb, Gertrude. 1991. *Poverty and Compassion*. New York: Knopf.

Hirota, Janice, Prudence Brown, and Nancy Martin. 1996. Building Community: *The Tradition and Promise of Settlement Houses*. Chicago: Chapin Hall Center for Children at the University of Chicago.

Hirota, Janice, Prudence Brown, William Mollard, and Hannah Richman. 1997. *Pathways to Change: Settlement Houses and the Strengthening of Community*. Chicago: Chapin Hall Center for Children at the University of Chicago.

Hirschman, Albert. 1991. *The Rhetoric of Reaction*. Cambridge: Harvard University Press.

Horne, Martha. "Gearing School Curricula to Public Welfare Needs." 1953. *Public Welfare* 11 (July): 92–94.

Hull, Ida. 1924. "Casework Among Foreign Born Families." *The Family* 5 (4): 75–82.

Husock, Howard. 1992. "Bring Back the Settlement Movement." *Public Interest* (Fall): 53–72.

Ignatieff, Michael. 1985. *The Needs of Strangers*. New York: Viking.

Institute for Educational Leadership, 1994. Lessons from San Diego's New Beginnings. IEL Policy Exchange. Washington, D.C.

Johnson, Alexander. 1926. "Social Microbe Hunters." *The Family* 7 (8): 231–233.

Joint Commission on the Mental Health of Children. 1970. *Crisis in Child Mental Health: Challenge for the 1970s*. New York: Harper and Row.

Jones, Hettie. 1969. "Overview of Services to Individuals and Families." In H. Weissman, ed., *Individual and Group Services in the Mobilization for Youth Experience*. New York: Association.

———. "Neighborhood Service Centers." In ibid.

Jones, Hettie and Harold Weissman. 1969. "Psychological Help for the Poor." In H. Weissman, ed., *Individual and Group Services in the Mobilization for Youth Experience*. New York: Association.

Jordan, Bill. 1979. *Helping in Social Work*. London. Routledge and Kegan Paul.

Kahn, Alfred. 1964. "A Coordinated Pattern of Services: Shibboleth or Goal?" In C. Cella and R. Lane, eds., *Basic Issues in Coordinating Family and Child Welfare Programs*. Philadelphia: University of Pennsylvania Press.

———. 1966. *Neighborhood Information Centers*. New York: Columbia University School of Social Work.

———. 1969. *Studies in Social Policy and Planning*. New York: Russell Sage.

———. 1976. "Service Delivery at the Neighborhood Level: Experience, Theory, and Fads." *Social Service Review* 50 (1): 23–55.

———. 1979. *Social Policy and Social Services*. New York: Random House.

Kahn, Dorothy. 1928. "The Future of Family Social Work." *The Family* (October): 185–188.

Kamerman, Sheila. 1996. "The New Politics of Child and Family Policies." *Social Work* 41 (5): 453–65.

Kamerman, Sheila and Alfred Kahn. 1989. *Social Services for Children, Youth, and Families in the United States*. New York: Annie E. Casey Foundation.

Kamerman, Sheila and Alfred Kahn, eds. 1996. *Children and Their Families in Big Cities*. New York: Columbia University School of Social Work.

Kardiner, Abram. 1936. *The Role of Economic Security in the Adaptation of the Individual*. 17 (6): 187–197.

Karger, Howard. 1987. *The Sentinels of Order: A Study of Social Control and the Minneapolis Settlement House Movement, 1915–1950*. Lanham, N.H.: University Press of America.

Katz, Michael. 1983. *Poverty and Policy in American History*. New York: Academic Press.

———. 1989. *The Undeserving Poor*. New York: Pantheon.

———. 1993. "Surviving Poverty in Early Twentieth-Century Century America." In Ronald Hirsch and Raymond Mohl, eds., *Urban Poverty in Twentieth-Century America*. New Jersey: Rutgers University Press.

———. 1995. *Improving Poor People*. Princeton: Princeton University Press.

Keith-Lucas, Alan. 1957. *Decisions About People in Need*. Chapel Hill: University of North Carolina Press.

Kelly, M. Patricia. 1995. "Minding Other Peoples' Children." *Johns Hopkins Magazine* 6 (June).

Kennedy, David. 1996. The price of immigration. *Atlantic Monthly* (November): 55–68.

Kessler-Harris, Alice. 1982. *Out to Work: A History of Wage-Earning Women in the U.S.* New York: Oxford University Press.

Kirschner, Don. 1986. *The Paradox of Professionalism.* New York: Greenwood.

Kissman, Kris. 1995. "Divisive Dichotomies and Mother-Headed Families: The Power of Naming." *Social Work* 40 (20): 151–153.

Koos, Earl. 1946. *Families in Trouble.* New York: King's Crown.

Kravitz, Sanford. 1964. *Social Crisis: Do We Plan or React?* New York State Welfare Conference.

Kravitz, Sanford and F. Kolodner. 1969. "Community Action: Where has It Been? Where Will It Go?" *Annals of the American Academy of Political and Social Science* 385: 30–40.

Kubisch, Anne, eds. 1995. *Voices from the Field: Learning From Comprehensive Community Initiatives.* New York: Aspen Institute.

Kubisch, Anne, Carol Weiss, Lisbeth Schorr, and James Connell. 1995. "Introduction." In J. Connell, A. Kubisch, L. Schorr and C. Weiss, eds., *New Aproaches to Evaluating Community Initiatives: Concepts, Methods, and Contexts.* New York: Aspen Institute.

Kunzel, Regina. 1993. *Fallen Women, Problem Girls: Unmarried Mothers and the Professionalization of Social Work, 1890–1945.* New Haven: Yale University Press.

Kusmer, Kenneth. 1973. "The Functions of Organized Charity in the Progressive Era: Chicago as a Case Study." *Journal of American History* 60 (3): 657–678.

Ladd-Taylor, Molly. 1994. *Mother-Work: Women, Child Welfare and the State, 1890–1930.* Urbana, Ill.: University of Illinois Press.

Lampman, Robert. 1971. "Foreword." In Joel Handler and Elaine Hollingsworth, *The Deserving Poor: A Study of Welfare Administration.* Chicago: Markham.

Landy, David. 1965. "Problems of the Person Seeking Help in Our Culture." In M. Zald, ed., *Social Welfare Institutions.* New York: Wiley.

Lane, James. 1973. "Jacob Riis and Scientific Philanthropy During the Progressive Era." *Social Service Review* 47 (1): 32–48.

Lane, Lionel. 1952. "The Aggressive Approach in Preventive Casework with Children's Problems." *Social Casework* 33: xxxx Feb. Xxx

Lane, Rodney. 1964. "The Problem of Welfare Coordination." In C. Cella and R. Lane, eds., *Basic Issues in Coordinating Family and Child Welfare Programs.* Philadelphia: University of Pennsylvania Press.

Larson, Magali. 1977. *The Rise of Professionalism.* Berkeley: University of California Press.

Lasch, Christopher. 1965. *The New Radicalism in America, 1889–1963.* New York: Knopf.

———. 1977 *Haven in a Heartless World.* New York: Basic Books.

———. 1995. *The Revolt of the Elites and the Betrayal of Democracy.* New York: Norton.

Leacock, Eleanor. 1971. *The Culture of Poverty: A Critique*. New York: Simon and Schuster.

Leiby, James. 1978. *A History of Social Work and Social Welfare in the United States*. New York: Columbia University Press.

Lemann, Nicholas. 1991. *The Promised Land: The Great Black Migration and How It Changed America*. New York: Knopf.

Lenrow, Peter. 1982. "The Work of Helping Strangers." In H. Rubenstein and M. Bloch, eds., *The Things That Matter: Influences on Helping Relationships*. New York: MacMillan.

Lescohier, Ilana. 1978. "Experiences in the Work Incentive Program." In C. Garvin, A. Smith, and W. Reid, eds., *The Work Incentive Experience*. Montclair, N.J.: Allenheld, Osman.

Levine, Daniel. 1971. *Jane Addams and the Liberal Tradition*. Madison: State Historical Society of Wisconsin.

Levine, Murray and Adeline Levine. 1992. *Helping Children: A Social History*. New York: Oxford University Press

Lewis, Oscar. 1961. *The Children of Sanchez*. New York: Random House.

Lindsey, Duncan. 1994. *The Welfare of Children*. New York: Oxford University Press.

Lipsky, Michael. 1980. *Street-Level Bureaucracy*. New York: Russell Sage.

———. 1984. "Bureaucratic Disentitlement in Social Welfare Programs." *Social Service Review* 58: 3–27.

Lissak, Rivka. 1989. *Pluralism and Progressives*. Chicago: University of Chicago Press.

Lourie, Ira. 1994 (May). *Principles of Local System Development*. Chicago: Kaleidoscope.

Lowell, Josephine. 1884. *Public Relief and Private Charity*. New York: Putnam and Sons (Reprinted by the Arno Press, 1971).

Lubove, Roy. 1965. *The Professional Altruist*. Cambridge: Harvard University Press.

MacDonald, Heather. 1994. "The Ideology of Family Preservation." *Public Interest* (Spring): 45–60.

Marcus, Grace. 1935. "The Status of Social Casework Today." *Proceedings of the National Council of Social Workers*. Chicago: University of Chicago Press.

Marris, Peter and Martin Rein. 1973. *Dilemmas of Social Reform*. London: Routledge and Kegan Paul.

Massey, Douglas and Nancy Denton. 1993. *American Apartheid: Segregation and the Making of the Underclass*. Cambridge: Harvard University Press.

May, Edgar. 1964. *The Wasted Americans*. New York: Harper and Row.

May, Mark. 1936. "Is There a Science of Human Relations?" *The Family* 17 (3): 139–144.

Mayer, Philippe. 1977. *The Child and The State: The Intervention of the State in Family Life*. London: Cambridge University Press.

McElvaine, Robert. 1994. *The Great Depression: America 1929–1941*. Madison: Wisconsin Policy Research Institute Report, vol. 8.

McGowan, Brenda (with Alfred Kahn and Sheila Kamerman). 1990. Social Services for Children, Youth, and Families: The New York City Study. New York: Columbia University School of Social Work.

McKnight, John. 1995. *The Careless Society: Community and Its Counterfeits.* New York: Basic Books.

———. 1996. The Future of Low Income Neighborhoods . . . .

Mead, Lawrence. 1986. *Beyond Entitlement: The Social Obligations of Citizenship.* New York: Free Press.

———. 1994. "Poverty: How Little We Know." *Social Science Review* (September): 322–50.

Mead, Lawrence. 1995. *The New Paternalism in Action: Welfare Reform in Wisconsin.* Madison: Wisconsin Policy Research Institute Report, vol. 8.

Meyer, Carol. 1976. *Social Work Practice: The Changing Landscape.* New York: Free Press.

Mikulecky, Thomas. 1974. *Human Services Integration.* Washington, D.C.: American Society for Public Administration.

Miles, Arthur. 1954. *American Social Work Theory: A Critique and a Proposal.* New York: xxxx.

Mills, C. Wright. 1943. "The Professional Ideology of Social Pathologists." *American Journal of Sociology* 49: 165–180.

Milton Eisenhower Foundation. 1993. "Doing What Works to Revise the Betrayal of American Democracy." Washington, D.C.

Mink, George. 1978. "The Organization of WIN and its Impact on Participants." In Garvin, Smith, and Reid, eds., *The Work Incentive Experience.*

Mink, Gwendolyn. 1995. *The Wages of Motherhood: Inequality in the Welfare State, 1917–1942.* Ithaca: Cornell University Press.

Minuchin, Salvador. 1995. "Foreword." In Adams and Nelson, eds., *Reinventing Human Services.*

Monkkonen, Eric. 1993. "Nineteenth-Century Institutions: Dealing With the Urban Underclass." In M. Katz, ed., *The Underclass Debate: Views From History.* Princeton: Princeton University Press.

Moore, 1927

Moroney, Robert. 1986. *Shared Responsibility.* New York: Aldine.

Morton, Marian. 1993. *And Sin No More: Social Policy and Unwed Mothers in Cleveland, 1855–1990.* Columbus: Ohio State University Press.

Moynihan, Daniel. 1965. *The Negro Family: The Case for National Action.* Washington, D.C.: Department of Labor.

Mullen, Edward, Chazin, Robert and David Feldstein. 1972. "Services for the Newly Dependent: An Assessment." *Social Service Review* 46 (3): 309–322.

Musick, Judith and Fran Stott. 1990. "Paraprofessionals, Parenting and Child Development: Understanding the Problems and Seeking Solutions." In S. Meisels and J. Shonkoff, eds., *Handbook Of Early Childhood Intervention.* New York: Cambridge University Press.

National Commission on Children. 1991. *Beyond Rhetoric*. Washington, D.C.

Nelson, Douglas. 1991. 'The Public Policy Implications of Family Preservation." In Kathleen Wells and David Biegel, eds., *Family Preservation Services*. Newbury Park, Cal. Sage.

——. 1995 (October). The Path of Most resistance: Lessons from New Futures. Handsnet.

New Beginnings. Undated. "Background Materials." San Diego: Department of Social Services, Community Initiatives for Children and Families.

Nightingale, Carl.1993. *On the Edge: A History of Poor Black Children and Their American Dreams*. New York: Basic Books

Normanda, Carmen. 1972. "Characteristics and Roles of Indigenous Workers." In Lowenberg and Dolgoff, eds., *The Practice of Social Intervention*.

North, Cecil. 1931. *Community and Social Welfare*. New York: McGraw Hill.

"Notes and Comments." 1972. "Selection from President Nixon;s Message to Congress, January 24, 1972." *Social Service Review* 46 (2): 263–66.

——. 1972. "Prospectus for Change at the Community Service Society." Ibid 46 (4): 205–211.

——. 1972. "Brownie Point Welfare." Ibid 46 (1): 111-113.

——. 1973. Elizabeth Wickenden, cited. Ibid. 47 (1): 102.

——. 1973. "What Kind of Federalism?" Ibid. 47 (2): 278–285.

——. 1973. "Sharing or Paring?" Ibid. 47 (1): 95–102.

O'Donnell, Edward and Marilyn Sullivan. 1972. "Service Delivery and Social Action Through the Neighborhood Center." In Lowenberg and Dolgoff, eds., *The Practice of Social Intervention*.

O'Looney, John. 1996. *Redesigning the Work of Human Services*. Westport, Conn.: Quorum.

Obama, Barack. 1995 (Summer). Cited in "COFI Notes." Chicago: Community Organizing and Family Issues.

Olasky, Marvin. 1992. *The Tragedy of American Compassion*. Washington, D.C.: Regnery Gateway.

Ooms, Theodora. 1996. "Where is the Family in Comprehensive Community Initiatives for Children and Families?" Washington, DC: Family Impact Seminar.

Orfield, Gary. 1991. "Cutback Policies, Declining Opportunities, and the Role of Social Service Providers." *Social Service Review* 65: 516–530.

Orfman, Kay. 1996. "A Rural View of Mothers' Pensions: The Allegan County, Michigan Mothers' Pension Program, 1913–1928." *Social Service Review* (March): 98–119.

Orland, Martin and Anna Danegger and Ellen Foley. 1995. *Creating More Comprehensive community-Based Support Systems: The Critical Role of Finance*. Washington, D.C.: The Finance Project.

Overton, Alice and Katherine Tinker. 1959. *The Casework Notebook*. St. Paul, Minnesota: Family-Centered Project.

Palevsky, Mary. 1926. "The Share of the Family Care Agency in Raising the Standards of Parenthood." *The Family* 7 (3): 67–71.

Paradise, Viola. 1948. *Toward Public Understanding of Casework*. New York: Russell Sage Foundation.

Patterson, James. 1986. *America's Struggle Against Poverty, 1900–1985*. Cambridge: Harvard University Press.

Patton, Michael. 1993. The Aid to Families in Poverty Program: Themes, Patterns and Lessons Learned. Minneapolis, Minn.: The McKnight Foundation.

Pavensted, Eleanor and Viola Bernard. 1971. *Crises of Family Disorganization*. New York: Behavioral Publications.

Payne, James. 1996. "Absence of Judgment." *Policy Review* (November-December): 50–4.

Perez-Foster, Rose Marie. 1996. "What is a Multicultural Perspective for Psychoanalysis?" In R. Perez-Foster, M. Moskowitz, and R. Javier, eds., *Reaching Across Boundaries of Culture and Class: Widening the Scope of Psychotherapy*. Northvale, N.J.: Jason Aronson.

Perlman, Helen Harris. 1960. "Are We Creating Dependency?" *Social Service Review* 34: 323–333.

Perlman, Robert. 1975. *Consumers and Social Services*. New York: Wiley.

Philliber Research Associates. 1994. *Interim Evaluation Report on New Beginnings*. New York.

Philpott, Thomas. 1978. *The Slum and the Ghetto*. New York: Oxford University Press.

Piven, Frances and Richard Cloward. 1971. *Regulating the Poor: The Functions of Public Welfare*. New York: Vintage.

———. 1972. "How the Federal Government Causes the Welfare Crisis." In Lowenberg and Dolgoff, eds., *The Practice of Social Intervention*.

Polacheck, Hilda. 1991. *I Came a Stranger: The Story of a Hull House Girl*. Urbana: University of Illinois Press.

Polier, Justine Wise. 1989. *Juvenile Justice in Double Jeopardy*. N.J.: Lawrence Earlbaum.

Polsky, Andrew. 1991. *The Rise of the Therapeutic State*. Princeton, N.J.: Princeton University Press.

Posner, Wendy. 1995. "Common Human Needs: A Story From the Prehistory of Government by Special Interest." *Social Service Review* 69 (2): 188–225.

Preister, Steven. 1996. "Some Initial Reflections: Lessons Learned in Illinois." The Governors Task Force on Human Service Reform. Mimeo.

Prochner, Larry. 1996. "Quality of Care in Historical Perspective." *Early Childhood Research Quarterly* 11: 5–17.

Provence, Sally and Audrey Naylor. 1983. *Working With Disadvantaged Parents and Their Children: Scientific and Practice Issues*. New Haven: Yale University Press.

Pumphrey, Ralph. 1964. "Past Campaigns in the War on Poverty." In *Social Welfare Forum*. New York: Columbia University Press.

Putnam, Robert. 1993. "Social capital and Economic Growth." *Currents* 356 (October): 4–9.

Queen, Stuart. 1932. "What Is Unemployment Doing to the Family?" *The Family* 12 (10): 299–302.

Rees, Stuart and Allison Wallace. 1982. *Verdicts on Social Work.* London: Edward Arnold.

Rein, Martin. 1983. *From Policy to Practice.* Armonk, New York: M. E. Sharpe.

Reynolds, Bertha. 1932. "The Things That Cannot Be Shaken." *The Family* 13 (2): 51–54.

——. 1935. "Response to Grace Marcus." *Proceedings of the National Council of Social Workers.* Chicago: University of Chicago Press.

——. 1963. *An Uncharted Journey.* New York: Citadel.

Reynolds, Rosemary. 1931. "They Have neither Money Nor Work." *The Family* 7 (2): 35–39.

Rhoades, Winfred. 1925. "The Warp of the Specialist." *The Family* 6 (1): 19–23

Richman, Harold and Renae Ogletree. 1995 (July). *The Partnership for Neighborhood Initiative.* Chicago: Chapin Hall Center for Children at the University of Chicago.

Richman, Harold, Robert Chaskin, and Renae Ogletree. 1993. *Neighborhood and Family Initiative, Interim Evaluation Report.* Chicago: Chapin Hall Center for Children at the University of Chicago.

Richmond, Mary. 1917. *Social Diagnosis.* New York: Russell Sage.

——. 1922. *What Is Social Casework?* New York: Russell Sage.

——. 1922. "Some Relations of Family Casework to Social Progress." *The Family* 3 (5): 99–104.

Robinson, Virginia. 1930. *A Changing Psychology in Social Work.* Chapel Hill: University of North Carolina Press.

Rochefort, David. 1984. "Progressive and Social Control Perspectives on Social Welfare." *Social Service Review* 55 (4): 568–592.

Rothman, David. 1978. "The State as Parent . . ." In W. Gaylin, I. Glasser, S. Marcus, and D. Rothman, eds., *Doing Good.* New York: Pantheon.

Rubenstein, Hrasura and Mary Bloch. 1978. "Helping Clients Who Are Poor: Worker and Client Perceptions of Problems, Activities, and Outcomes." *Social Service Review* 52: 69–84.

Rupert, Ethel. 1929. "Philadelphia, 1900–1909." *The Family* 90 (10): 326–335.

Ryerson, Ellen. 1978. *The Best Laid Plans: America's Juvenile Court Experiment.* New York: Hill and Wang.

Sandel, Michael. 1996. "Dewey Rides Again." *New York Review of Books.* May 9, pp. 35–38

Scheper-Hughes, Nancy. 1987. "Child Abuse and the Unconscious in Popular American Culture." In N. Scheper-Hughes, ed., *Child Survival.* New York: Reidel.

Schlossman, Steven. 1978. "The Parent Education Game: The Politics of Child Psychology in the 1970s." *Teachers College Record* 78 (4): 788–808.

Schorr, Alvin. 1986. *Common Decency.* New Haven: Yale University Press.

Schorr, Lisbeth. 1988. *Within Our Reach: Breaking the Cycle of Disadvantage.* New York: Anchor.

———. 1997. Common Purpose: Strengthening Families and Communities to Rebuild Urban America. New York, Anchor.

Schuerman, John, Tina Rzepnicki, and Julia Littel. 1994. *Putting Families First: An Experiment in Family Preservation.* New York: Aldine de Gruyter.

Scott, Daryl. 1996. "The Politics of Pathology: The Ideological Origins of the Moynihan Controversy." *Journal of Policy History* 8 (1): 81–105.

Sears, Amelia. 1926. "The Resistive Zone and the Social Program." The Family 6 (9): 255–258.

Sexton, Joe. 1996. "Child Welfare Chief Provides a Glimpse of Decentralization." *New York Times*, pp. 1, 22.

Sheppard, Harold. 1972. "The Social Geography of Poverty." In Lowenberg and Dolgoff, eds., *The Practice of Social Intervention.*

Silberman, Deanna. 1990 (April). *Chicago and its Children: A Brief History of Social Services for Children in Chicago.* Chicago: Chapin Hall Center for Children at the University of Chicago.

Silver, Abba. 1932. *The Crisis in Social Work: Proceedings of the National Conference of Social Work.* Chicago: University of Chicago Press.

Silverstein, Bally and R. Krate. 1975. *Children of the Dark Ghetto.* New York: Praeger.

Skerry, Peter. 1983. "The Charmed Life of Head Start." *The Public Interest* 73: 18–39.

Skocpol, Theda. 1992. *Protecting Soldiers and Mothers.* Cambridge: Harvard University Press.

———. 1993 (January). "African Americans in U.S. Social Policy." Paper presented at a workshop on Race, Ethnicity, representation and Governance, Harvard University.

Smith, Adam. 1759. *Theory of Moral Sentiments.* (Reprinted by Oxford University Press, 1976).

Smith, John. 1946. "Understanding the Negro Client." *Journal of Social Casework* 27 (3): 87–95.

Sosin, Michael. 1990. "Decentralizing the Social Service System: A Re-Assessment." *Social Service Review* 64: 617–636.

Spalter-Roth, Roberta and Heidi Hartmann. undated. *Dependence on Men, The Market, or the State: The Rhetoric and Reality of Welfare Reform.* Washington, D.C.: Institute for Women's Research.

Spano, Rick. 1982. *The Rank and File Movement in Social Work.* Washington, D.C.: University Press of America.

Spock, Benjamin. 1946. *Baby and Child Care.* New York: Dutton.

Stadum, Beverly. 1990. "A Critique of Family Caseworkers 1900–1930: Women Working With Women." *Journal of Sociology and Social Welfare* Xxxxx.

———. 1992. *Poor Women and Their Families: Hard-Working Charity Cases.* Albany: State University of New York Press.

Stangler, Gary. 1995. (November). *Life Boats and Safety Nets*. Handsnet, Children, Youth and Families Forum.

Stark, Rodney. 1987. "Deviant Places: A Theory of the Ecology of Crime." *Criminology* 25 (4): 893–909.

Steiner, Gilbert. 1981. *The Futility of Family Policy*. Washington, D.C.: Brookings Institution.

Stokely, Jan. 1996. *The Emerging Role of California's Family Support Programs in Community Economic Development*. Oakland, Cal.: National Economic Development and Law Center.

Stone, Michael. 1992. "A Few Good Men and Women." *New York Magazine*. December 14: 44–69.

Stone, Rebecca, ed. 1995. *Core Issues in Comprehensive Community-Building Initiatives*. Chicago: Chapin Hall Center for Children at the University of Chicago.

Sullivan, William. 1995. *Work and Integrity*. New York: Harper Business.

Sutton, John. 1988. *Stubborn Children*. Berkely: University of California Press.

Sviridoff, Mitchell and William Ryan. 1996. "Investing in Community: Lessons and Implications of the Comprehensive Community Revitalization Program." Mimeo.

——. 1996. (January). *Prospects and Strategies for Community-Centered Family Service*. Milwaukee: Family Service America.

——. 1997. "Community-Centered Family Service." *Families in Society* 78 (2): 128–139

Swift, Linton. 1925. "The Chest and the Family Society." *The Family* 6 (5): 119–124.

Taylor, James and Jerry Randolph. 1975. *Community Worker*. New York: Jason Aronson.

Taylor, Lea. 1935. "Social Settlements." *Social Work Yearbook*. New York: Russell Sage.

Taylor, Robert. 1958. "The Social Control Function of Casework." *Social Casework* 34 (1): 17–20.

Testa, Mark. 1985 (October). *Child Welfare in Sociological and Historical Perspective*. Chicago: Chapin Hall Center for Children at the University of Chicago.

Thomas, George. 1994. *Travel in the Trenches Between Child Welfare Theory and Practice*. New York: Haworth.

Thomas, William and Dorothy Thomas. 1928. *The Child in America*. New York: Knopf.

Todd, Arthur. 1927. "Some Industrial Management Aspects of Married Women's Work and Their Bearing on the Family." *The Family* 8 (3): 88–92.

Towle, Charlotte. 1973. *Common Human Needs*. London: Arlen and Unwin.

Trolander, Judith. 1975. *Settlement Houses and the Great Depression*. Detroit: Wayne State University Press.

——. 1987. *Professionalism and Social Change*. New York: Columbia University Press.

Tyson, Katherine. 1995. *New Foundations for Scientific Social and Behavioral Research*. Boston: Allyn and Bacon.

Valentine, Charles. 1968. *Culture and Poverty*. Chicago: University of Chicago Press.

——. 1971. "The Culture of Poverty: Its Scientific Significance and Application." In

Eleanor Leacock, ed., *The Culture of Poverty: A Critique*. New York: Simon and Schuster.

Valentine, Margarite. 1994. "The Social Worker as Bas Object." *British Journal of Social Work* 24: 71–86.

Van Galen. 1993.

Van Waters, Miriam. 1925 (October). The Juvenile Court as an Agency in Parent Education. Bronxville, New York: Child Study Association of America, Conference on Parental Education.

Vobejda, Barbara and Judith Haveman. 1997. "Success After Welfare?" *Washington Post Weekly*, January 13: 6–7.

Waite, Florence. 1931. "What Has Been Happening?" *The Family* 12 (5): 142–146.

———. 1936. "A Little Matter of Self-Respect." *The Family* 17 (March): 12–13

Weick, Karl. 1986. "Small Wins." In E. Seidman and J. Rapaport, eds., *Redefining Social Problems*. New York: Plenum.

Weir, Margaret. 1993. "Urban Policy and Persistent Urban Poverty." Background Memo for Policy Conference on Persistent Urban Poverty. New York: Social Science Research Council.

Weiss, Robert. 1973. "Helping Relationships: Relationships of Clients with Physicians, Social Workers, Priests, and Others." *Social Problems* 20 (3): 319–328.

Weiss, Heather and Robert Halpern. 1988 (April). *Community Based Family Support and Education Programs: Something Old or Something New?* New York: National Center for Children in Poverty, Columbia University.

Weissbourd, Richard. 1996. *The Vulnerable Child: What Really Hurts America's Children and What We Can Do About It*. Reading, Mass.: Addison-Wesley.

Weissman, Harold. 1978. Integrating Services for Troubled Children. San Francisco: Jossey Bass.

Wenocur, Stanley and Michael Reisch. 1989. *From Charity to Enterprise: The Development of American Social Work in a Market Economy*. Urbana: University of Illinois Press.

White, Julie and Gary Whelage. 1995. "Community Collaboration: If It Is Such a Good Idea, Why Is It so Hard to Do?" *Educational Evaluation and Policy Analysis* 17 (1): 23–38.

Wickenden, Elizabeth. 1976. "A Perspective on Social Services: An Essay Review." *Social Service Review* 50 (4): 570–585.

Wiltse, Kermit. 1954. "Social Casework Services in the Aid to Dependent Children Program." *Social Service Review* 28 (2): 173–185.

———. 1958. "The Hopeless Family." Social Welfare Forum. New York: Columbia University Press.

Wofford, John. 1969. "The Politics of Local Responsibility: Administration of the Community Action Program." In J. Sundquist, ed., *On Fighting Poverty*. New York: Basic Books.

Wukas, Mark. 1991. *The Worn Doorstep*. Chicago: Northwestern University Settlement Association.

Wulczyn, Fred. 1996. "Child Welfare Reform, Managed Care and Community Rein-
vestment." In Kahn and Kamerman, eds., *Children and their Families in Big Cities*.

Ylvisaker, Paul. 1973 (September). Interviewed by Charles Morrissey for the Ford
Foundation Oral History project. New York: Ford Foundation Archives.

Zalenski, John. 1996. "Patch Approach Is Leading Reform." Handsnet, Child Welfare Forum.

Zigler, Edward and Susan Muenchow. 1992. *Head Start*. New York: Basic Books.

Zmora, Nurith. 1994. *Orphanages Reconsidered: Child Care Institutions in Progressive
Era* Baltimore, Pa.: Temple University Press.

Zurcher, Louis. 1969. *From Dependency to Dignity: Individual and Social Consequences of a Neighborhood House*. New York: Behavioral Publications.